Learn Hmong

the

Jay Way

Learn Hmong the Jay Way

1st Edition

Date Published: ***July 20, 2012***

International Standard Book Number (ISBN): **0-9726964-2-3**

To Order This Book

Please visit **www.HmongDictionary.com**

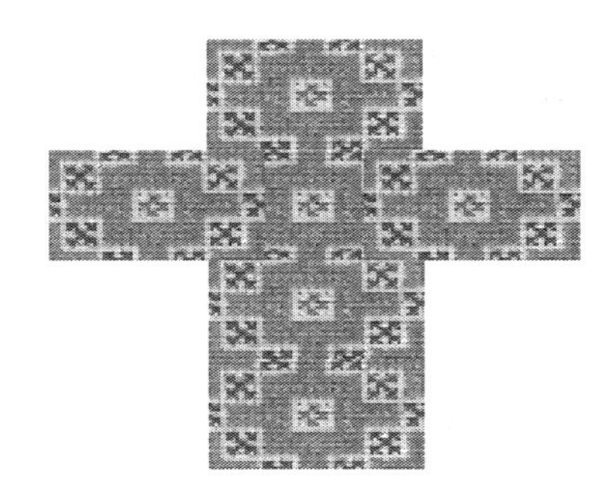

To My Loving Parents

Txoov Neeb Xyooj
&
Ntxhi Tsab Xyooj

Parents-in-law

Txhiaj Foom Yaj
&
Phuab Kwm Yaj

My Family

Rena Yang Xyooj,
Tiffany, Timothy,
Thomas, and Anthony

About the Author

Jay Xiong, Hmong: Zeb Xyooj, is the author of the **Hmong Dictionary** called "**Lus Hmoob Txhais**", and also the **owner** and **author** of the ***www.HmongDictionary.com***. Mr. Xiong is also one of the key contributors to the ***www.MicrosoftTranslator.com*** where he provided this dictionary with more than 6,000 Hmong entries to help kick start the translation engine in November 2011. Mr. Xiong also has taught many Hmong classes to children and adults in the past.

Mr. Xiong has a great passion to preserve, improve and educate the Hmong language by offering his service freely to the world at **www.HmongDictionary.com** since 2003.

Mr. Xiong received an Associate Degree in Mechanical Design from Lakeshore Technical College. His professional work experience includes 10+ years in Geographic Information System (GIS) and Mapping, GIS application programming, and 11+ years in Database Design and Database Management, Website Design and Computer Programming. Mr. Xiong speaks and writes Hmong, Laos and English.

You can visit his online dictionary at: **www.HmongDictionary.com**

B*elieving is not good enough, you have to accomplish it to prove to yourself – JX.*

A *hidden knowledge is like a hidden star, it shines nowhere – JX.*

I*f I focus on one thing long enough, I become the seed of that thing – JX.*

R*ua muag thiaj pom ntuj; qhib siab thiaj pom txuj – JX.*

Acknowledgments

I would like to thank the following people for their time and knowledge to help with this book. Without their help and invaluable suggestions, this book would be like a song without lyrics.

☆ **Travis Gore**	Hmong name is Peev Xwm xeem Khab. Chico, California. Business website: www.travisgore.com
☆ **Sarah Gore**	Hmong name is Nkauj Dawb xeem Khab. Chico, California.
☆ **Amy Ross**	Hmong name is Nkauj Hli, Music Teacher. Crescent City, California.
☆ **Paj Cai Xyooj**	Business Owner, B.S. in Civil Engineer and M.S. in Business. Melbourne, Australia.
☆ **Charles Tsu Vue**	Associate Director of Multicultural Affairs Office and Hmong Language Instructor – UW-Eau Claire, Wisconsin.
☆ **Dr. Douglas-Chuedoua Vue**	Professor, Ph.D. in Education. Milwaukee, Wisconsin.
☆ **Nick Poss, Ph.D.**	Columbus, Ohio.
☆ **Phong Yang**	Hmong Language Instructor, M.A. Linguistics. California State University, Fresno.
☆ **Yer T. Yang**	High School Teacher – Sheboygan, Wisconsin. Master of Education with emphasis on ELL Education

Last but not least, I want to thank God for his endless love, wisdom and forgiveness he has given me. When I was in doubt, he poured in more confidence; when I was hopeless, he blessed with his love, and when I sinned, he kindly disciplined.

CEEB TOOM

Phau ntawv no tsis yog siv los qhia txog kev kawm lus Askiv, tabsis yog sau los pab rau cov neeg uas paub lus Askiv zoo es xav kawm txog lus Hmoob xwb. Cov lus Askiv txhais thiab sau nyob hauv phau ntawv no yog txhais **raws** lus Hmoob, xws li: **Koj los pab kuv = You come help me.**
Es tsis sau tias:
You come *to* help me.
Tabsis lus Askiv tiag ces sau li kab uas *muaj "**to**" dhau los.*

DISCLAIMER

Although every precaution has been taken in the preparation and writing of this book, the author assumes no responsibility for errors, omisions, and/or incorrect translations. Furthermore, the author assumes no liability of any damages resulting from the use of the information contained herein. In addition, there are words referenced in here which may have multiple meanings; therefore, please check with other Hmong dictionaries, and consult with Hmong speakers for appropriate use. Last but not least is that some words and graphic images illustrated in this book may not be suitable for all ages; however, as an author, I want this book to be beneficial and comprehensive to the people who wish to learn the Hmong language as much as possible.

Hmong have this old saying, "*Xav luaj ntuj los xu luaj nyuj; xav luaj teb los xu luaj zeb.*" In English it simply means one can think and prepare as big as the universe, but still will miss something as big as a cow, and when one thinks or prepares as big as a farm, he still will miss something as big as a rock. In other words, human beings are not perfect no matter how hard we try.

Nov kuv yuav tham me ntsis lus Hmoob vim phau ntawv no sau los pab qhia rau cov neeg uas paub lus Askiv zoo lawm, tabsis lawv ho xav kawm lus Hmoob. Yog li, cov lus txhais ua Askiv ces **tsis yog** lossis **tsis sau raws li kev siv lus Askiv** nawb. Qhov no vim yog lus Hmoob tsis muaj ib cov lus li lus Askiv. Piv txwv li zaj lus hauv qab no:

Hmoob		**Askiv**
Kuv *nyiam* haus dej.	Txhais ua lus Askiv ces yog:	I *like* **to** drink water.

Sab lus Hmoob ces muaj **4** lo lus, tabsis sab lus Askiv ces muaj **5** lawm vim sab Askiv muaj lo lus "**to**" uas lus Hmoob tsis muaj. Yog li, kev txhais thiaj li sau li hauv qab no:

Hmoob yog: **Kuv *nyiam* haus *dej*.**
Askiv yog: **I *like* drink *water*.** Tus neeg paub lus Askiv zoo ces nws paub tias *yog "I like **to** drink water" lawm.*

Qhov txhais li no mas vim yog kuv xav kom cov neeg kawm lus Hmoob paub tias:
Kuv = ***I***, **nyiam** = ***like***, **haus** = ***drink***, **dej** = ***water***.

Tsis tag li no xwb, kev txhais lus Askiv los tseem muab *sau raws li lus Hmoob*, xws li: *Koj nyob qhov twg?* = ***You live where?*** Tabsis qhov yog lus Askiv tiag ces yog li no: **Where do you live?** Uas yog txhais ua lus Hmoob ces ho yog: *Qhov twg koj nyob?*

Contents

INTRODUCTION

The purpose of this book is to offer a different and non-linguistic approach to learning the Hmong language. By non-linguistic approach I meant from a person, me, who is not a linguist, but have a great desire to share with people who are interested to learn the Hmong language in a different way. Another reason that motivated me to write this book is the number of people who supported my effort and my website, www.HmongDictionary.com, since 2003, and their encouragement for writing this book.

The Hmong language, like many human languages, has pronouns, adverbs, verbs, conjunctions, adjectives, nouns and the likes; however, with its own morphology and syntax. A human language is no different than a computer language, and we need to know one, hopefully, our native language well before trying to learn a second one. With this being said, I hope you are fluent either in English or in Hmong because throughout this book there are many comparisons between them. In its simplistic term, a **human language** is a means *to converse* or *to speak*, and a **computer language** is a means *to execute* or *run* a specific program or command. For humans, the exact words a person converses or speaks to get his result might vary from person to person, and this variation happens because there are many different choices of words or synonyms to choose from when forming his/her instructions. For the most part, the Hmong language does not have many synonyms in comparison to the English language, and that is easy to learn, but it is extremely hard to explain and define.

Furthermore, the **Hmong language has two dialects**: Hmong Der (also known as White), and Hmong Leng or Hmong Joua (also known as Green). Many Hmong people who came from China many centuries ago spoke the Hmong Leng dialect. For the most part, my guess is, that 75 percent of the words from these two dialects are exactly the same – *both pronunciations and meanings*; however, there are a few words that have the same spellings and pronunciations but have different meanings. For example, the Hmong Der word "**txav**" means "***to move***" but it means "***to cut***" in Hmong Leng. However, this book covers only the Hmong Der dialect, and I want to apologize for not being able to cover both at this time – ***please see page 147*** for some basic differences between these two dialects.

Learning a new language both spoken and written forms at the same time can be done, but you have to be patient because you are being born into the new language. If you already know the spoken form and need to learn only the written form then it might be a few months; however, if you are trying to learn both at the same time, it will be a few years. However, the neat part about *knowing another language is like knowing another cooking recipe*. Therefore, I sincerely hope that the information I provided here is concise and useful enough that you will not only be able follow my recipe, but also be able to speak and write Hmong better than some native Hmong. Last but not least is that there are many words used throughout this book that have multiple meanings, and this is true not only for Hmong but also for English. Additionally, most translations may not be *proper English translation* but rather literal translation to help you understand the number of words used in both Hmong and English. For example:

	Hmong	English	
The Hmong sentence is correct.	*Kuv nyiam haus dej.*	*I like drink water.*	The English sentence is not correct because it is missing the "**to**" after the verb "like."
	And not	*I like **to** drink water.*	

In other words, **Kuv** = *I*, **nyiam** = *like*, **haus** = *drink*, and **dej** = *water*.

The Hmong People, Culture, and Language

The **Hmong** are an Asian ethnic group, *the majority are in China*, from the mountainous and many isolated regions of China, Vietnam, Laos, Burma, and Thailand. After the United States Secret War in Laos ended in 1975 many of the Hmong, estimated **100,000**+, had migrated to the United States, Canada, France, Japan, Argentina, Germany, New Zealand, and Australia. The **Hmong culture** is very much like many other cultures; however, one distinctive difference of the Hmong culture is that the Hmong people are organized into **18** last names or clans. Furthermore, the Hmong culture prohibits marriage between two people with the same last name. Hmong believe that those who have the same last name came from the same ancestors.

The **main religion** of the Hmong people prior to 1975 is mainly ***Shamanism*** – a belief and practice of the spiritual world. However, many of the Hmong people who now live in the United States have changed from Shamanism to Christianity. This change of religion has spread for many Hmong people around the globe today. *One can not choose to be a shaman*, however, but only the spirit can choose who can be a shaman, and either gender can become a shaman. Generally it does not cost anything to consult with a shaman regarding one's illness until his/her illness is cured.

Hmong did not have a written language where it was taught and learned openly until **1952** and **1953** when a Protestant missionary **Dr. Lindwood Barney**, a Roman Catholic missionary **Father Yves Bertrais** (better known as **Txiv Plig Nyiaj Pov**), and **Dr. William A. Smalley** who came to Laos to help create the Latin script for Hmong words. This Hmong language is what we currently use these days, also better known as the Romanized Popular Alphabet (RPA) system. Another popular Hmong script is called "**Pahawh**" which was invented by a Hmong *spiritual* and *highly respected* person named Shong Lue Yang, **Soob Lwj Yaj** in Hmong.

The **Hmong language** is considered a tonal language, and for the most part, about **90** percent of the words are monosyllabic. The language is spoken with open syllables. Similar to most human languages, the Hmong language also follows the ***subject-verb-object*** syntax structure. Unlike English, Hmong do not have the plural forms, "**-s, -en**" and verbs remain the same regardless of whether you use it to refer to the first, second, and third person. Additionally, there are no *participles* in Hmong, i.e., "**-ed**, **-ing**, and **-en**" and no *verbal nouns or gerunds*, i.e., the **writ*ing*** of this book. In addition, Hmong do not have **long** and **short vowels** – just *one pronunciation* for each vowel. Therefore, reading and writing Hmong is very consistent even words that you have never seen nor heard before *you can still write them correctly.* There are **seven distinctive tones** in the Hmong language and there are roughly about **13** vowels.

However, I believe there are more vowels/sounds than these that have not been identified due to the lack of adequate research into the Hmong spoken language. For example, the Hmong sound "**au**", as in the English word **L*ao***, and the Hmong sound "**oe**" as in the English word **t*oe*** do exist, but the Hmong people just use the "**au**" to represent both sounds. For example, the word "**oeb**" is commonly used as an exclamation. For example: ***Oeb**, koj tuaj thiab los?* And the Hmong word "**aub**" means a *dog* and it also means to *carry on the back* in Hmong Leng, and these two words clearly have two distinctive sounds or phonics; however, we will leave this topic for a different book.

Suggestion for Learning the Hmong Language

When learning a new language you need to train your ears to hear the different sounds and tones of that language so your hearing can steer your tongue and mouth to speak that new language correctly. This process will take time; however, I truly believe that most of us can learn any new language no matter how old we are. However, the trick of learning a new language is to have an attainable goal with simple steps so you can learn it properly from the start. Once you have gained some confidence and believe you can learn more, the rest is just a matter of time, commitment and to immerse yourself into that new language. Next is to repeat and practice pronouncing the words that you are not good at, and ask a lot of questions. Your mind is like a tool, the more times you sharpen it, the more sharp it will get. Lao people have a saying that, "*10 ears heard is not as good as one eye sees; ten eyes saw is not as good as one hand touches.*"

With that being said, reading and learning from this book alone without actually seeing how a native Hmong person talks and hearing the actual words being pronounced in front of you is not going to be the same; however, I believe you can learn a lot by reading and learning from a good book on your own. With that being said, if you **read through this book** and **fully comprehend what I presented here**, you should be able to ***read*** and ***write*** Hmong as well as be able to ***engage*** in simple Hmong conversation. Most importantly, I have provided audio for most of the important pages so it is like having a live Hmong instructor helping you any time you are ready to learn. Last but not least is try to focus on words that are easy, and you like the most. Not sure about you, but for me, I seem to learn the best when I like what I am learning the most.

Learning Strategies

1. **Learn the English alphabet**
2. **Learn the Hmong vowels**
3. **Learn to pronounce the single consonants**
4. **Learn the Hmong tones**
5. **Learn the rest of the polyconsonants**
6. **Learn the pronouns, verbs and adverbs**
7. **Learn the adjectives, conjunctions and prepositions**
8. **Learn the numbers, 1 to 100,000 and more**
9. **Learn some of the differences between English and Hmong**
10. **Learn the Hmong classifiers**
11. **Learn the Hmong Grammar**

For introduction to the Hmong language, you might want to teach as follows:
1. Consonants
2. Vowels
3. Tones
4. Pronouns, and
5. Simple Phrases

Please refer to *www.HmongDictionary.com/***learnhmong** for applicable audio and additional resources.

Last but not least is **to not skip** any lines or pages because everything I put in this book is imperatively helpful to your learning, and thank you for your interest in learning the **Hmongology** (my new word) – *the study of the Hmong people, culture, and language.*

Simplified Consonants and New Vowels

For your information only

Six of the following original consonants, **np, nts,** and **nk** have very similar phonics to the English letters **b, j,** and **g,** i.e., **b**aw, **j**aw, and **g**aw. For this reason, some Hmong people use these new consonants in place of the original ones. Below are some words in both the new and the original forms.

No	Original	New	Word with Original	Word with Simplified
1	np	b	**np**ua	**b**ua
2	npl	bl	**npl**ua	**bl**ua
3	nplh	blh	**nplh**aib	**blh**aib
4	nts	j	**nts**aum	**j**aum
5	ntsh	jh	**ntsh**ai	**jh**ai
6	nk	g	**nk**aum	**g**aum
7	nkh	gh	**nkh**aus	**gh**aus

Useful Information

Nasal-aspirated means *puffing air* through your *nose* like the word "**h**mm", and **mouth-aspirated** means *puffing air* through your *mouth* like the word "**Th**ai."

Soft means **no** puffing sound – *unaspirated,* i.e., the "**p**" in the word "s**p**y" is a ***soft P, and hard*** means there is a puffing sound – *aspirated,* i.e., the "**p**" in the word "**p**ie" is a ***hard P.***
The **K**, **P**, and **T** pronunciation in Hmong is always *soft – no puffing sounds*, as in s**k**y, s**p**y, and s**t**ay.

The reason I mentioned these simplified consonants here is so you are aware that some of the younger Hmong people, especially those that live in the United States, have used both forms interchangeably.

A new vowel I also created is the "**H**" which is a ***silent vowel***. This "h" vowel is being used at the end of other vowels only, i.e., **ohs** and **ohm.** For example: "*Koj puas noj os?*" is the current or old writing method, and the above question can mean as follows:

1. Do you want to eat ***ducks***?
2. Do you want to eat [*with a different sound but having the same spelling "**os**"*]

The new way with the "**h**" is as follows:

1. Koj puas noj **os**? Means "*Do you want to eat **ducks**?*"
2. Koj puas noj o**h**s? Means "Do you want to eat [*with the correct Hmong sound*]

To utter this new word "o**h**s", you have to utter the "os" + "hos" = "ohs" which it happens more toward the very back of your tongue. There are other vowels that I had used in my dictionary to accommodate some of the English and Lao sounds that don't exist in Hmong. However, don't worry about these new vowels yet.

These are for your information only!

io = As in English L***eo***
oe = As in English t***oe***
ue = Similar to the English sound **oo-ay.** Hmong example: ***Hueb***! Ua twg lawm?
ui = As in the English word q***ui***t. Hmong example: ***Uib***! Ua cas tsis pom lawm?
oi = Hmong example: ***Oib***, tsis txhob ua li hos! By Dr. Chuedoua Vue.
wa = Like the Lao word ***khib nywab*** (garbage), for example.

The English Alphabet

The ***R**omanized **P**opular **A**lphabet*, RPA, is a Latin-based script which you already know. What you will have to learn is just the *new pronunciations*. Each Hmong consonant has the English phonics "***aw***" as in the word l***aw***, i.e., the English "**daw**" has the same pronunciation as the Hmong letter **D**.

No	Letter	English phonics	Hmong usage
1	A	**ah**, or **a** as in word ***a**bout*	vowel
2	B*	**b***aw*	tone marker. Also a simplified consonant
3	**C**	*no equivalent – learn later*	consonant – *you will learn this later*
4	D	**d***aw*	consonant – exactly like English D
5	E	**ay**, as in word *d**ay***	vowel
6	F	**f***aw*	consonant – exactly like English F
7	G*	**g***aw*	tone marker. Also a simplified consonant
8	H	**h***aw*	consonant – exactly like English H
9	I	**ee**, as in word *b**ee***	vowel
10	J*	**j***aw*	tone marker. Also a simplified consonant
11	K	**k***aw – soft k, like "s**kaw**"*	consonant – exactly like English ***soft*** K as in s***ky***
12	L	**l***aw*	consonant – exactly like English L
13	M	**m***aw*	consonant – exactly like English M
14	N	**n***aw*	consonant – exactly like English N
15	O	**aw**, as in word *l**aw***	vowel. This sounds exactly like the English word "**awe**"
16	P	**p***aw – soft p, like "s**paw**"*	consonant – exactly like English ***soft*** P, as in s*pin*
17	**Q**	*no equivalent – learn later*	consonant – *you will learn this later*
18	**R**	*no equivalent – learn later*	consonant – *you will learn this later*
19	S	**sh***aw, s =* ***sh*** *in English*	consonant – exactly like English "sh" as in **sh**e
20	T	t***aw*** *– soft t, like "s**taw**"*	consonant – exactly like English ***soft*** T as in s*tay*
21	U	**oo**, as in word *z**oo***	vowel
22	V	**v*aw***	consonant – exactly like English V
23	W	vowel **w** like "hmm" sound →	Pinch your nose tight, open your mouth and say "**hmm**" similar to "***ah***" but with the "**hmm**" sound. No puffing!
24	X	**s***aw, x =* ***s*** *in English*	consonant – exactly like English S
25	Y	**y***aw*	consonant – exactly like English Y
26	Z	**zh***aw – like in "mea**saw**"*	consonant – like syllable "**-sion**" of the word vi***sion*** – vi***saw***

The English word "**tasty**" has two **T***s*. The first **T** is uttered with a *puff of air – aspirated*, but not the second **T.** The first **T** is called a ***hard T***, and the second **T** is called a ***soft T***.

The Hmong k, p, t are uttered without *the puff of air.*

* Some people use "**b**" to replace "np", "**g**" to replace "nk" and "**j**" to replace "nts"

Now you are ready to learn the rest of the **Hmong vowels,** but don't worry because some of these vowels do follow the same English phonetical methodology. Furthermore, there are *no short and long vowels* in Hmong. In other words, there is only *one type of pronunciation* for each vowel.

Hmong Vowels and English Equivalent Sounds

No	Hmong Vowel	English phonics	As in English word
1	a	***ah***	**a**bout
2	***ai***	***ai***	Th**ai**
3	au	***ao***	L**ao**
4	aw	***er***	p**er**. **Do not curl** your tongue for the "r", however.
5	e	***ay***	d**ay**
6	ee	***eng***	**Eng**lish
7	i	***ee***	b**ee**
8	***ia***	***ia***	k**ia**
9	o	***aw***	l**aw**
10	oo	***ong***	am**ong**
11	u	***oo***	z**oo**
12	ua	***oua***	M**oua**
13	w	***w***[1] Letter for this sound	*This vowel has the sound of the English "**hmm**" but don't utter the "h" with your mouth open – see above.*
14	aa*	***ung***	l**ung**. *This is a Hmong Leng vowel.

To utter the Hmong **W** vowel:

1. Pinch your nose tight.
2. Open your mouth and act like you're going to say "ah" but instead utter "hmm" or "ewh" with your mouth open.

[1] From now on, we will be using the letter **w** to represent the English "**hmm**" sound as well as the Hmong **w** vowel.

Each of the Hmong words below has three parts: *consonant + vowel + the **S** tone.* The **S** tone has a similar pitch to the first musical note "**Do**" as in "***Do*** *Re Mi Fa So La Ti.*" Also, I considered this "S" tone the ***mid*** or ***neutral*** tone. From now on, we will spell "Do" like "**Doe**" instead.

No	Hmong words with the "s" tone – *"Doe" pitch.*													
1	English **phonics**	*dah*	*dai*	*dao*	*der*	*day*	*deng*	*dee*	*daw*	*dong*	*doo*	*doua*	*dw*	*dung*
2	*Hmong*	das	dais	daus	daws	des	dees	dis	dos	doos	dus	duas	dws	daas
3	**phonics**	*nah*	*nai*	*nao*	*ner*	*nay*	*neng*	*nee*	*naw*	*nong*	*noo*	*noua*	*nw*	*nung*
4	*Hmong*	nas	nais	naus	naws	nes	nees	nis	nos	noos	nus	nuas	nws	naas
5	**phonics**	*lah*	*lai*	*lao*	*ler*	*lay*	*leng*	*lee*	*law*	*long*	*loo*	*loua*	*lw*	*lung*
6	*Hmong*	las	lais	laus	laws	les	lees	lis	los	loos	lus	luas	lws	laas

The Hmong word "**d*es***" sounds exactly like the English word "**d*ay***" with the "***Doe***" pitch.

Please circle the English sound on the right column that has the sound of the Hmong vowel on the left column. Make a few copies of this page and study ***until you know them all***.

Hmong Vowel	English Sound	Hmong Vowel	English Sound	Hmong Vowel	English Sound	Hmong Vowel	English Sound
a	ao ah ay	**i**	ao ee ay	**u**	ao oo ay	**o**	ee *aw* ao
ee	ao ee *eng*	**e**	*ay* ee eng	**oo**	ao ee *ong*	**ia**	ee aw *ia*
i	ee ay ah	**ai**	ia ay ai	**i**	ee ay ah	**e**	oo ay ee
oo	oo ong aw	**aw**	oo ong er	**w**	w ong aw	**a**	ah oo aw
ua	oo oua aw	**au**	oo oua ao	**u**	oo oua aw	**w**	w oo ee
w	ao ay w	**oo**	ao ong ew	**ai**	ao ai ew	**u**	oo ee ay
ai	ai ia ah	**a**	ai ia ah	**o**	ai aw ah	**ia**	oo ia ai
e	ay ee oo	**ee**	eng ee oo	**ai**	ay ai oo	**w**	w ay ee
aw	ee ay er	**i**	ee ay er	**e**	ee ay er	**u**	ay ee oo
w	aw w ay	**o**	aw ee ay	**a**	aw ew ah	**o**	aw oo ee
ua	oua aw ao	**ia**	oua aw ia	**aw**	oua er ao	**ua**	oo oua ay
o	aw oua ao	**w**	w oua ao	**u**	aw oo ao	**o**	ee oo aw
u	oo aw ee	**ua**	oo oua ee	**a**	oo aw ah	**i**	oo ee ay
oo	ong ung ay	**o**	ong ung aw	**ee**	eng ung ay	**aw**	er aw oo
ia	ia ai ee	**i**	ia ai ee	**ai**	ee ai oo	**u**	oo ee ah
w	ai w oo	**aw**	ai er oo	**o**	ai ew aw	**aa**	ah ung oo
u	oo ai ia	**a**	oo ah ia	**ua**	oo oua ia	**o**	aw oo ee
a	oo ah ee	**ia**	oo ah ia	**w**	oo ah w	**ai**	oo ai aw
oo	ai ay ong	**o**	ai aw ong	**u**	ai oo ong	**ee**	ee ay eng
ai	ia ee ai	**ia**	ia ee ai	**oo**	ia ong ai	**i**	ee ay oo
e	ee ay ao	**ee**	ee ay eng	**ai**	ee ay ai	**w**	ee oo w
ai	ai ia oo	**a**	ai ah oo	**w**	w ia oo	**u**	ee oo ay
w	oo w aw	**aw**	oo er aw	**ua**	oua ew aw	**a**	oo ee ah
ua	ao oua oo	**u**	ao oua oo	**a**	ao oua ah	**o**	ee aw oo
ee	eng oo ee	**aw**	eng oo er	**e**	eng oo ay	**ai**	ee ai oo
a	ah ee ay	**u**	ah oo ay	**ia**	ah ee ia	**e**	aw ay oo
aw	er oo oua	**aa**	ung oo oua	**o**	er oo aw	**u**	aw oo oua

Before we learn more Hmong words, let's recite the **K**, **P**, and **T** letters again to make sure you understand the way I expect you to pronounce certain sound segments from certain words. In English there is a "*puff of air*" uttered after the consonants **k**, **p**, and **t** such as words **key**, **pie**, and **tay**. In Hmong we omit this "*puff of air*" and pronounce the **k**, **p**, and **t** consonants like in words "s**ki**, s**py**, and s**tay**" but without the "s" instead. In other words, "**tay**" has the "*puff of air*" but when you add the "**s**", "stay", the "*buff of air*" goes away. The "*puff of air*" consonants do exist in Hmong, but we add the "**h**" *after* these consonants, i.e., **k***h*, **p***h*, and **t***h* to indicate such a "*puffing*" utterance. Therefore, the Hmong ***kh***, ***ph*** and ***th*** have the same pronounciations like the English *hard* **k**, **p**, and **t** – thanks to Dr. Nick Poss for this.

With that being said, I have recorded two words, "**stay**" and "**Tay**", *see below*, and the "**tay**" sound segments from these two words are the same. The purpose of this graph is to show you that when I ask you to utter "**tay**" like the word "s**tay**" it means you pronounce "**tay**" the same way as the "**-tay**" of the word "stay." In other words, you only mute the "**s**" from the word "s**tay**." For example, the Hmong word "**tes**" has the exact phonics or sound like the "*-tay*" of the English word "s**tay**", and "**tes**" means *a* **hand** in Hmong.

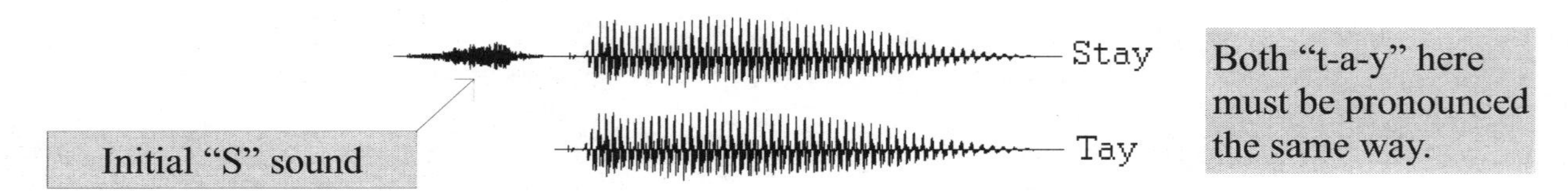

The purpose of this exercise is to train you in advance because we will be borrowing many sound segments from many English words to help you pronounce some of the Hmong words and consonants.

Below are more detailed explanations of how you should pronounce the **K**, **P**, **T**, and **Z** in Hmong.

Hmong	English pronunciation and remark
K kos = *kaw*	Utter this **K** as in the English word "s**ky**" – *soft* K. In other words, only pronounce the "**ky**" exactly as how you say "**-ky**" in the word "s**ky**." Now say the word "s**kaw**" as how you say "**sky**" but mute the "s" and only say "**kaw**."
P pos = *paw*	Utter this **P** as in the English word "spy" – *soft* P. In other words, only pronounce the **"py"** exactly as how you say "**-py**" in the word "s**py**." Now say the word "s**paw**" as how you say "s**py**" but mute the "s" and only say "**paw**." The Hmong word "**pos**" has the same phonics like the "**-paw**" of the English word "spaw."
T tos = *taw*	Utter this **T** as in the English word "s**tay**" – *soft* T. In other words, only pronounce the "**tay**" exactly as how you say "**tay**" in the word "s**tay**." Now say the word "s**taw**" as how you say "s**tay**" but mute the "s" and only say "**taw**." The Hmong word "**tos**" has the same phonics like the "**-taw**" of the English word "staw."
Z zos = *zaw*	Utter this **Z** as in the English word "mea**sure**" – like **zher**. In other words, the "**-sure**" must be pronounced like in the word "mea**sure**." Now replace mea***sure*** with mea***saw*** (***zhaw***) and the "**-saw**" syllable or sound segment is exactly like the Hmong "**zos**." **Do not** say the "**z**" of the word "**z***aw*" as in the English word "zip", however.

Another letter I want to cover again is the Hmong vowel "**w**". This Hmong vowel has the sound segment of the English word "**hmm**" but without the "**h**" – *nasal-aspirated* and without the "**mm**" – *closed lips*. Here is how to utter this Hmong "**w**" vowel. First, **pinch your nose tight** and **open your mouth**, and then utter the English word "***ah***" and then the word "*hmm*", but *don't puff any air through your mouth*, however, and *with your mouth open*. If you do this correctly, what you uttered should be the the Hmong "**w**" sound. Again, transfer the "**a**-" as in **a**bout to "**w**" as in word "hmm" only.

Now let's finish learning the remaining single consonants, **C**, **Q**, and **R**. The first letter we are going to learn is the "**C**", pronounced "**cos**." To help you learn even better, I have provided a partial and side view of how your tongue, teeth, and mouth are working together to produce the Hmong consonant "**cos**." To further help you learn Hmong or any new language for that matter is to understand that your mouth, tongue and teeth are like a musical instrument that it can play just about any musical notes; however, playing a new note requires a new tongue and mouth movement. Below is an image showing how you should form your mouth to say the Hmong consonant "**C**".

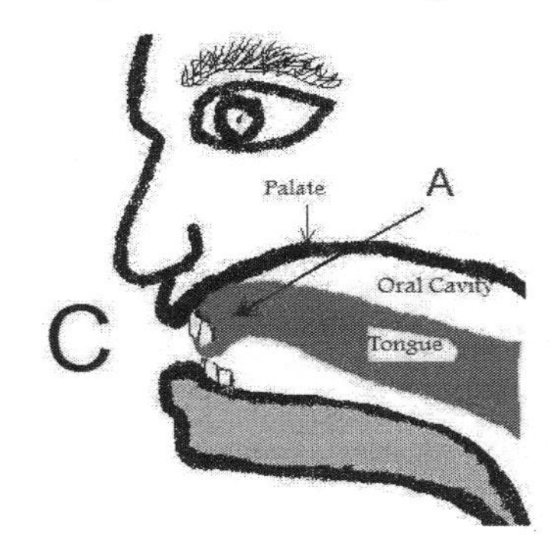

A sound segment we can use is from the English word *situation*. The sound segment we need is the capitalized letters of the word si**TU**ation. Make sure you don't say "**TU**" as **CH**OO, but without the "**H**" and that would be very close to the Hmong sound "**cus.**" In other words, the phonics spelling is "si-**tu**-Ay-shuhn" and not as "si-**choo**-Ay-shuhn." If you stick your tongue past your two teeth like the picture on the left ***without*** **aspirating** the "**h**" then the "C*H*OO" will sound like "**cus**" in Hmong.

Another English word that has the parts we need to learn the Hmong "**C**" is perhaps the word "**itch**" but end without aspirating the "*h*", i.e., i**tc**. Now let's create a new word "**itc*h*aw**" but say this word like "*itcaw*" and the syllable "*-caw*" of this word should be close to the Hmong "**cos**" sound. The other word you can try is the word "**speec*h***" but not aspirating the "*h*". In other words, say it like "spee**c**" by ending the "**c**" with your mouth and tongue looking like the image above. Make sure not uttering "speec" like "spee**k**", however. This Hmong **C** perhaps is difficult for most English speakers because the **C** letter alone sounds either like a K, **k**it, or like an S as in **c**ell. So try saying the words **chat** and **child** without aspirating the "h" and by making your mouth and tongue looking like the image above and see if it helps you. Make sure you place your tongue between both teeth very similar to how you say the English word "**th**at", but *bend your tongue* and *press it against your teeth* like **point A**.

It is helpful for me to think about pressing my tongue against the back of my teeth to pronounce "cos" – Dr. Nick Poss.

The English pronunciation for words such as **key**, **pie** and **tay** are considered "***hard***" *k, p,* and *t* also known as *aspirated*. For example, the word "**tas**ty" has two "Ts". The first **T** – "*-tas*" has the *audible puff of breath* uttered after, but not the second **T** – "*-ty*." The second T's pronunciation is called the ***soft T*** – *unaspirated*. In Hmong, an "h" is placed after the consonant, i.e., kh, ph and th to indicate the "*puff of air*." And without the "h" placed after, the pronunciation is always **soft** or **unaspirated**.

How to Pronounce the Consonant Q

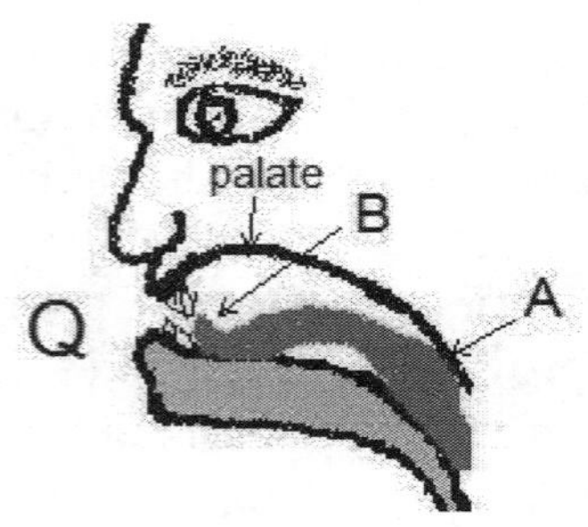

The pronunciation of this consonant *perhaps* only exists in the Hmong language because Hmong used to live close to too many frogs in the past. Other than that, I can't think of any words in English that would come close to this "**Q**", pronounced "**qos.**" But let's not give up because if frogs can say it, we can, too. So let's try this. First, open your mouth but close your *oral cavity*, **point A**, so that the back of your tongue is blocking all air and is touching both sides of your oral cavity. Then make the tip of your tongue curve and touch the bottom teeth as shown in **point B.** In other words, say this consonant "Q" from the back of your throat by lowering your tongue at **point A**. You **might have to gag** the first few tries, but don't give up because we know it can be done.

1. Once you are able to make your mouth and tongue looking like the picture above, you are now ready to call the most beautiful **Miss Frog** ever! Who?
2. Okay, are you ready? Making sure you are *ready to gag* and then utter the word "**who**" but **do not** let any air escape through your nose nor your mouth. That is it. If you can do this, you can go call Miss Frog **Who!** – "**quj**" in Hmong, and she might even *nyiam* koj, *like* you.

How to Pronounce the Consonant R

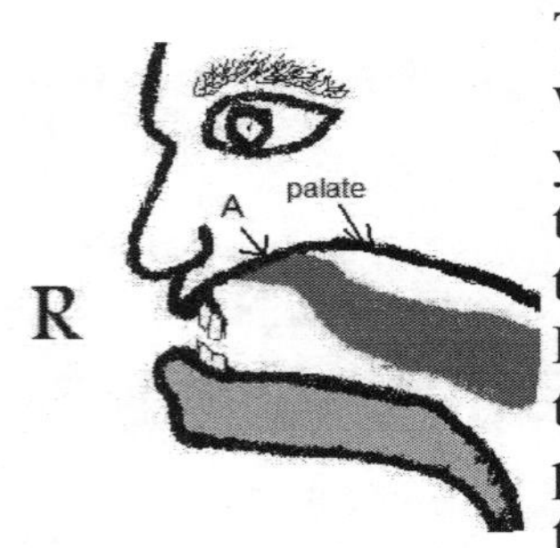

The closest English word to this Hmong **R**, pronounced "ros", is perhaps the word "**true**." Now say this word "**true**" a few times and pay close attention to your tongue forming position. The tip of your tongue should look very close to the image on the left. In other words, you are saying the "**tr**" near the tip and top part of your tongue, **point A**, ***without puffing*** like the normal word "**true**." Meaning make your tongue and mouth ready to utter the word "**true**" but only to drop your tongue almost like saying the English word "**do**." The English phonics of the word "**true**" sounds very close to the Hmong word "**rhuj"** and the subtle difference is the Hmong word "**rhuj**" is being uttered by merely opening or lowering the tip of the tongue at **point A** from your palate with ***a puffing*** sound to form the "h" only. In other words, place your tongue in a position to say the word "true", but then *slightly curl* the tip of your tongue, *point A*, so that it is pressing against the ridge on the roof of the mouth when uttering the Hmong "ros." Try saying the word "**tr̲aw**" with a *soft T*, unaspirated, to see if that helps you.

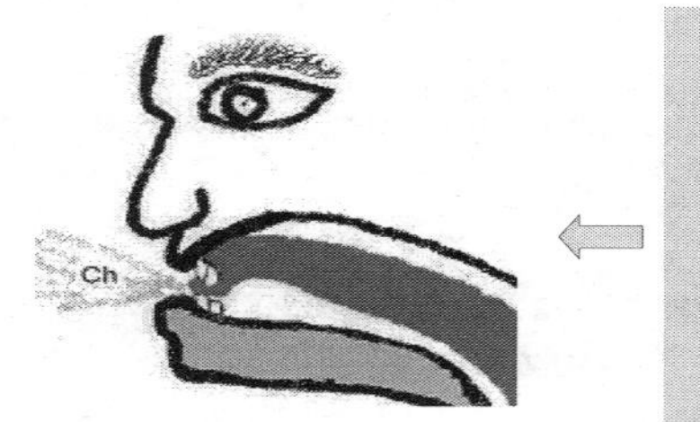

Mouth-aspirated means exhale thru your mouth after other letters, i.e., "C" as in C**h̲ay**.

Nasal-aspirated means exhale thru your nose to form the "**H**" sound, i.e., "hmm" before the rest, i.e., *mong* as in the word **H̲**mong.

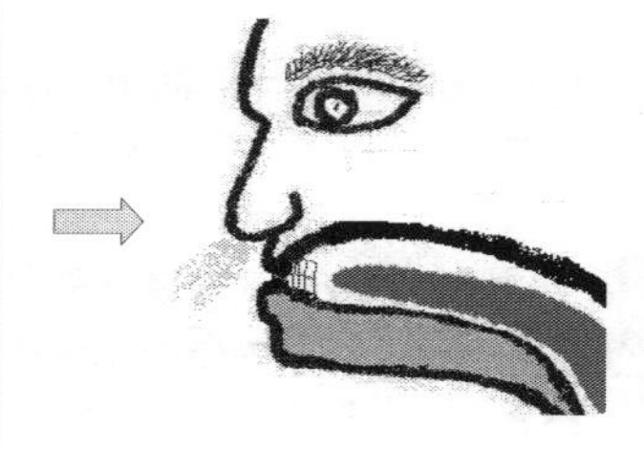

Letters such as the **L**, **M**, and **N** are *unaspirated consonants* – no puffing sounds.

Hmong Tones

What is a tone? In human language, a tone is a **pitch** stressed *with* a particular word or a syllable of word. For example, the English word "**yo-yo**" has two pitches or *tones* – "**YO**-yo", *high* pitch to *low* pitch respectively. A tone is then similar to the English musical notes "***Do Re Me So Fa Ti***." With that said, we are going to use the first note "**Do**", spelled "**Doe**" from here on which has the same pitch as the Hmong "**S**" tone marker. This "**S**" tone marker is called the *cim **Mus***, and the English phonics for the Hmong word "**mus**" is "**moo**." Okay, now you sound like a cow. **:)** Make sure you utter "**moo**" with the same "**Doe**" pitch or like the pitch of the syllable "**a**-" as in word "**a**bout", and not like "**moo**!"

Below are some simple words ending with the "**S**" tone marker with no particular meanings.

No														
1	**English**	dah	dai	dao	der	day	deng	dee	dia	daw	dong	doo	doua	dw
2	*Hmong*	*das*	*dais*	*daus*	*daws*	*des*	*dees*	*dis*	*dias*	*dos*	*doos*	*dus*	*duas*	*dws*
3	**English**	mah	mai	mao	mer	may	meng	mee	mia	maw	mong	moo	moua	mw
4	*Hmong*	*mas*	*mais*	*maus*	*maws*	*mes*	*mees*	*mis*	*mias*	*mos*	*moos*	*mus*	*muas*	*mws*
5	*Hmong*	*nas*	*nais*	*naus*	*naws*	*nes*	*nees*	*nis*	*nias*	*nos*	*noos*	*nus*	*nuas*	*nws*

If without the "s" tone marker, words "**dai** and **dia**" would have the same spelling and pronunciation in both Hmong and English. The Hmong word "**dai**" means *to hang,* and *"dia"* means *a spoon, i.e., ib dia mov – a spoon of rice*. Let's see what some of these Hmong words mean in English.

Hmong	English	Hmong	English	Hmong	English	Hmong	English	Hmong	English
daws	**to untie**	dos	**onion**	mis	**breast**	mos	**young**	mus	**to go**
muas	**to buy**	nas	**squirrel**	nees	**horse**	nias	**push**	nus	**brother**

Single Consonants and Vowels

Below is a table with single consonants and the 13 vowels with the "**S**" tone – ***Doe** pitch*.

English	*ah*	*ai*	*ao*	*er*	*ay*	*eng*	*ee*	*ia*	*aw*	*ong*	*oo*	*oua*	*w*
1	ba*s*	ba*is*	ba*us*	ba*ws*	be*s*	bee*s*	bi*s*	bi*as*	bo*s*	boo*s*	bu*s*	bu*as*	bw*s*
2	cas	cais	caus	caws	ces	cees	cis	cias	cos	coos	cus	cuas	cws
3	das	dais	daus	daws	des	dees	dis	dias	dos	doos	dus	duas	dws
4	fas	fais	faus	faws	fes	fees	fis	fias	fos	foos	fus	fuas	fws
5	gas	gais	gaus	gaws	ges	gees	gis	gias	gos	goos	gus	guas	gws
6	has	hais	haus	haws	hes	hees	his	hias	hos	hoos	hus	huas	hws
7	jas	jais	jaus	jaws	jes	jees	jis	jias	jos	joos	jus	juas	jws
8	kas	kais	kaus	kaws	kes	kees	kis	kias	kos	koos	kus	kuas	kws
9	las	lais	laus	laws	les	lees	lis	lias	los	loos	lus	luas	lws

10	mas	mais	maus	maws	mes	mees	mis	mias	mos	moos	mus	muas	mws
11	nas	nais	naus	naws	nes	nees	nis	nias	nos	noos	nus	nuas	nws
12	pas	pais	paus	paws	pes	pees	pis	pias	pos	poos	pus	puas	pws
13	qas	qais	qaus	qaws	qes	qees	qis	qias	qos	qoos	qus	quas	qws
14	ras	rais	raus	raws	res	rees	ris	rias	ros	roos	rus	ruas	rws
15	sas	sais	saus	saws	ses	sees	sis	sias	sos	soos	sus	suas	sws
16	tas	tais	taus	taws	tes	tees	tis	tias	tos	toos	tus	tuas	tws
17	vas	vais	vaus	vaws	ves	vees	vis	vias	vos	voos	vus	vuas	vws
18	xas	xais	xaus	xaws	xes	xees	xis	xias	xos	xoos	xus	xuas	xws
19	yas	yais	yaus	yaws	yes	yees	yis	yias	yos	yoos	yus	yuas	yws
20	zas	zais	zaus	zaws	zes	zees	zis	zias	zos	zoos	zus	zuas	zws

Okay, I sure hope you have mastered the "**S**" tone by now because we are going to add two more tones to this boring "**Doe**" pitch. These two new tones have the highest and lowest pitches in the Hmong language, and the closest English word that has these two pitches is the English word "**yo-yo**." The first syllable "**YO-**" has the higher pitch and that is equivalent to the Hmong tone "B" – *cim **Siab***. The second syllable "**-yo**" has the lower pitch which is equivalent to the Hmong tone "M" – *cim **Niam***. Now let's say this word "**YO-**yo" a few times from high to low pitches. Now read the below table starting from the left column, **YO-**, -yo, then **niab**, **niam** to **lab** and la*m*. Then read by row starting from syllable YO-, nia**b**, na**b** to la**b** – *b tone marker,* and then *-yo, niam to lam.*

Tone	**Pitch**					**Hmong words with tones**							
highest -b	**YO-**	nia^b	na^b	ne^b	nu^b	ni^b	dia^b	da^b	de^b	du^b	do^b	dee^b	la^b
lowest -m	-yo	nia$_m$	na$_m$	ne$_m$	nu$_m$	ni$_m$	dia^m	da$_m$	de$_m$	du$_m$	do$_m$	dee$_m$	la$_m$

Tone	**Pitch**					**Hmong words with tones**							
highest -b	**YO-**	A^b	YA^b	E^b	ye^b	yi^b	yia^b	nia^b	ye^b	yau^b	yo^b	yee^b	yai^b
lowest -m	-yo	A$_m$	YA$_m$	E$_m$	ye$_m$	yi$_m$	yia^m	nia$_m$	ye$_m$	yau$_m$	yo$_m$	yee$_m$	yai$_m$

Now let's add the mid tone **S** in between the *cim Siab* (b) and the *cim Niam* (m). Now read each column *from top to bottom*, i.e., "**YO-**, Doe, and -yo" and then "**sia**^{b}, nias, nia$_m$" etc...

Tone	**Pitch**					**Hmong words with tones**							
highest -b	**YO-**	n*ia*^{b}	***nab***	neb	nub	nib	diab	dab	deb	dub	dob	deeb	lab
mid -s	Doe	n*ias*	***nas***	nes	nus	nis	dias	das	des	dus	dos	dees	las
lowest -m	-yo	n*ia*$_m$	***nam***	nem	num	nim	diam	dam	dem	dum	dom	deem	lam

Make sure you say the syllable "**YO-**" the same way as in "**YO**-yo", and say the "-yo" the same way as in "**YO**-yo." This word "**YO**-yo" is your secret to learning the Hmong tones "sia**b**-nia**m**." In other words, "**YO**-yo" and "**YIA**-yia" do have the same pitches like the Hmong words "Sia**b** Nia**m**."

Please fill in the correct tones for the Hmong words on the right column for each English pitch on the left, *syllable*, column using our new word "a-**YO**-yo."

Pitch	Word	Pitch	Word	Pitch	Word	Pitch	Word	Pitch	Word
a-	mus	YO-	na__	-yo	de__	a-	me__	-yo	no__
YO-	sia^{b}	a-	na__	YO-	de__	YO-	me__	a-	no__
-yo	nia$_{m}$	-yo	na__	a-	de__	-yo	me__	YO-	no__

See if you can pronounce this Hmong writing, "**dis laim**" – English phonics: **dee lai**. Well, these two words are Lao words and it means "**very good**." See now you even learn another language, too. And another Lao word some Hmong people use a lot is "**pais**" – soft p, and it means to "**go**."

Now let's use just the three tone markers and see if you are still able to read the following words.

as	mus	dab	nam	yeb	dem	nas	meb	lom	hib	mus	nom
yau^{b}	sia^{b}	dam	nas	yem	des	yam	mes	los	his	mub	nob
yau$_{m}$	nia$_{m}$	das	nab	yes	deb	yab	mem	lob	him	mum	nos

Now let's learn some simple words that have these three tones.
Some of these words do have multiple meanings, however.

No	Hmong	English	No	Hmong	English
1	mus	to go	16	tob	deep
2	hais	to say or speak	17	mem	pen or pencil
3	paub	to know	18	nom	official
4	pom	to see	19	pib	begin, start
5	los	to come, to return	20	kim	expensive
6	deb	far	21	kib	to fry
7	dib	cucumber	22	kis	1. gap. 2. to spread
8	dam	to break	23	lis	to take care or work on
9	lem	to turn	24	lim	to filter
10	teb	to answer, respond	25	nab	snake
11	cem	to yell, scold	26	tam	to reserve (without pay)
12	ces	then	27	tas	done, finished
13	peb	we, three	28	lom	to poison
14	tos	to wait for	29	lob	to grab or take
15	tom	to bite, allege	30	zes	a nest

Well, with just three tones, we can't really create any meaningful Hmong songs so let us add two more tones, and their pitches are similar to the English word "**section**." Now, let's say this word "**SEC**-tion" like this: "**SEC**-" with an *upward pitch*, and then "**-tion**!" with a *downward or falling pitch.* The "**SEC**-" pitch is similar to the Hmong "**V**" tone – **cim Kuv**, and the "**-tion**" pitch is similar to the "**G**" tone – **cim Neeg**. So say this word "SEC-tion" a few times and then practice these words: **SEC**-tion and then with the Hmong tones **sec**^{v} **-tion**^{g} and then **da**^{v} **da**^{g} **de**^{v} **de**^{g} dov **dog** and **nav nag**.

Now read the following table, from left column "**SEC**-" to "-tion", "nav nag" and "nev neg" to the last column. Then read by row, starting "**SEC**-, nav, nev" to "lov", and then "-tion", nag to log.

No	**Pitch**	**Tone**	**Hmong words with tones**											
1	SEC-	v	na^v	nev	nov	duv	mev	div	nuv	liv	tiv	dev	deev	lov
2	-tion	g	na$_g$	neg	nog	dug	meg	dig	nug	lig	tig	deg	deeg	log

Now please fill in the appropriate Hmong tone markers.

Pitch	Word	Pitch	Word	Pitch	Word	Pitch	Word	Pitch	Word
SEC-	mu^v	-tion	na__	SEC-	de__	SEC-	me__	-tion	no__
-tion	mu$_g$	SEC-	na__	-tion	de__	-tion	me__	SEC-	no__

Now let's read the following table using the same system, starting from left column, "YO-, SEC-, a-, -tion, and -yo" and then "da*b* da*v* da*s* dag da*m*" etc... When you are done, read words by row starting from left to right, i.e., YO-, dab, daib to dwb.

No	**Pitch**	**Tone**	**Hmong words with tones**										
1	YO-	b	da^b	dai^b	dau^b	daw^b	de^b	dee^b	di^b	dia^b	do^b	du^b	dw^b
2	SEC-	v	dav	daiv	dauv	dawv	dev	deev	div	diav	dov	duv	dwv
3	a-	s	das	dais	daus	daws	des	dees	dis	dias	dos	dus	dws
4	-tion	g	dag	daig	daug	dawg	deg	deeg	dig	diag	dog	dug	dwg
5	-yo	m	da$_m$	dai$_m$	dau$_m$	daw$_m$	de$_m$	dee$_m$	di$_m$	dia$_m$	do$_m$	du$_m$	dw$_m$

Please fill in the corresponding Hmong tone for each English syllable.

No	pitch	tone	pitch	tone	pitch	tone	pitch	tone	pitch	tone	pitch	tone
1	YO-	*b*	-tion		YO-		a-		YO-		YO-	
2	SEC-	*v*	-yo		SEC-		-tion		YO-		SEC-	
3	a-	*s*	YO-		a-		-yo		SEC-		a-	
4	-tion	*g*	SEC-		-tion		YO-		a-		-tion	
5	-yo	*m*	a-		-yo		SEC-		-yo		-yo	

Okay, now you have learned five tones out of eight, and so let's learn some Hmong words that have these tones. Read each row from left to right, and then each column from top to bottom.

No	Hmong	English	Hmong	English	Hmong	English	Hmong	English	Hmong	English
1	da*b*	ghost	de*b*	far	ze*s*	nest	tua*b*	thick	tee*b*	light
2	da*v*	wide	de*v*	dog	pe*v*	up there	tua*v*	hold	cee*v*	fast
3	pa*s*	a stick	na*s*	rat	lo*s*	come	mua*s*	buy	lee*s*	admit
4	da*g*	lie	na*g*	rain	ta*g*	done	mua*g*	sell	tua*g*	die
5	da*m*	to break	he*m*	scare	pa*m*	blanket	mua*m*	sister	tua*m*	kick

The last two tones you are going to learn are very simple. The first one is similar to the musical note "**Re**" – cim **Zoo**. This tone has no marker; therefore, any words ending with just vowels, i.e., z**oo**, **ua**, p**a**, d**ua** etc... means they have the "**Re**" musical pitch. The other tone is equivalent to the English word "**hey!**" or any interjection words, i.e., **hey!** This is called the "**J**" tone – *cim **Koj***.

No	**Pitch**	**Tone**					**Hmong words with tones**						
1	hey!	j	duj	daij	dauj	dawj	**dej**	deej	dij	diaj	doj	duj	dwj
2	"Re"	*blank*	du	dai	dau	daw	**de**	dee	di	dia	do	du	dw

The above word "**dej**" means *water*, and "**de**" means *to pinch*. Below is a table of words that have the seven tones. So read from left column from top to bottom row, starting from "YO- hey! SEC- Re Doe -tion and -yo." Again, you must maintain the original pitch of each English syllable.

No	**Pitch**	**Tone**					**Hmong words with tones**						
1	YO-	b	da^{b}	dai^{b}	dau^{b}	daw^{b}	de^{b}	dee^{b}	di^{b}	dia^{b}	do^{b}	du^{b}	dw^{b}
2	hey!	j	daj	daij	dauj	dawj	dej	deej	dij	diaj	doj	duj	dwj
3	SEC-	v	dav	daiv	dauv	dawv	dev	deev	div	diav	dov	duv	dwv
4	"Re"		da	dai	dau	daw	de	dee	di	dia	do	du	dw
5	"Doe"	s	das	dais	daus	daws	des	dees	dis	dias	dos	dus	dws
6	-tion	g	dag	daig	daug	dawg	deg	deeg	dig	diag	dog	dug	dwg
7	-yo	m	da$_{m}$	dai$_{m}$	dau$_{m}$	daw$_{m}$	de$_{m}$	dee$_{m}$	di$_{m}$	dia$_{m}$	do$_{m}$	du$_{m}$	dw$_{m}$

Now you have learned the seven tones that cover most of the Hmong words. The only tone left is the **D** tone, and you will learn that later. To learn the Hmong tones, try to memorize this Hmong line:

English Pitch:	Hey!	Doe	SEC-	-yo	-tion	YO-	Re	n/a
Hmong Tone:	**Koj**	**Mus**	**Kuv**	**Niam**	**Neeg**	**Siab**	**Zoo**	**Tod**
English phonics:	*kaw*	*moo*	*koo*	*nia*	*neng*	*shia*	*zong*	*taw*

Phrase to remember:	*Koj*	*Mus*	*Kuv*	*Niam*	*Neeg*	*Siab*	*Zoo*	*Tod*
Equivalent English phonics:	***kaw***	***moo***	***koo***	***nia***	***neng***	***shia***	***zong***	***taw***

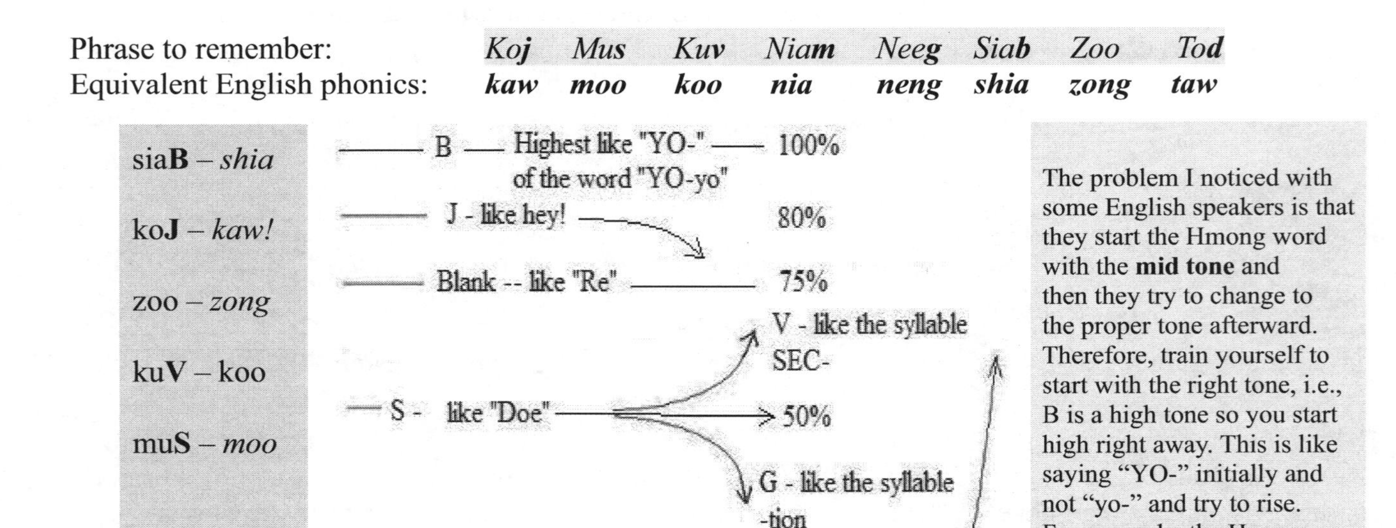

Looking at the graph of tones above you see that the highest tone is the **B** which is equivalent to the syllable "**YO-**" of the word **YO-yo**. And the lowest possible pitch you can make is the **M** tone which is equivalent to the second syllable "**-yo**" of the word "YO-**yo**." And the mid tone is the **S** which I put it at 50% pitch between tones **B** and **M**. So the **S** tone has the equivalent pitch to the musical note "**Doe**." Branching from this **S** mid tone are the **G** and **V** tones that we have learned earlier, and that the V tone is equivalent to the syllable "SEC-" and the G tone is equivalent to the syllable "-tion" of the word "section." The **G** tone starts roughly from the **S** tone, but it drops downward similar to the syllable "-**tion**." The **V** tone starts from the **S** tone but it rises upward like the syllable "**SEC-**" The next tone is the "**blank**" tone which has no marker after the vowels. This tone is very close the the pitch of the musical note "**Re**." The last tone is the **J** and its pitch is very close to the word "**hey!**" Now let's put these tone markers or pitches into English phrase to see if we can compare them to the Hmong tones.

English Pitch:	**Hey!**	Doe	**SEC-**	-yo	-tion	**YO–**	Re
Hmong Tone:	Koj	Mus	Kuv	Niam	Neeg	Siab	Zoo
Hmong a:	ka*j*	ma*s*	ka*v*	na*m*	nag	sa*b*	za
Hmong e:	ke*j*	me*s*	ke*v*	ne*m*	neg	se*b*	ze

Huh, I sure hope you have learned something from these examples and illustration. Now I know why people take live music lessons and not by learning from books. If you need to hear the sounds of these tones, please go to my website, **www.HmongDictionary.com.** You have to memorize, be able to spell and pronounce the Hmong tonal line, "**Koj Mus Kuv Niam Neeg Siab Zoo Tod**" correctly if you want to speak Hmong because this is the musical/tonal notes of the Hmong language. The **D** tone is nothing more than starting with the **M** tone and then rise like a **V** tone, i.e., to*d* = to*m+v*.

Let us learn some simple Hmong phrases.

Hmong	English transliterated	Hmong	English transliterated
1. Koj tuaj los.	1. You come (greeting).	11. Noj mov.	11. Eat rice or eat.
2. Kuv zoo siab.	2. I am happy.	12. Mus pw.	12. Go sleep.
3. Koj haus dej.	3. You drink water.	13. Tuaj pab.	13. Come help.
4. Ua li koj hais.	4. Do like you say.	14. Los saib.	14. Come see.
5. Yog lawm.	5. Correct or right.	15. Dag xwb.	15. Joking only.
6. Leej twg?	6. Person who *or who*?	16. Ua li cas?	16. What happens?
7. Koj paub.	7. You know.	17. Vim tias.	17. Because.
8. Koj pab.	8. You help.	18. Piav los.	18. So explain.
9. Kuv pom.	9. I see.	19. Tag lawm.	19. Done already.
10. Zoo **heev**.	10. **Very** good.	20. Koj muaj.	20. You have.

Hmong	English transliterated
21. Kuv xav tuaj pom koj.	21. I want to come see you.
22. Koj puas kam?	22. Do you allow?
23. Kuv yog tib neeg.	23. I am human.
24. Koj noj ab tsi?	24. You eat what? *Or what are you eating?*
25. Nej tuaj pab peb.	25. You come to help us.
26. Ua rau peb zoo heev.	26. Make us happy.
27. Yog li, peb tuaj pab nej.	27. Therefore, we come to help you.
28. Yog nej xav tau kev pab.	28. If you need assistance.
29. Nej hais rau peb paub.	29. You let us know. *You tell us.*
30. Peb yuav tuaj saib nej.	30. We will come to see you.
31. Nej puas yuav?	31. Do you want to buy?
32. Koj puas noj?	32. Do you want to eat?
33. Leej twg paub?	33. Who knows? *Who would know?*
34. Wb mus pw.	34. We go sleep. (*two persons only*)
35. Koj zoo siab heev.	35. You are very happy.
36. Kuv pom koj *ib leeg* xwb.	36. I see you *one person* only.
37. Yav tag los.	37. In the past.
38. Tus neeg zoo.	38. A good person.
39. Nees noj zaub.	39. Horse eats vegetables.
40. Nas los haus dej.	40. Squirrel comes drink water.
41. Dev mus caum dab.	41. Dog goes chase ghost.
42. Nas noj paj.	42. Squirrel eats flowers.
43. Koj puas da dej?	43. Do you take a bath?
44. Los peb mus ua si.	44. Come we go play?
45. Leej twg hu koj?	45. Who calls you?
46. Koj puas xav kawm?	46. Do you want to learn?
47. Koj puas paub kuv?	47. Do you know me?
48. Koj puas mus?	48. Are you going?

Same word with different tones

nee***s*** = horse
nee***g*** = humans
nee***b*** = shamanism
nee***j*** = life
no = cold
no***j*** = eat
no***v*** = here
no***m*** = officials
no***g*** = load

Therefore, pronouncing each Hmong tone **correctly** is very important. For example: *Kuv **noj** means **I eat**, and Kuv **no** means **I am cold**.*

However, when Hmong people sing the "kwv txhiaj", the tones may not always be correct. For example: **Leem nias leem txi.** Means "***Leej niam leej txiv***." So how do you know? Well, when you're good enough to "hais" the Hmong "kwv txhiaj" then you will know. **:)** – *content-based that is!*

Below please circle the English sound (vowel) that corresponds to the Hmong vowel. For example, the Hmong word "d**a**b" has the Hmong "**a**" vowel which is equivalent to the English "***ah***" sound, and the Hmong word "l**i**s" has the English equivalent "*ee*" sound.

Hmong Word	English Sound	Hmong Vowel	English Sound	Hmong Vowel	English Sound	Hmong Vowel	English Sound
dab	ao ah ay	**lis**	ao ee ay	**dub**	ao oo ay	**tos**	ee aw ao
seev	ao ee eng	**tes**	ay ee eng	**noob**	ao ee ong	**diab**	ee aw ia
ib	ee ay ah	**dais**	ia ay ai	**zib**	ee ay ah	**eb**	oo ay ee
zoo	oo ong aw	**laws**	oo ong er	**lws**	w ong aw	**av**	ah oo aw
dua	oo oua aw	**bua**	oo oua aw	**mus**	oo oua aw	**pw**	w oo ee
wb	ao ay w	**roob**	ao ong ew	**pais**	ao ai ew	**tub**	oo ee ay
sai	ai ia ah	**nab**	ai ia ah	**pom**	ai aw ah	**cia**	oo ia ai
peb	ay ee oo	**teeb**	eng ee oo	**pais**	ay ai oo	**cw**	w ay ee
dawb	ee ay er	**pib**	ee ay er	**zeb**	ee ay er	**pub**	ay ee oo
wb	aw w ay	**noj**	aw ew ay	**yaj**	aw ew ah	**pom**	aw oo ee
dua	oua aw ao	**luaj**	oua aw ao	**laws**	oua er ao	**ua**	oo oua ay
noj	aw oua ao	**nws**	w oua ao	**ru**	aw oo ao	**nov**	ee oo aw
hu	oo aw ee	**pub**	oo aw ee	**fab**	oo aw ah	**iv**	oo ee ay
moo	ong ung ay	**mob**	ong ung aw	**kee**	eng ung ay	**laws**	er aw oo
sia	ia ai ee	**zib**	ia ai ee	**miv**	ee ai oo	**dub**	oo ee ah
lwj	ai w oo	**hws**	ai w oo	**nom**	ai ew aw	**aa**	ah ung oo
tu	oo ai ia	**kuj**	oo ai ia	**cua**	oo oua ia	**os**	aw oo ee
pa	oo ah ee	**zia**	oo ah ia	**hwm**	oo ah w	**hais**	oo ai aw
moo	ai ay ong	**zos**	ai aw ong	**yus**	ai oo ong	**ceev**	ee ay eng
tais	ia ee ai	**sai**	ia ee ai	**moo**	ia ong ai	**ci**	ee ay oo
ze	ee ay ao	**ze**	ee ay ao	**tais**	ee ay ai	**cw**	ee oo ew
tais	ai ia oo	**pab**	ai ah oo	**dws**	w ia oo	**cub**	ee oo ay
tw	oo w aw	**pw**	oo w aw	**puas**	oua ew aw	**cam**	oo ee ah
sua	ao oua oo	**huv**	ao oua oo	**pas**	ao oua ah	**nom**	ee aw oo
keev	eng oo ee	**daws**	eng oo er	**lees**	eng oo ee	**nai**	ee ai oo
zab	ah ee ay	**tu**	ah oo ay	**cia**	ah ee ia	**neb**	aw ay oo
hawm	er oo oua	**qaa**	ung oo oua	**cos**	er oo aw	**muab**	aw oo oua

Now that you know how to pronounce the single consonants and vowels you are now ready to learn how to link each letter to a Hmong word and picture. This is very similar to English "**A**" for **a**pple and "**B**" for **b**ird etc... However, before we do that, let's make sure you understand the keys and methodology that I am using.

Keys to Understand

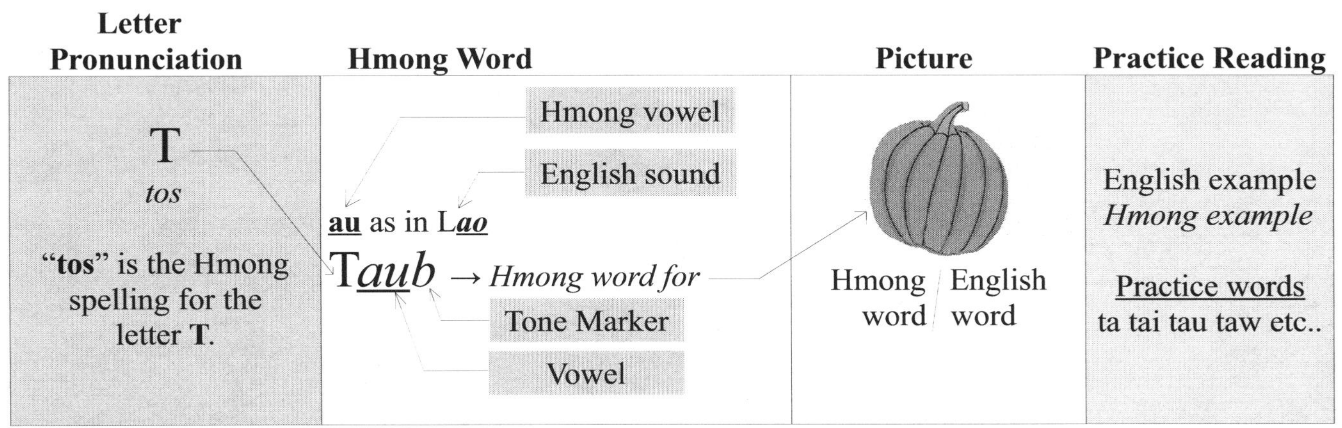

The Hmong "**os**" phonics is exactly as the English word "**awe**" or like "**aw**" as in word l**aw**. Therefore, the Hmong letter **T** pronounced "**tos**" is equivalent to the English "**taw**", *soft t*, as in word "s**taw**." The "**au**" phonics is similar to the "**ao**" of the word L**ao**, and "**tau<u>b</u>**" has the highest tone – *cim **Siab***.

Below is the letter **D,** pronounced "d<u>os</u>" in Hmong having the English phonics "**daw**." The Hmong word for the letter **D** here is "**dev**" having the equivalent English phonics "**day**" with a Hmong **V** tone. Below the picture is the Hmong word "**Dev**", and to the right is the English word for the picture – **dog**.

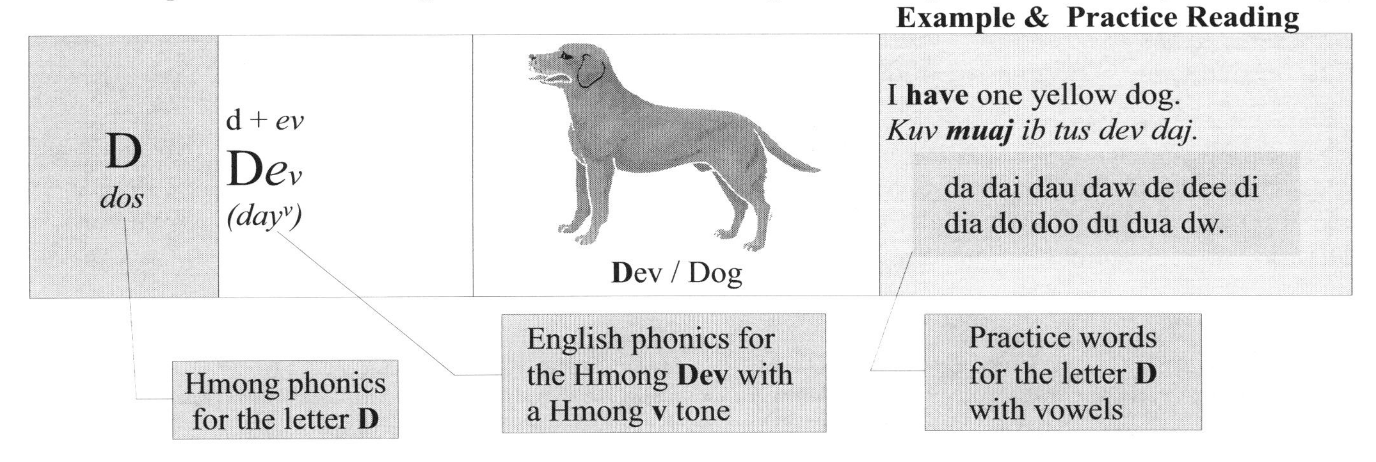

The Hmong word "**ib**" means **one**, and since there are no articles in Hmong, the syntax, "*ib classifier*" is equivalent to the English article. For example, *kuv muaj* ***<u>ib tus</u>*** *dev = I have* ***<u>a</u>*** *dog* or *I have* ***<u>one</u>*** *dog.* Withtout a number in front of a classifier, i.e., **<u>tus</u>** *dev daj* means **<u>the</u>** *yellow dog*, and **<u>tus</u>** *dev* means **<u>a</u>** or **<u>the</u>** *dog*. And with a number, for example, **ob** tus *<u>dev</u>* means **two** *<u>dogs</u>*.

Single Consonants

Consonant	Word	Picture	Example & Practice Reading
B* *bos*	b + *ua* B*ua* (b*o*ua) English phonics	**B**ua / Pig	I see <u>one</u> **pig**. *Kuv pom <u>ib tus</u> **bua**.* **<u>Practice Words</u>** ba bai bau baw be bee bi bia bo boo bu bua bw. *Bai mus caum bua.* ***Bau taws** means **upset** or **angry**.* ***Tus bauj baim** means **a butterfly**.*
C *cos*	c + *uam* C*ua*$_m$ (*coua*$_m$)	**C**uam / Gibbon	This is a <u>white</u> **gibbon**. *Nov yog tus **cuam** <u>dawb</u>.* ca cai cau caw ce cee ci cia co coo cu cua cw. *Cia tus cuam zaum. Let the gibbon sits. Tus cuam <u>saib</u> koj. The gibbon <u>looks</u> at you.*
D *dos*	d + *ev* D*e*$_v$ (*day*^{v})	**D**ev / Dog	I have one <u>yellow</u> **dog**. *Kuv muaj ib tus **dev** <u>daj</u>.* da dai dau daw de dee di dia do doo du dua dw. *Tus dev <u>los</u> haus dej. The dog <u>comes</u> to drink water. The word "**ces yog**" = **means**.*

* Some people use "**B**" in place of the "**np**" consonant, i.e., "**bua**" instead of "**npua**."

<u>Practice Reading</u>

Due to the above three consonants, we are limited to very few words here. And to help you understand the Hmong words and the equivalent English words, the following are transliterated English. Pay no attention to its grammar, but just the Hmong words and their phonics.

	Hmong	English	Hmong	English
1.	Bua da dej.	*Pig take bath.*	Dev caum bua.	*Dog chase pig.*
2.	Cuam dag dev.	*Gibbon tease dog.*	Dev daj da dej.	*Dog yellow take bath.*
3.	Dev de cuam.	*Dog pinch gibbon.*	Dab dag dev.	*Ghost tease dog.*
4.	Bua de dib.	*Pig pick cucumber.*	Dev dua dab doog.	*Dog tear ghost bruise.*
5.	Cuam cem dev.	*Gibbon yell dog.*	Bua da av dub.	*Pig take dirt black bath.*
6.	Cuam dawm dev.	*Gibbon stumble dog.*	Cuam cuab bua.	*Gibbon call pig.*

Tus bua caum tus dev. The pig chases the dog. **Tus cuam cab tus dev.** The gibbon pulls the dog.

Single Consonants

Consonant	Word	Picture	Example & Practice Reading
F *fos*	f + *wj* Fw*j*	Fwj / Bottle	You have <u>one</u> **bottle** of alcohol. *Koj muaj <u>ib</u> **fwj** cawv.* fa fai fau faw fe fee fi fia fo foo fu fua fw. *Foom haus dej. Fong drinks* **water**. ***Faib** ces yog **share**.*
G* *gos*	g + *oj* G*oj* *(gaw!)*	Goj / Boat	People use **boats** for fishing. *Neeg siv **goj** los nuv jes.* ga gai gau gaw ge gee gi gia go goo gu gua gw. *Gauj caij lub goj mus ua si hauv dej. Peb pom <u>ib lub</u> goj. We see <u>one</u> boat.*
H *hos*	h + *aus* H*aus* *(hao)*	Haus / Drink	You **drink** alcohol. *Koj **haus** cawv.* ha hai hau haw he hee hi hia ho hoo hu hua hw. *Huab haus ib fwj dej. Koj zaum haus dej. You sit to drink water. Hais lus = speak or talk.* ***Hais lus loj** ces yog **talk big**.*

* Some people use "**g**" in place of "**nk**" consonant, i.e., "*goj*" instead of "*nkoj.*"

Practice Reading

The following are transliterated English. Pay no attention to its grammar, but only focus on reading the Hmong words with the correct *vowel* and *tone*.

No	Hmong	English	Hmong	English
1.	Dev haus dej.	*Dog drink water.*	Cuam caij goj.	*Gibbon ride boat.*
2.	Bua dag dev haus.	*Pig trick dog drink*	Dev faib fwj dej	*Dog divide bottle water.*
3.	Goj da dej.	*Boat take bath.*	Bua cuam dev.	*Pig gibbon dog.*
4.	Haus fwj dej.	*Drink bottle water.*	Dev caum dab.	*Dog chase ghost.*
5.	Dev caum dab.	*Dog chase ghost.*	Dab dim.	*Ghost escape.*
6.	Huab dub.	*Cloud black.*	Dev de cuam.	*Dog pinch gibbon.*

Tus dev haus dej. The dog drinks water. **Tus dab dag tus dev.** The ghost tricks the dog.
Dev da dej. *Dog takes a bath*. **Bua haus fwj cawv**. *Pig drinks a bottle of alcohol.*

Single Consonants

Consonant	Word	Picture	Example & Practice Reading
J* *jos*	j + *es* Jes *(jay)*	**J**es / Fish	Do you have **fish**? *Koj puas muaj **jes**?* ja jai jau jaw je jee ji jia jo joo ju jua jw. *Foom xav noj jes. Fong would like to eat fish.*
K *kos*	k + *auv* Kauv *(kao^{v}) – soft k like skao but without the s*	**K**auv / Deer	I see one small **deer**. *Kuv pom ib tus **kauv** me.* ka kai kau kaw ke kee ki kia ko koo ku kua kw. *Kaub mus caum kauv. Tus kauv tig los saib peb. The deer turns to look at us. **Kaum** yog **ten**.*
L *los*	l + *iab* Liab *(lia^{b})*	**L**iab / Monkey	You know one *yellow* **monkey**. *Koj paub ib tug **liab** daj.* la lai lau law le lee li lia lo loo lu lua lw. *Tus liab xav los **haus** dej. The monkey wants to come **drink** water. Lauj liam liab tias nws dag. **Leeg twg** ces yog **who**?*

* Some people use "**J**" in place of the "**nts**" consonant, i.e., "**jes**" instead of "**ntses**."

Practice Reading

	Hmong	**English**	Hmong	**English**
1.	Kauv los haus dej.	*Deer come drink water.*	Liab hu jes los.	*Monkey call fish come.*
2.	Liab hais lus.	*Monkey say words.*	Dev caum liab.	*Dog chase monkey.*
3.	Kauv pw hauv goj.	Deer *sleep in boat.*	Dev kov tus kauv.	*Dog touch the deer.*
4.	Lauj haus fwj dej.	***Lauj** drink bottle water.*	Koj los haus cawv	*You come drink alcohol.*
5.	Jes haus dej heev.	*Fish drink water much.*	Liab saib tus kauv.	*Monkey watch the deer.*
6.	Koj haus dej.	*You drink water.*	Dev hais liab haus dej.	*Dog tell monkey drink water.*
7.	Jes kauv liab.	*Fish deer monkey.*	Liab liam tus kauv.	*Monkey accuse the deer.*

8. Tus dev los haus dej = The dog comes to drink water. **Tus kauv haus dej** = The deer drinks water.

Please fill in the missing tone markers and missing words.
Tus **lia**__ caum tus **cua**__ ces tus **kau**__ los da dej. **Je**__ , **lia**__, **kau**__ ces yog *fish*, *monkey* and *deer*. A *fish* yog tus _______. A *deer* yog tus ________, and a *monkey* yog tus ___________.

Single Consonants

Consonant	Word	Picture	Example & Practice Reading
M *mos*	m + *iv* M*iv* *(mee^{v})*	Miv / Cat	The cat <u>chases</u> the **squirrel**. *Tus miv <u>caum</u> tus **nas**.* ma mai mau maw me mee mi mia mo moo mu mua mw. *Mab muaj <u>ntau</u> tus miv. Ma has <u>many</u> cats. Hais kom **meej** = say it **clear**.*
N *nos*	n + *ees* N*ees* *(neng)*	Nees / Horse	The **horse** eats <u>my</u> flowers. *Tus **nees** noj <u>kuv cov</u> paj.* na nai nau naw ne nee ni nia no noo nu nua nw. *Kuv niam muaj **peb** tus nees. My mother has **three** horses. Nab noj nas ces nees noj zaub.*
P *pos*	p + *aj* P*aj* *(pah!) – soft p like s<u>pa</u> – but without the <u>s</u>*	**P**aj / Flowers	I plant **flowers**. *Kuv cog **paj**.* pa pai pau paw pe pee pi pia po poo pu pua pw. *Koj muaj paj <u>liab</u>. You have <u>red</u> flowers. Pab peb pav paj. Puag ta peb pom Paj mus pw.*

<u>Practice Reading</u>

No	Hmong	English
1.	Tus miv dag tus dev mus caum kauv.	*The cat trick the dog to chase the deer.*
2.	Dab liam miv tias nws noj tus nas.	*Ghost accuse the cat that he eat the squirrel.*
3.	Dev pom tus nees noj lub paj liab.	*Dog see the horse eat the red flower.*
4.	Koj paub miv zoo heev.	*You know cat well.*
5.	Koj puas mus pw?	*Are you going to sleep?*
6.	Tus nees mus da dej.	*The horse go take a bath.*
7.	Tus miv kov lub paj daj.	*The cat touch a yellow flower.*
8.	Tus dev mus hu tus nees los haus dej.	*The dog go call the horse to come drink water.*

Hmong	Please translate to English
Ib lub paj	______________________
Ob tus nees	______________________
Tus miv los haus dej.	______________________
Tus miv dag tus nees noj paj?	______________________ (tricks)

Hmong vowel(English sound), **a**(ah) **ai**(ai) **au**(ao) **aw**(er) **e**(ay) **ee**(eng) **i**(ee) **ia**(ia) **o**(aw) **oo**(ong) **u**(oo) **ua**(oua) **w**(w)

 Hmong tone markers: ko**J** mu**S** ku**V** nia**M** nee**G** sia**B** zoo to**D**

Single Consonants

Consonant	Word	Picture	Example & Practice Reading
Q *qos*	q + *av* Q*av*	**Q**av / Frog	You see <u>one</u> **frog**. *Koj pom <u>ib tus</u>* ***qav****.* qa qai qau qaw qe qee qi qia qo qoo qu qua qw. *Tus qav* ***tos*** *peb. The frog* ***waits*** *for us. Tus qav quaj tom lub pas dej tuaj. Lub qe qaib qus.*
R *ros*	r + *auj* R*auj*	**R**auj / Hammer	Give the **hammer** <u>to</u> me. *Muab rab* ***rauj*** *<u>rau</u> kuv.* ra rai rau raw re ree ri ria ro roo ru rua rw. *Ib rab rauj. One hammer. Kuv <u>xav tau</u> ib rab rauj. I <u>would to have</u> a hammer. Riam raug tes.*
S *sos*	s + *ai* S*ai* *(shai)*	**S**ai / Mountain goat	The **mountain goat** looks at us. *Tus* ***sai*** *saib peb.* sa sai sau saw se see si sia so soo su sua sw. *See dag sai <u>los</u> saib peb. Sheng tricks the mountain goat to <u>come</u> look at us. Tuaj sai = come hurry. Sim saj seb puas siav.*

<u>Practice Reading</u>

Cov qav quaj ua rau sai ceeb loj heev li. Peb mus ua si ces peb pom nws da dej. Lawv muaj ib lub pas jes loj heev. Nej puas kam peb siv nej rab rauj. Kauv li kauv mus noj paj ua si. Neeg dag mus haus cawv ces nws los hais lus ua dog ua dig. Koj mus da dej dag peb los sav. Ua cas nej ho muab peb cov paj dam ua si lawm. Bua los noj lawv cov pob kws ces peb mus pab lawv caum. Sai saib mus, saib los ua rau nws mus kev poob qab ke. Nej lam hais lus Hmoob seb peb ho puas paub dog dig.

Lawv yog ib pab neeg muaj meej mom. Peb pub noob paj rau lawv coj mus cog. Nej los haus dej. Koj los noj mov. Nej rau siab kawm lus Hmoob heev. Nej puas paub hais lus Hmoob. Hmoob muaj ob hom lus. Lus Hmoob Dawb *hab lug Moob Leeg*. Kuv yuav los pab nej kawm lus Hmoob kom nej hais lus Hmoob meej heev. Maj mam kawm ces koj yeej yuav paub xwb. Ua siab loj.

Koj puas paub hais lus Hmoob? *Do you know how to speak Hmong?* Kuv paub me~, *me me*, xwb. *I know a little only.* ***Qaib*** *ces yog chicken.* ***Qab*** *ces yog delicious.* ***Rau*** *ces yog six, and* ***raum*** *ces yog kidney.* ***Siav*** *means cooked, and it also means "life", too.* ***Siab*** *means tall or high.*

Single Consonants

Consonant	Word	Picture	Example & Practice Reading
T *tos*	t + *aub* T*aub* *(tao^b) – soft t like stao but without the s*	Taub / Pumpkin	This **pumpkin** is very big. *Lub **taub** no loj heev.* ta tai tau taw te tee ti tia to too tu tua tw. ***Teem taub** ces yog **short**. **Teeb meem** ces yog **problems**. Tau kov ces yog have touched. Tau tuaj = have come. Tej zaum = maybe, perhaps.*
V *vos*	v + *aub* k + *ib* V*aub* k*ib* *(vao^b kee^b)*	Vaub kib / Turtle	This **turtle** walks slow. *Tus **vaub** kib no mus kev qeeb.* va vai vau vaw ve vee vi via vo voo vu vua vw. *Vaub kib mus kev qeeb dua tib neeg. Turtles walk slower than humans. Vim yog vauv Vaj.*
X *xos*	x + *ov* X*ov* *(saw^v)*	Xov / Threads	People use **threads** to sew clothes. *Neeg siv **xov** los xaws khaub ncaws.* xa xai xau xaw xe xee xi xia xo xoo xu xua xw. *Ib lub lig xov ces yog a spool of threads. Xia xaws ris.*

Practice Reading

Bua mus da av dub tag. Dev haus fwj cawv du lug. Peb caij lub goj mus nuv jes. Kauv los noj lawv cov dib tas mus li. Liab los laij puv nws daim teb. Miv los caum tom tus nas. Peb mus cog noob paj tim lawv daim qub teb. Qaib qus qua teb qaib dib. Suav muag ib cov riam kim heev li. Cov neeg laus hau taub dag los noj tas mus li. Vaub kib paub mus hauv pas dej. Nej xa xov tuaj rau peb paub. Yaj mus dag sai poob qab ke. *Teem taub* ces yog short *as not tall*. *Vauv* ces yog son-in-law. *Xeev* ces yog state.

Simple Phrase

No	Hmong	English transliterated
1.	Koj puas **muaj** taub dag?	*Do you **have** pumpkins?*
2.	Kuv pom ib tus vaub kib hauv lub **pas dej**.	*I see one turtle in the **pond.***
3.	Koj puas **muaj** xov liab lawm nab?	*Do you **have** any red threads?*
4.	Tus vaub kib **los** noj lub taub dag tas lawm.	*The turtle **come** eat the pumpkin all gone.*
5.	Kuv siv xov los **pav** tus vaub kib rau lub taub.	*I use threads to **tie** the turtle to a pumpkin.*
6.	***Tag kis** koj puas ua ab tsi?*	***Tomorrow** are you doing anything?*

Single Consonants

Consonant	Word	Picture	Example & Practice Reading
Y *yos*	y + *aj* Y*aj* *(yah!)*	**Y**aj / Sheep	You have <u>two</u> **sheep**. *Koj muaj <u>ob</u> tus **yaj**.* ya yai yau yaw ye yee yi yia yo yoo yu yua yw. *Yeeb **hu** yaj los pw. Yeng **calls** sheep to come sleep. **Yaj yuam** ces yog **peacock**.*
Z *zos*	z + *aj* Z*aj* *(zhah!)*	**Z**aj / Dragon	I see a **dragon** <u>in</u> the water. *Kuv pom tus **zaj** <u>hauv</u> dej.* za zai zau zaw ze zee zi zia zo zoo zu zua zw. *Tus zaj <u>ua luam dej</u>. A dragon <u>swims</u>. Zab dag zaj los zaum **ze** peb zuj zus. **Ze** yog **near**.*

Practice Reading

Zaj los noj zaub hauv lub pas dej xiav. Yaj pom tus zaj ces yaj sawv saib xwb. Zoo siab uas nej xav kawm lus Hmoob. Bua cuam dev fwj goj haus jes kauv liab miv nees paj qav rauj sai taub vaub kib xov paj yaj zaj puav leej yog lus Hmoob. Zaj loj dua miv ces bua loj dua liab. Nees haus dej loj ces dev tom tus sai. Bua da av yaj noj paj miv caum nas fwj dej jes nees pom qav. *Koj mus kuv niam neeg siab zoo tod.* Koj kawm tag cov lus hais no zoo lawm. Tus bua ces yog pig. Tus cuam ces yog gibbon. Tus dev ces yog dog. Fwj ces yog a bottle. Goj ces yog lub boat. Dev haus dej ces yog *dog drinks water.* Kuv mus nuv jes ces yog *I go fishing*. Koj puas paub hais lus Hmoob? *Do you know how to speak Hmong?* Kuv paub me me thiab. *I know very little.* Zoo heev. *Very good.*

Koj yuav tau rov kawm cov suab thiab cim ib lwm dua. *You have to learn the vowels and tones one more time.* Yog koj tsis paub. *If you don't know.* Saib hauv qab ces koj pom lawm. *Look at the bottom then you will see.* Nws muaj *a, ai, au, aw, e, ee, i, ia, o, oo, u, ua, w.* Hos cov cim ne? *How about tones?* Nws muaj yim tus cim. *There are eight tones.* Koj puas paub? *Do you know?* Kuv paub kawg los mas. *I sure do know.* Just remember, "*Koj mus kuv niam neeg siab zoo tod*" xwb. Zoo li koj paub zoo kawg lawm tiag. *Looks like you know pretty well.* Yog li, kuv pab koj zoo siab. *Therefore, I am happy for you.*

Okay, my sagacious Grasshopper. You have come a long way, and I want to congratulate you for not giving up. You see, once you know Hmong and English equally well, you can say something like this: Kuv *like* koj *very much* nawb. Vim koj yog *a good person*. Weird? No, this is one human language with many synonyms! **Teachers**, please read each of the single consonants, i.e, **Cos, Dos**, and have your students write them down on a piece of paper. Next, you read the name of each picture, i.e., **Zaj, Taub**, and have them write down the **correct consonant** for each word you read. Once they are good, you might ask them to write down the Hmong word for each picture instead. And then you read the English words and have your students write the equivalent Hmong words.

The Single Consonants and Pictures

bua **c**uam **d**ev **f**wj **g**oj **h**aus **j**es **k**auv **l**iab **m**iv **n**ees **p**aj **q**av **r**auj **s**ai **t**aub **v**aub kib **x**ov **y**aj **z**aj

Make a copy of this page and erase the Hmong words, and give each student a copy. Now you read the English word and have your students write down the equivalent Hmong word, i.e., ***cat*** = ***miv***.

Single Consonants and Vowels

The table below consists of 20 single consonants and 13 vowels. First, read by row starting from left to right, and then by column. Make sure you are able to pronounce each word correctly before you move on. The correct pitch or tone of these words are equivalent to the musical note "**Re**" since there is no tone marker. This is called the *cim* ***Zoo*** *– Zhong.*

1	b*a*	b*ai*	b*au*	b*aw*	b*e*	b*ee*	b*i*	b*ia*	b*o*	b*oo*	b*u*	b*ua*	b*w*
2	ca	cai	cau	caw	ce	cee	ci	cia	co	coo	cu	cua	cw
3	da	dai	dau	daw	de	dee	di	dia	do	doo	du	dua	dw
4	fa	fai	fau	faw	fe	fee	fi	fia	fo	foo	fu	fua	fw
5	ga	gai	gau	gaw	ge	gee	gi	gia	go	goo	gu	gua	gw
6	ha	hai	hau	haw	he	hee	hi	hia	ho	hoo	hu	hua	hw
7	ja	jai	jau	jaw	je	jee	ji	jia	jo	joo	ju	jua	jw
8	ka	kai	kau	kaw	ke	kee	ki	kia	ko	koo	ku	kua	kw
9	la	lai	lau	law	le	lee	li	lia	lo	loo	lu	lua	lw
10	ma	mai	mau	maw	me	mee	mi	mia	mo	moo	mu	mua	mw
11	na	nai	nau	naw	ne	nee	ni	nia	no	noo	nu	nua	nw
12	pa	pai	pau	paw	pe	pee	pi	pia	po	poo	pu	pua	pw
13	qa	qai	qau	qaw	qe	qee	qi	qia	qo	qoo	qu	qua	qw
14	ra	rai	rau	raw	re	ree	ri	ria	ro	roo	ru	rua	rw
15	sa	sai	sau	saw	se	see	si	sia	so	soo	su	sua	sw
16	ta	tai	tau	taw	te	tee	ti	tia	to	too	tu	tua	tw
17	va	vai	vau	vaw	ve	vee	vi	via	vo	voo	vu	vua	vw
18	xa	xai	xau	xaw	xe	xee	xi	xia	xo	xoo	xu	xua	xw
19	ya	yai	yau	yaw	ye	yee	yi	yia	yo	yoo	yu	yua	yw
20	za	zai	zau	zaw	ze	zee	zi	zia	zo	zoo	zu	zua	zw

For teachers, you might want to select a particular row and read from left to right with a different tone. For example, row 20: *Zab, zaib, zaub, zawb to zwb.* And then do the same thing for certain column, i.e., **column 7**, beeb, ceeb, deeb, feeb to zeeb. Next is to select certain row but then mix each word with a different tone, i.e., row 20: Za**m**, zai**s**, zau**b**, zaw**v** to zw**g**. If you are learning on your own, try to put the seven tones, Ko**j** Mu**s** Ku**v** Nia**m** Nee**g** Sia**b** Zoo, with any row. For example, row 20: za*j* zai*s* zau*v* zaw*m* ze*g* zee*b* zi zia*j* zo*s* zoo*v* zu*m* zua*b* zw.

Hmong Vowels with Tones

To help speed things, I created a new word called "**vitch**" – vowel and tone (*pitch*).

	Koj	Mus	Kuv	Niam	Neeg	Siab	Zoo	Tod
1	**aj**	**as**	**av**	**am**	**ag**	**ab**	**a**	**ad**
2	**aij**	**ais**	**aiv**	**aim**	**aig**	**aib**	**ai**	**aid**
3	**auj**	**aus**	**auv**	**aum**	**aug**	**aub**	**au**	**aud**
4	**awj**	**aws**	**awv**	**awm**	**awg**	**awb**	**aw**	**awd**
5	**ej**	**es**	**ev**	**em**	**eg**	**eb**	**e**	**ed**
6	**eej**	**ees**	**eev**	**eem**	**eeg**	**eeb**	**ee**	**eed**
7	**ij**	**is**	**iv**	**im**	**ig**	**ib**	**i**	**id**
8	**iaj**	**ias**	**iav**	**iam**	**iag**	**iab**	**ia**	**iad**
9	**oj**	**os**	**ov**	**om**	**og**	**ob**	**o**	**od**
10	**ooj**	**oos**	**oov**	**oom**	**oog**	**oob**	**oo**	**ood**
11	**uj**	**us**	**uv**	**um**	**ug**	**ub**	**u**	**ud**
12	**uaj**	**uas**	**uav**	**uam**	**uag**	**uab**	**ua**	**uad**
13	**wj**	**ws**	**wv**	**wm**	**wg**	**wb**	**w**	**wd**

For teachers, please select one or more rows from the table above and then select your favorite single consonant to go with these **vitches**. For example, row 12, and the letter "d + *uaj*" = d*uaj*, d*uas* to the last vitch "*uad*." You must ***memorize*** the above *vitches* in order to read Hmong rapidly.

Below is a table with 10 rows and 13 columns. Read each word from left to right starting from row number 1 to row 10. Then read from top row first word **naj** to bottom row **mas**. Again, only focus on your phonics and tones. More importantly, the correct *vitch.*

1	naj	nias	nauv	nawm	neg	neej	nis	niam	nog	nooj	nug	nuaj	nwv
2	cas	cias	cauv	cawm	ceg	ceeb	cis	ciav	cog	coob	cus	cuab	cws
3	dam	diav	dauv	dawm	deg	deeb	dij	diav	dom	doob	du	duav	dw
4	fag	fiav	faum	fawm	feg	feeb	fis	fia	fom	foog	fuj	fuaj	fwm
5	pav	piab	paus	pawg	peg	peeb	piv	pia	po	poog	pub	puas	pws
6	ham	hias	hau	hawj	heb	heeb	him	hia	hov	hoo	hub	hua	hwv
7	tag	tiag	tauj	tawj	te	tee	tig	tia	tog	too	tu	tua	tw
8	kab	kiam	kaub	kaw	kes	keeb	kij	kiaj	kom	koo	ku	kua	kw
9	lab	liav	lauv	law	leb	leev	lig	lias	los	loo	lua	lua	lw
10	mas	miab	mauj	maws	mej	meeg	mim	miam	mov	moov	mu	mua	mw

Simple Phrase with Single Consonants

No	Hmong	English	Hmong Example	English (*you is one person*)
1	bua*	*pig*	*Tus bua noj **zaub.***	*The pig eats **vegetables.***
2	cia	*let, allow*	*Kuv cia koj mus.*	*I let you go.*
3	dawb	*white*	*Kuv lub **ris** dawb.*	*My white **pants**.*
4	faus	*bury*	*Koj faus **noob** taum.*	*You bury bean **seeds.***
5	gaum*	*hide*	*Koj gaum **hauv** zos.*	*You stay **in** town.*
6	haus	*drink*	*Koj puas xav haus **dej**?*	*Would you like to drink **water**?*
7	jaum*	*ant*	*Kuv **pom** ib pab jaum.*	*I **see** a colony of ants.*
8	kub	*hot*	*Ib **tais** dej kub.*	*One **bowl** of hot water.*
9	liab	*monkey*	*Tus liab tom kuv **tes.***	*The monkey bites my **hands.***
10	miv	*cat*	*Tus miv **tom** tus nas.*	*The cat **bites** the squirrel.*
11	noj	*eat*	*Koj noj mov **xwb**.*	*You eat rice **only**.*
12	pw	*sleep*	*Kuv **mus** pw.*	*I **go** sleep.*
13	quaj	*cry*	*Tus **ab me** quaj taug heev.*	*The **baby** cries a lot.*
14	rau	*six*	*Koj muaj **rau** tus miv.*	*You have **six** cats.*
15	sau	*write*	***Koj** sau lus Hmoob.*	***You** write in Hmong.*
16	teeb	*light*	*Pab **tua** lub teeb.*	*Help **turn off** the light.*
17	vau	*fall*	*Koj vau los raug **kuv.***	*You fall on **me.***
18	xa	*send*	*Koj **xa** daim duab tuaj.*	*You **send** the picture in.*
19	yeem	*agree*	*Kuv **yeem** kawm lus Hmoob*	*I **agree** to learn Hmong.*
20	zoo	*good*	*Koj yog tug neeg **zoo.***	*You are a **good** person.*
21	muab	*give*	*Koj **muab** rau kuv.*	*You **give** to me.*
22	mus	*go*	*Koj mus **zaum.***	*You go sit.*
23	hu	*call*	*Kuv **mam li** hu koj.*	*I **will** call you.*

* Simplified consonants

Practice Reading

Cuam kau ua rau peb sawv los noj mov. Miv pom nas ces ua rau miv caum tus nas mus poob lub pas dej. Koj yog ib tus neeg xav paub lus Hmoob zoo. Koj puas paub hais lus Hmoob? Kuv paub me~ xwb. Hos koj ne? Kuv paub sau xwb. Zoo heev li los mas. Maj mam kawm ces koj yeej yuav tau xwb. Koj yeej meem kawm. *You keep on learning.* Mus zoo koj. *Goodbye to you.* Zoo siab kawg = *very happy.*

Double Consonants

The Hmong double consonants phonology follows the same English methodology. For example, when you combine **d** + **r** = **dr** for word such as **"dr***ive***"**, **p** + **l** = **pl** for **pl***ay*, and **t** + **r** = **tr** for **tr***ay* etc... Of course, Hmong have different phonics, but the logic is the same. To help you learn, I even put some beautiful pictures, **:()**, so you can remember things better. Unlike English, Hmong has consonants that have "**H**" prefix* and suffix, and they exist for a good phonetical reason. Consonants with "h" prefix mean they are *nasal-aspirated consonants* like the English word "<u>h</u>mm." For example:

1	H*ma*	Aspirating the "H" through *your **nose*** before uttering the "ma"	H + *ma* = hma
2	H*na*	Aspirating the "H" through *your **nose*** before uttering the "na"	H + *na* = hna
3	H*la**	*Puffing the "H" through your **mouth** before uttering the "la"*	H + *la* = hla

Let's put the above examples in a slow motion. The word "**hma**" is really being pronounced like this: Hmm... ma, and the word "**hna**" is like hmm... na. To say "**hna**", form your tongue as if you are going to say the word "**na**" and *hold your tongue there then **exhale** through your nose* – a heavy breathing sound similar to how you say the "**h**mm" and then finish uttering the "na." The word "**hla**" is easy because it is a mouth-aspirated. So try to say "ha la" very fast but making sure you really puff out the "ha" loud and then softly end with the "la." When you don't see any "H" prefix it means you can *pinch your nose tight* and you are still able to pronounce the word correctly. For example:

1	Ma	M as in **m**om, and **a** as in <u>a</u>bout
2	Na	N as in **no**
3	La	L as in **la**w
4	Pa	P as in s**p**in – *soft* P
5	Ka	**k** as in s**k**in – *soft* K

* This is a mouth-aspirated consonant because you can pinch you nose tight and still able to utter this word correctly. Therefore, just utter the "h" then the rest through your mouth, i.e., **hla, hle** etc...

What about the "H" suffix? Good thing you remember, Grasshopper! If an "H" is placed after other consonants, it is called a *mouth-aspirated consonants, i.e.,* like the English words "**T***h*ai and **C***h*at." Make sure you ***really puff*** out the "h" sound otherwise words such as "**k<u>h</u>au** and **kau**" might sound the same to some people. The word "**khau**" sounds like the English word "***cow***", and the word "**kau**" sounds like "s<u>**kao**</u>" but without the "s" sound. Below are some consonants with the "h" suffix:

1	K*h*	as in **ke**y – English *hard K, i.e., kay, kit.*	Aspirating the "h" after the K
2	P*h*	as in **p**in – English *hard P, i.e., pie, pan.*	Aspirating the "h" after the P
3	T*h*	as in **Th**ai or tie – English *hard T, i.e., tie.*	Aspirating the "h" after the T

The "**Th**" in Hmong does not sound like the "th" as in English ***<u>th</u>****igh*, but exactly as "**Th**ai or **tie**."

Double Consonants

There are 26 double consonants. However, four of them are new and/or used by some people. These double consonants were put/combined together based on the Hmong phonics of each of the single consonants, i.e., **t**os + **h**os = **th***os* → *English phonics taw + **h**aw =* ***th**aw* *(**th** as in **Th**ai).*

No	How to combine	Consonant	Hmong word	Equivalent English
1	b + *h*	b*h**	bhoo / nphoo	to shake, i.e., shaking peppers or salt
2	b + l	bl*	blooj / nplooj	leaf
3	c + *h*	c*h*	cheb	to sweep
4	d + *h*	d*h*	dhia	to jump
5	g + h	g*h**	ghaus	curvy, crooked
6	h + l	**h**l	hlua	rope – this is a **mouth**-aspirated.
7	h + m	**h**m	hma	fox – this is a **nasal**-aspirated.
8	h + n	**h**n	hnub	sun – this is a **nasal**-aspirated.
9	j + *h*	j*h**	jhiab / ntshiab	clear, like a **clear** bottle of water.
10	k + *h*	k*h*	khau	shoe. This is the English *hard k*, i.e., ***kao***.
11	m + l	ml	mluav	dented in
12	n + c	nc	nceb	mushroom
13	n + k	nk	nkoj	boat
14	n + p	np	npua	pig
15	n + q	nq	nquab	pigeon
16	n + r	nr	nraj	pheasant
17	n + t	nt	ntoo	tree
18	n + y	ny	nyuj	cow
19	p + *h*	p*h*	phom	gun. This is the English *hard p*, i.e., ***paw***.
20	p + l	pl	plas	owl
21	q + *h*	q*h*	qhiav	ginger
22	r + *h*	r*h*	rho	to pull, like pulling weed.
23	t + *h*	t*h*	thoob	bucket. This is the English *hard t*, i.e., ***tong***.
24	t + s	ts	tsov	tiger
25	t + x	tx	txiv	fruits
26	x + y	xy	xyoob	bamboo

* Simplified consonants

How to Pronounce the Hmong Double Consonants

The Hmong double consonants follow a similar English phonetical letter combining methodology. For example, if we take the English letters "**c** + **h**" it would be **ch**, for **ch***ild*, and letters "**t** + **h**" would be **th**, for **Th***ai*, and letters "**b** + **l**" = **bl**, for **bl**aw etc... However, you must have mastered the Hmong single consonants in order to properly combine more consonants in a phonetical way.

The consonant C*h*

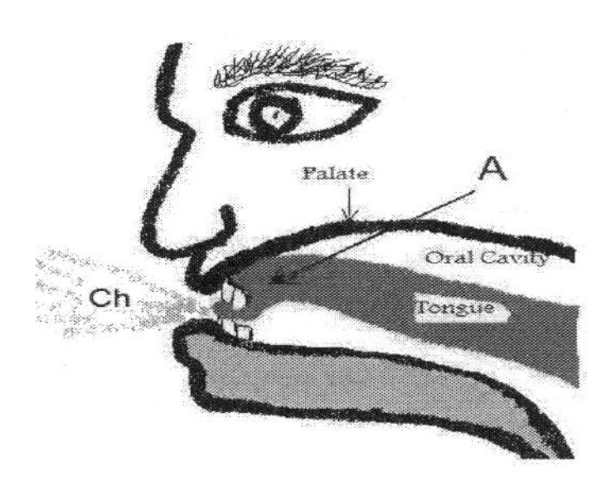

This consonant is very close to the "C" you have learned previously except it has the mouth-aspirated "h". Try saying the English word "itch" but make sure when you utter the "ch", the tip of your tongue is ***outside of your teeth*** as shown on the left. If not, you might be saying the English "ch" as in "child" or the Hmong consonant "tsh" instead.

The consonant "**Ch**", pronounced "**chos**", is the "C + h", a mouth-aspirated consonant. So let's try this. Say the "**Cos**" firmly and then form your tongue as shown above, and try to thrust the tip of your tongue, *at point A*, forward with a slight puffing, almost like spitting, to create the "h" sound. Make sure you say the "Cos" in Hmong and not like English "**see.**" This "chos" sound is very close to the English "chaw", except the utterance is happening *at the tip* and *on top of your tongue* by pressing it against the back of your upper teeth like ***point A*** above. Therefore, *cos + hos = chos.*

The consonant "**Dh**", pronounced "dhos", is easy because you already can say the "D" as in "Day." Now try to say "day" as having the *mouth-aspirated* "h" after the "d" like "**dhay**." Better yet, try to say the word "**Th**ai and **Dh**ai" and see if that helps you. Therefore, *dos + hos = dhos.*

The consonant "**Hm**", pronounced "hmos", is a phonetic combination of the "h + m" and it is exactly like the English "hmm." So saying the word "Hm*ong*" is nothing more than saying "h + mong", but uttering them in *one utterance* and *not like* "ha + mong". To say the word "Hmong" correctly, you would exhale about 30% through your nose to create the *nasal sound* "**h**" *prior to* uttering both "**Hmong**" in one utterance. If you pinch your nose tight, no nasal-aspirated "h", you can't utter the word "Hmong." All you can say is either "**Mong**" or "**mmm** + **hong**." Therefore, *hos + mos = hmos.*

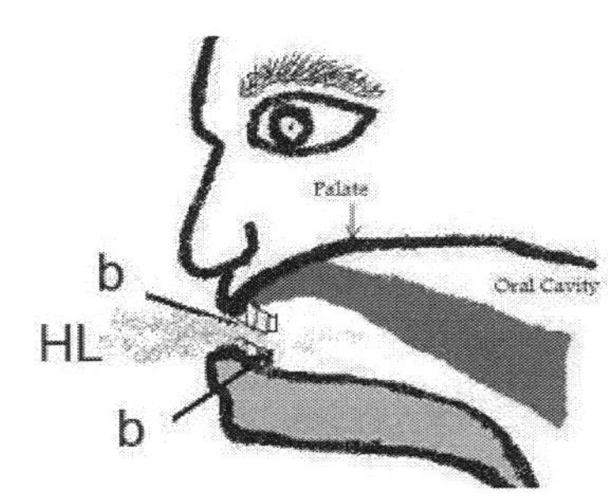

The consonant "**HL**", pronounced "hlos", is a phonetic combination of the "h + l." First, make your tongue, teeth and mouth look like the image on the left. Then puff some air on both sides of your mouth, ***small b***, while keeping the tip of your tongue intact with the upper front part of you mouth and then utter the "l" like the English word "**l**aw." This is a **mouth-aspirated** consonant even though the "**h**" is before the "l". In other words, even when you pinch your nose tight, you can still say words, "hlub, hlos, hlua and hle" etc... Therefore, *hos + los = hlos.*

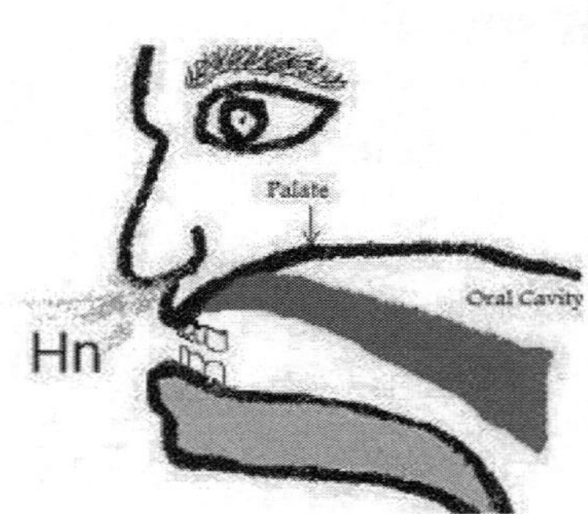

The consonant "**Hn**", pronounced "hnos", is a phonetic combination of the "h + n", and this is a *nasal-aspirated* consonant. First, start saying the word "**hmm**" a few times. Now change "**hm**" to "**hn**" and try to say the English word "**hn***aw*" instead. In other words, your tongue is in the **N** position but exhale about 30% through your nose to create the "**h**" *nasal sound prior* to uttering the word "**hnos.**" If you pinch your nose tight, you can't utter this consonant. For example, the word **hnab** would sound like **nab** only. The equivalent English phonics for this Hmong word "hnos" is "*hnaw.*" Therefore, *hos + nos = hnos.*

The consonant "**Kh**", pronounced "khos", is really the *hard* pronunciation of the English **K** as in **k**ey. So try to say "**key**" and then replace the "**ey**" with "**aw**" so your new English word is "**k**aw" and that is how the Hmong consonant "**khos**" sounds like. Therefore, *kos + hos = khos.*

The consonant "**ML**", pronounced "mlos", is a phonetic combination of the "m + l." Here is the English phonetic: *Maw + Law* = mlaw. The "m" is just a way to close your mouth before saying the "law" because you can say the word "law" with your mouth open. Do not *aspirate through your nose* otherwise this would become the Hmong consonant "hml" instead. Therefore, *mos + los = mlos.*

The consonant "**Nc**", pronounced "ncos", is a phonetic combination of the "n + c." What that means is you start your mouth at the "**nos**" position and then utter the "**c***os.*" Do not puff any air forward otherwise you would be saying the consonant "nc*h*" instead. Therefore, *nos + cos = ncos.*

The consonant "**Nk**", pronounced "nkos", sounds exactly or very close to the English "**gaw**". Do not puff any air forward otherwise this would become the consonant "nk*h*" instead.
Therefore, *nos + kos = nkos.*

The consonant "**Np**", pronounced "npos", sounds exactly or very close to the English "**baw**". So if you can say "**bee** or **baw**" then you can easily say "**npos**." Do not puff any air forward otherwise you would be saying the consonant "np*h*" or "bh" instead. Therefore, *nos + pos = npos → English "**baw.**"*

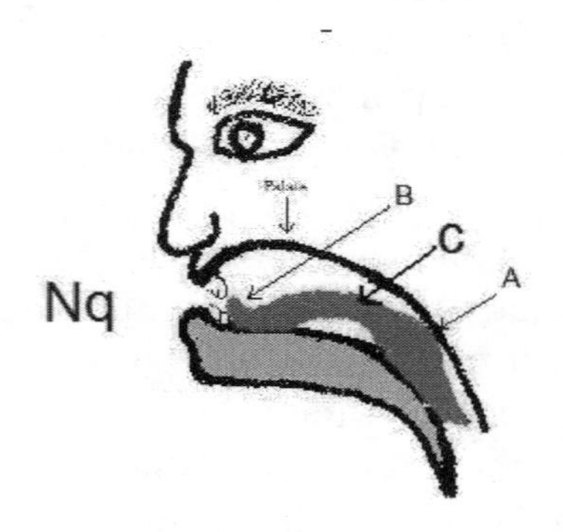

The consonant "**Nq**", pronounced "nqos", is a combination of the phonetic consonants "n + q". See image on the left.
First, place the tip of your tongue and make it look like **point B**, and then close your throat so that the back of your tongue is touching both sides of your throat like **point A**. Now utter "nqos" like you are going to gag by lowering your tongue at **point C** as to open up **point A**. If you lower the back of your tongue too much, you will be saying the "qos" itself without the "nos". Think of it this way, point **B** is "nos" and point **A** is "qos", but the sound is being blocked by point **C**. So by lower point **C**, your tongue can play the note "nqos" you are looking for. And be careful not to puff any air through your mouth otherwise it will sound like you are saying the consonant "nq*h*" instead. Therefore, *nos + qos = nqos.*

The consonant "**Nr**", pronounced "nros", is a combination of the phonetic consonants "n + r", and it is very close to the English word "**draw**"; however, the tip of your tongue is placed at the "**nos**" position, and *curl the tip* of your tongue just behind the *alveolar ridge* (the area right behind your top teeth) – thanks to Dr. Nick Poss for this, then utter "nos + ros" as one utterance. It is almost like if you are saying the English "naw + draw" but stressing *just one beat* of the "raw" sound.
Therefore, *nos + ros = nros.*

The consonant "**Nt**", pronounced "ntos", is similar the English word "**the**", but place your tongue like the picture below and not like how you say the normal "**the**" in English. However, don't stick out your tongue past your teeth, but just enough to form the beginning sound of "**the**" only. Do not puff or thrust any air forward otherwise this would sound like the consonant "nt*h*" instead.
Therefore, *nos + tos = ntos.*

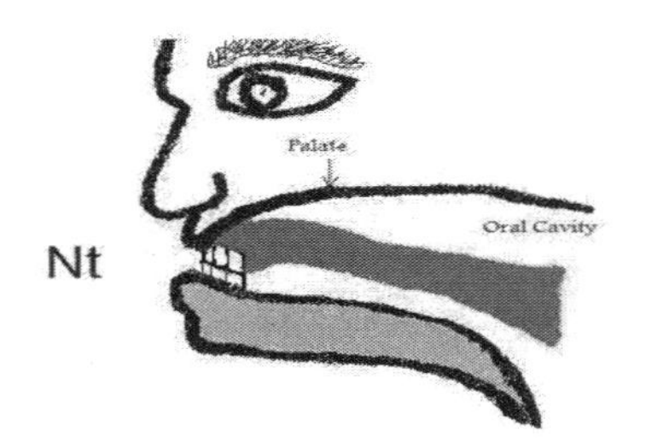

Try this. Bite your teeth together tight like image on the left and say the word "**the**" without any puff of air as to eliminate the "h" sound, and without opening your mouth at all. This very sound is then similar to the Hmong word "**nt**aws" instead.

The consonant "**Ny**", pronounced "nyos", is a phonetic combination of the "n + y", and its phonics is similar to the "**ny**" of the English word "ca**ny**on" – thanks to *Sarah Gore* for this word. Now let us replace the English word "ca***ny**on*" with "ca***nyaw***" and the "***nyaw***" of English phonics is exactly the same as the Hmong "***nyos***." Another English word that has this "**ny**" sound is o***n**ion*.

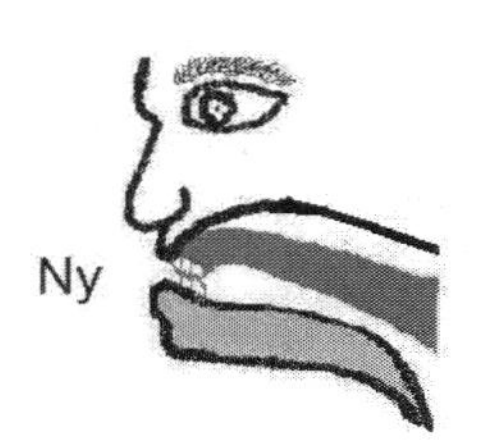

Another English word which has the "ny" is the word "u**n**ion." So if you replace "u*nion*" with "u***naw***" and mute the "u" you should have the Hmong phonics "nyos" as well.

So to say the Hmong "nyos", you would not aspirate or let any air through your nose, like "hmm" or you will be saying the Hmong consonant "h**ny**" instead. Again, utter the English phonics "naw" and "yaw" a few times and then put your tongue as shown above then say the word "**nyos.**" Again, pay close attention to your tongue when you say the "nos" because by dropping the tip of your tongue to create the "yos" sound is going to phonetically create the "nyos" phonics. Therefore, *nos + yos = nyos.*

The consonant "**Ph**", pronounced "phos", is a combination of the phonetic "p + h" like the English word "**p**aw" – *hard* **P**. Therefore, the Hmong word "***phos***" and English "***paw***" do have the exact phonics or very close to each other. So you don't need a picture for this consonant; just remember that the Hmong "**ph**" is the English *hard* **p**, and **not like** the *ph* of a "*ph*one" because this word sounds like "**f**one" instead. Therefore, *pos + hos + phos.*

The consonant "**PL**", pronounced "plos", is easy to learn because English has that already. However, you must do exactly as I tell you and not like what you are used to. The "**PL**" as in the English word "dis**PL**ay" is the exact sound I want you to utter whenever you see the "**PL**" in Hmong. Now say my new English word, "dis**PL**aw", *aw* as in l*aw*. Now mute the "*dis*" and only say the "**Plaw"** – don't you sound like English the word "**play**" game because that is incorrect – it has the aspirated "h" like "p**h**lay" instead. In other words, **P** in Hmong is a *soft P* as in s**p**y, s**p**ade. Make sure you don't puff any air because that would sound like the Hmong word "pl**h**os" instead. The Hmong word "plhes" has the same phonics like the English word "play." Therefore, *pos + los = plos.*

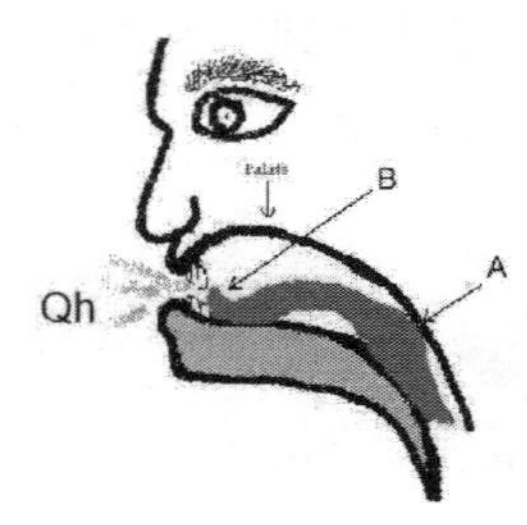

The consonant "**Qh**", pronounced "qhos", is a phonetic combination of the "q + h" and we have learned the Hmong Q before. So then all is left is the puffing or aspirated sound of the "h" suffix. See image shown on the left.
Meaning that you say the "**qos**" first and then puffing the "hos" as the ending sound like coughing, and you have it. Just like gagging with a friendly cough. Therefore, *qos + hos = qhos.*

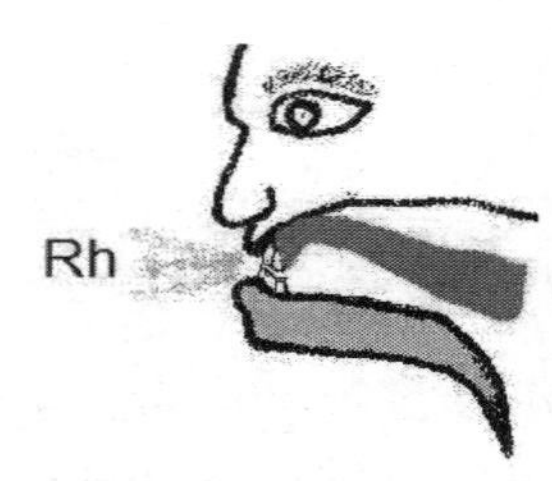

The consonant "**Rh**", pronounced "rhos", is a combination of the phonetic "r + h" and you have learned the **R** already. So the "h" is nothing more than the puffing sound uttered after the "R". The "rh" pronunciation is very close to the English "**tr**" as in **tr**ue or "traw", but the utterance happens more at the tip of your tongue and at the "**ros**" position, and it is without the tongue vibration as in the English word "**r**ing." Therefore, *ros + hos = rhos.*

The consonant "**Th**", pronounced "**thos**" is a phonetic combination of the "t + h" – the English *hard* **T**, and this is another easy one to learn. If you can say the English word "**Th***ai*" or "**tie**" then it is the same thing. And if you don't know the word "**Thai**" sounds like then you definitely need to travel to **Th**ailand or go try some **Th**ai noodle *pho.* So the English "**taw**" sounds like the Hmong "**thos**."

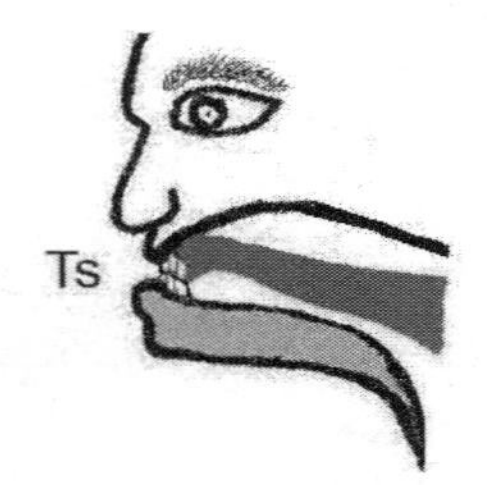

The consonant "**Ts**", pronounced "**tsos**", is a combination of the phonetic "t + s", and it is very close to the English "**Ch**" as in **ch**at and **ch**aw; however, without puffing the "**h**". In other words, it almost seems like you're saying the "**j**aw" but with the word "**ch**aw." To start, bite your teeth while placing your tongue behind your teeth like the image on the left. Now just utter the word "**ch**aw" by dropping the bottom jaw without puffing the "**h**" sound. Be careful *not to puff any air* otherwise you will be saying the Hmong consonant "ts***h***" instead. Therefore, *tos + sos = tsos.*

The Hmong consonant "**tsh**", pronounced "***tshos***" has a very close or exact phonics as the English "***chaw.***" For example, the Hmong word "**tsh**iab" – English phonics "*chia*" with a "b" tone – "YO-" pitch means ***new***, and the Hmong word "**tsh**uaj" – English phonics "*choua!*" means ***medicines***.
We will learn this consonant more later on.

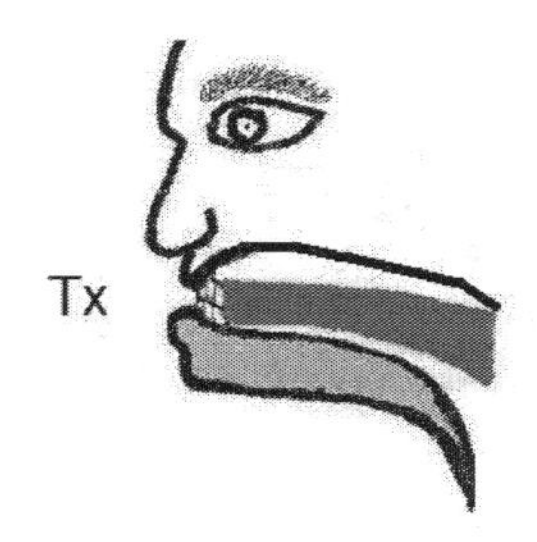

The consonant "**Tx**", pronounced "txos", is a combination of the phonetic "t + x". Perhaps the closest English word that has this sound is the "da**d's**" – thanks to **Sarah Gore** for this suggestion. Indeed the ending sound of "**d's**" is very close to the Hmong word "**txis**." Sarah also mentioned that this "**tx**" is like the sound of air leaking from a tire. If you form your mouth and tongue as illustrated left, *tos + xos,* you should be able to utter the Hmong "**txos**." Notice the tip of the tongue needs to be placed in the *center* of both teeth.

Now begin to place your tongue at the "tos" position as shown above. Now mix the Hmong "tos" with the English "*siss*" sound and then uttering the English word *awe.* This should give you the pronunciation of the Hmong "txos." Do not puff any air or you will be saying the Hmong "tx***h***os" consonant instead. Therefore, *tos + xos = txos.*

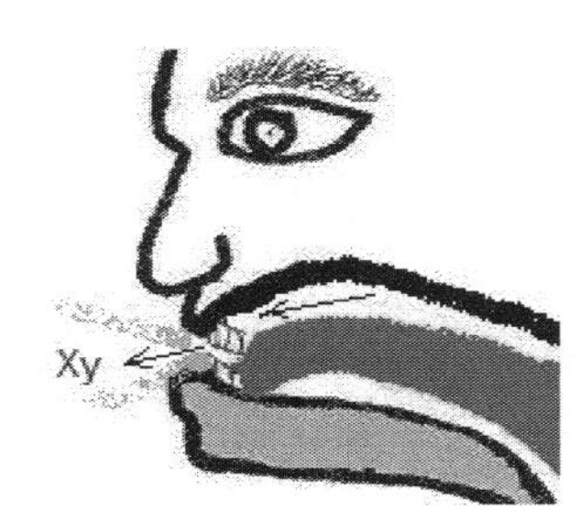

The last consonant "**Xy**", pronounced "xyos", is a phonetic combination of the "x + y." Make sure the tip of your tongue is placed at the bottom of your lower teeth and bending it forward so a part of your tongue is touching the top teeth. However, you need to leave a little room above your tongue, *see arrows*, so you can puff a little air to create the "**hiss**" sound before uttering the word "xyos." The tip of your tongue *barely moves* while uttering words with this consonant. Now place your tongue as shown on the right and say the English phonics "***see + yaw** or even **saw + yaw***" – through the opening indicated by the arrows without moving your tongue, and open your mouth slightly only for the "**yaw.**" Now say the English phonics "**syaw**" very fast but with same tongue position mentioned above and this sound should be very close to the Hmong **xyos**. Therefore, the Hmong phonics is *xos + yos =* ***xyos.*** Another way to learn this "xyos" word is perhaps try the English word "thaw." Now replace the "t" with a "y" so your new word is "**y**haw" instead. In other words, the "Y" or "yaw" is your starting point and then puff the "h" ending *mouth-aspirated* sound effect which is similar to the word "thaw" as in Thai. Again, making sure you are able to pronounce each of the single consonants correctly before learning the double consonants.

Practice Reading

Hmong	English	Hmong	English	Hmong	English	Hmong	English	Hmong	English
chim	upset	**dhia**	jump	**hlub**	love	**hma**	fox	**hnub**	sun
kho	fix	**mloog**	listen	**nce**	climb	**nkaum**	hide	**npaj**	prepare
nqa	bring	**nruas**	drum	**ntog**	fall	**nyob**	live	**phim**	match
plaub	hair	**qhia**	tell	**rhiab**	ticklish	**them**	pay	**tsev**	house
txaus	enough	**xyaum**	practice	**hluas**	young	**hmoo**	luck	**hnav**	wear
choj	bridge	**dhau**	past	**khau**	shoe	**ncaj**	straight	**nka**	skinny
plas	owl	**qhuas**	admire	**theem**	stop	**tsau**	full	**tsav**	drive

Double Consonants with Pictures

Consonant	Word	Picture	Example & Practice Reading
Bh* *bhos*	bh + *oo* Bh*oo* *(bhong!)*	**Bh**oo / Shake	**Shake** black peppers <u>on</u> my pho. ***Bhoo** hwj txob <u>rau</u> kuv tais fawm.* ***Practice Words*** bha bhai bhau bhaw bhe bhee bhi bhia bho bhoo bhu bhua bhw. *Bhuab bhoo hwj txob ntau dhau.*
Bl* *blos*	bl + *ooj* Bl*ooj* *(blong!)*	**Bl**ooj / Leaf	You have <u>a</u> **leaf**. *Koj muaj <u>daim</u> **blooj**.* bla blai blau blaw ble blee bli blia blo bloo blu blua blw. *Blias hu tuaj **qhia** koj. Blia calls to **tell** you. Kuv xav noj **mov blaum**. I would like to eat **sticky rice**.*
Ch *chos*	ch + *eb* Ch*eb* *(ch**ay**ᵇ)* ***ay** as in **day***	**Ch**eb / Sweep	You **sweep** the dirt. *Koj **cheb** av.* cha chai chau chaw che chee chi chia cho choo chu chua chw. *Cheeb <u>tuaj pab</u> cheb. Cheng <u>comes to help</u> sweep. **Cheem** means **stop**.*
Dh *dhos*	dh + *ia* Dh*ia*	**Dh**ia / Jump	This kangaroo **jumps** so <u>high.</u> *Tus kangaroo no **dhia** <u>siab</u> heev.* dha dhai dhau dhaw dhe dhee dhi dhia dho dhoo dhu dhua dhw. *Koj dhia **siab dua** kuv. You jump **higher than** me.*

* Some people use "**bl**" in place of of the "**npl**" consonant, i.e., "blooj" instead of "nplooj."

<u>Practice Reading</u>

Blooj poob los rau hauv pem teb – *ground*. Koj pab kuv cheb av. Koj dhia siab dua kuv. Ua cas koj chim rau kuv? Koj puas pom tus kauv dhia ua twg lawm? Rab *khaub ruab* ces yog rab "*broom*" xwb.

Double Consonants

Consonant	Word	Picture	Example & Practice Reading
Hl *hlos*	hl + *ua* Hl*ua* *(hloua)*	**Hl**ua / Rope	You have **ropes**. *Koj muaj **hlua**.* hla hlai hlau hlaw hle hlee hli hlia hlo hloo hlu hlua hlw. *Hli hlub <u>nws tus</u> txiv. Hlee loves <u>her</u> husband. Hle khau = take off shoes.*
Hm *hmos*	hm + *a* Hm*a* *(hm**a**)*	**Hm**a / Fox	The **fox** wants to <u>drink</u> water. *Tus **hma** xav <u>haus</u> dej.* hma hmai hmau hmaw hme hmee hmi hmia hmo hmoo hmu hmua hmw. ***Muaj hmoo** ces yog **have luck**.* ***Noj hmo** ces yog **eat dinner**.*
Hn *hnos*	hn + *ub* Hn*ub* *(hnoo^{b})*	**Hn**ub / Sun	I see the sun **rise**. *Kuv pom lub hnub **tuaj**.* hna hnai hnau hnaw hne hnee hni hnia hno hnoo hnu hnua hnw. *Hnub no = today. Hnub hnav daim tiab liab. Hnue wears a red dress.*
Kh *khos*	kh + *au* Kh*au* *(kao) – hard k*	**Kh**au / Shoe	You **have** <u>one</u> shoe only. *Koj **muaj** <u>ib sab</u> khau xwb.* kha khai khau khaw khe khee khi khia kho khoo khu khua khw. *Khau khiab = sandal, sandle shoes*

<u>Practice Reading</u>

Hma hla dej los tom qaib. Kuv pom lub hnub ci puag tim lub roob tuaj. Koj muaj ib sab khau xwb. Koj puas pom ib tus hma los nov. Kuv pom ib tus hma los kwv sab khau khiav rau tom hav zoo lawm. Cia koj los da dej tag es koj mam li rov mus ua num. Yog koj kawm tiag ces lus Hmoob kuj yooj yim heev nawb. Cuam kau ua rau peb kho siab zim xwb. Koj puas kam sawv los ua mov rau peb noj. Zoo siab tau paub koj mog. Mus zoo koj nawb.

Koj puas pom tus hma? *Did you see the fox?* Kuv siv hlua los khi tus hma. *I use ropes to tie the fox.* Ib nkawm khau. *One pair of shoes.* Lub hnub tawm tuaj. *The sun comes up or rises.* Koj puas xav kawm lus Hmoob? *Would you like to learn Hmong?*

Double Consonants

Consonant	Word	Picture	Example & Practice Reading
Ml *mlos*	ml + *uav* Ml*uav*	**Ml**uav / Dent	The **kettle** was dented. *Lub **hwj kais** mluav.* mla mlai mlau mlaw mle mlee mli mlia mlo mloo mlu mlua mlw. *Peb mloog koj hais lus.* *We listen to you talk.*
Nc *ncos*	nc + *eb* Nc*eb*	**Nc**eb / Mushroom	People pick **mushroom** to sell. *Neeg de **nceb** los muag.* nca ncai ncau ncaw nce ncee nci ncia nco ncoo ncu ncua ncw. *Dib nce tus ntaiv. Dee climbs a ladder. Ncaj means straight*
Nk *nkos*	nk + *oj* Nk*oj* *(gaw!)*	**Nk**oj / Boat	People use **boats** to go in water. *Neeg siv **nkoj** mus hauv dej.* nka nkai nkau nkaw nke nkee nki nkia nko nkoo nku nkua nkw. *Paj yog ib tus hluas nkauj.* *Pa is a young girl – unmarried.*

Practice Reading

Neeg siv nkoj mus hauv dej. Nceb liab noj ces tuag xwb nawb. Ua zoo koj ua raug kuv lub hwj kais mluav nawb. Kuv caij nkoj ces nws ua rau kuv xeev siab. Hma mag neeg muab hlua khi. Lub hnub ci ua rau kuv sawv los noj mov. Leej twg lub nkoj no? Koj puas xav haus dej? Koj puas *muag* dej?

No	Hmong	English
1	Lub nceb liab qaij mus rau lub nkoj.	*The red mushroom leans toward the boat.*
2	Lub hwj kais mluav sab xis.	*The kettle was dented on the right side.*
3	Kuv caij lub nkoj mus hauv dej.	*I ride on a boat to go in the water.*
4	Lub nkoj muaj ib cov pa dub dub.	*The boat has some very black smoke.*
5	Neeg mus de nceb los muag.	*People go pick mushrooms to sell.*

Double Consonants

Consonant	Word	Picture	Example & Practice Reading
Np *npos*	np + *ua* Np*ua* *(boua)*	**Np**ua / Pig	The **pig** comes to eat corn. *Tus **npua** los noj pob kws.* npa npai npau npaw npe npee npi npia npo npoo npu npua npw. *Npauj los pub npua.* *Bao comes to feed pigs.*
Nq *nqos*	nq + *uab* Nq*uab*	**Nq**uab / Pigeon	**Pigeons** can **fly** fast. ***Nquab** muaj peev xwm **ya** ceev.* nqa nqai nqau nqaw nqe nqee nqi nqia nqo nqoo nqu nqua nqw. *Nquab ya **ceev dua** qaib.* *Pigeons fly **faster than** chickens.*
Nr *nros*[1]	nr + *aj* Nr*aj*	**Nr**aj / Pheasant	This pheasant is very **pretty.** *Tus nraj no **zoo nkauj** heev.* nra nrai nrau nraw nre nree nri nria nro nroo nru nrua nrw. *Nraj **qab dua** qaib. Pheasants **taste better than** chickens.*

* Some people use "**b**" in place of the "**np**", for example, **bua** instead of "**npua.**"

Practice Reading

Nquab pom tus npua ua rau nws ya ceev heev mus piav rau tus nraj kom nws khiav mus nkaum. Nraj li nraj xav mus noj kooj xwb. Neeg xav noj nqaij npuas ci nrog mov blaum. Nraj pom npua ua rau nraj khiav mus nkaum. Tus nquab ya los noj blej. Koj puas pom ib tus npua khiav los nov. Kuv yeej paub tias tus npua loj dua tus nraj. Npua li npua xav da av tas hnub xwb. Koj xov tau ib lub nkuaj los kaw koj cov npua. Kuv ua tau ib lub cooj los kaw kuv cov nquab. Kuv pom ib tus nraj los noj kab puag tim roob. Koj muab siab kawm lus Hmoob tiag ces koj yuav paub hais lus Hmoob zoo dua kuv nawb.

Sis jib dua – *See you later.*
Koj lub npe hu li cas? *What is your name?*
Koj puas kam tuaj pab kuv? *Do you mind come to help me?*
Koj puas paub hais lus Askiv? *Do you know how to speak English?*
Kuv paub me me xwb. *I know very little only.*
Mus zoo. *Goodbye.*

Double Consonants

Consonant	Word	Picture	Example & Practice Reading
Nt *ntos*	nt + *oo* Nt*oo*	**Nt**oo / Tree	You have two **trees**. *Koj muaj ob **tus* ntoo**.* nta ntai ntau ntaw nte ntee nti ntia nto ntoo ntu ntua ntw. *Neeg siv ntoo los ua tsev.* *People use trees to build houses.*
Ny *nyos*	ny + *uj* Ny*uj*	**Ny**uj / Cow	**Cows** provide milk for humans. ***Nyuj** muaj kua mis rau tib neeg.* nya nyai nyau nyaw nye nyee nyi nyia nyo nyoo nyu nyua nyw. *Nyuj nyiam nyob tom teb xwb.* *Cows like to live at the farm only.*
Ph *phos*	ph + *om* Ph*om* *(paw$_m$) – hard p*	**Ph**om / Gun	People use **guns** during wars. *Neeg siv **phom** lub caij muaj rog.* pha phai phau phaw phe phee phi phia pho phoo phu phua phw. *Phuab xav yuav phau ntawv no.* *Phoua wants to buy this book.*
Pl *plos*	pl + *as* Pl*as*	**Pl**as / Owl	**Owls** can see at night. ***Plas** pom kev hmo ntuj.* pla plai plau plaw ple plee pli plia plo ploo plu plua plw. *Lub **plab** ces yog a **stomach**.* ***Ploj** ces yog **disappear**.*

* The proper classifier is "*tsob*" instead of "*tus*"

Practice Reading

Tus plas plam taw ces nws poob los rau hauv pem teb ua rau tus nyuj dhia los nyob hauv qab ntoos. Nws nkaum hauv ib pliag ces Hmoob tua phom nrov tim roob tuaj ua rau nyuj ras los hem plas poob plig tas li lawm. Plas xav mus tom nas los noj xwb. Lo lus neeg ces yog leej tib neeg xws li koj thiab kuv. Nyob rau lub caij ntuj nag mas ua rau tej nroj thiab ntoo hlav blooj thiab tawg paj zoo nkauj heev. Tabsis dhau mus rau lub caij ntuj no ces ho ua rau tej nroj los yog ntoo zeeg blooj tag li lawm.
Kawg no, kuv nrog koj zoo siab uas koj xav los kawm peb Hmoob tej lus nawb mog.
Koj kawm ntawv Hmoob puas nyuaj? *Is it hard for you to learn Hmong?* Yooj yim heev – *very easy.*

Double Consonants

Consonant	Word	Picture	Example & Practice Reading
Qh *qhos*	qh + *iav* Qh*iav*	**Qh**iav / Ginger	Would you like to eat **ginger**? *Koj puas xav noj **qhiav**?* qha qhai qhau qhaw qhe qhee qhi qhia qho qhoo qhu qhua qhw. *Peb **qhia** lus Hmoob rau nej.* *We **teach** Hmong to you.*
Rh *rhos*	rh + *o* Rh*o* *(traw)*	**Rh**o / Pull	**Pull,** like pulling weed. You pull the **grass.** *Koj rho cov **nyom.*** rha rhai rhau rhaw rhe rhee rhi rhia rho rhoo rhu rhua rhw. *Koj rho kuv cov nyom. You pull my grass.*
Th *thos*	th + *oob* Th*oob* *(tong^b^) – hard t*	**Th**oob / Bucket	A **bucket** of blue water. *Ib **thoob** dej xiav.* tha thai thau thaw the thee thi thia tho thoo thu thua thw. *Kuv xav mus tim Thaib teb.* *I would like to go to Thailand.*

Practice Reading

Ua ntej koj yuav tau qhiav los noj, koj yuav tau muaj ib daim teb, thiab muaj ib lub thoob uas yog siv los nqa dej mus ywg rau cov qhiav kom lawv thiaj li loj thiab hlob taus tuaj mus. Thaum ywg dej tag rau daim av ces nws yuav muaj nyom tuaj thiab. Yog li, koj yuav tau rho thiab dob tej nyom tawm mas koj tej qoob loo thiaj li yuav zoo tuaj. Yog li, ua ntej koj yuav noj ib yam khoom twg, koj yuav tau kawm kom koj paub tias nws cog thiab tu nyuaj npaum li cas. *And when you know this.* Ces thaum koj paub li no. *You then know how hard the growers had worked.* Koj thiaj li paub tias cov neeg cog tau khwv npaum li cas. Ua cas koj muab lus Askiv sau nrog lus Hmoob lawm? *Why did you write English with Hmong?* Vim kuv xav kom koj paub txhais lus Hmoob mus ua lus Askiv. *Because I want you to know how to translate Hmong into English.* Vim li cas koj ho xav kawm lus Hmoob? *Why do you want to learn Hmong?* Rau qhov hais lus Hmoob ces yus tsis tas kaw yus lub qhov ncauj li. *Because speaking Hmong one does not have to close his mouth.* Tabsis ceev faj mov dhia tawm mus rau lwm tus neeg lub phaj nawb. *But be careful rice might jump out to another person's plate.* Koj thiab kuv mam li tham dua lwm zaus ohs mog. *You and I will chat again next time.* Kuv hlub koj – *I love you.* Hos koj ne? *How about you?* Tej zaum. *Maybe.* Mus zoo. *Goodbye.*

Double Consonants

Consonant	Word	Picture	Example & Practice Reading
Ts *tsos*	ts + *ov* Ts*ov*	**Ts**ov / Tiger	**Tigers** like to eat <u>raw</u> meat. ***Tsov*** *nyiam noj nqaij <u>nyoos</u>.* tsa tsai tsau tsaw tse tsee tsi tsia tso tsoo tsu tsua tsw. *Kuv pom ib tus tsov loj.* *I see one big tigger.*
Tx *txos*	tx + *iv* Tx*iv*	**Tx**iv / Fruits	I <u>like to</u> eat **fruits**. *Kuv <u>nyiam</u> noj **txiv**.* txa txai txau txaw txe txee txi txia txo txoo txu txua txw. *Cov txiv liab no qab zib heev.* *These red fruits are very sweet.*
Xy *xyos*	xy + *oob* Xy*oob*	**Xy**oob / Bamboo	People use bamboo to **build** houses. *Neeg siv xyoob los **ua** tsev.* xya xyai xyau xyaw xye xyee xyi xyia xyo xyoo xyu xyua xyw. *The year 2012 was very hot. Lub xyoo 2012 sov heev. We practice reading Hmong. Peb xyaum nyeem ntawv Hmoob. Xyeej = available.*

<u>Practice Reading</u>

Puag thaum ub Hmoob tseem nyob rau pem tej toj roob thiab hav zoo mas muaj tsov los tom lawv tej tsiaj heev li. Tsov yog ib hom tsiaj uas muaj nyob rau tom hav zoo xwb vim lawv txawj mus caum lwm hom tsiaj thiab tom los noj. Thaum tsov nkees ces tsov mus pw hauv tej qhov chaw uas muaj xyoob thiab ntoo ntau kom neeg tsis pom. Nyob rau teb chaws yaj sab, *bucolic*, mas muaj ntau hom txiv hmab thiab txiv ntoo. Tsis tag li, tseem muaj ntau hom tsiaj qus uas xws li liab, cuam, kauv, thiab hma ltn...

Peb ua neeg nyob, peb yuav tsum paub hlub tsis yog tsiaj xwb, tabsis xyoob ntoo mus rau ntau hom tsiaj nyob rau hauv dej huv tib si. Tej no puav leej yog Tswv Ntuj tsim thiab lawv yeej muaj nqis tib yam nkaus li tib neeg. Yog li, peb yuav tau xyaum cog xyoob, ntoo thiab pab txuag tej txiv hmab, txiv ntoo kom tej tsiaj qus thiaj li tau chaw nyob vim lawv tsis paub cog thiab ua tsev li tib neeg nawb mog. Kawg no, thov kom Vaj Tswv foom koob hmoov zoo rau nej cov xav kawm lus Hmoob kom nej tsuas yim kawm los yim txawj; yim huab xyaum los yim huab tau zoo zuj zus xwb mog.

The Double Consonants with Pictures

The "jh" consonant is not listed here. See the "*ntsh*" on page 59.

Make a copy of this page and erase the Hmong words, and give each student a copy. Now you read the English words and have your students write down the equivalent Hmong words. Then read the Hmong words and have your students write down the English words.

Simple Phrase with Double Consonants

The Hmong double consonants are a bit confusing at first, but once you fully understand its phonology, you will always remember them. Here are some simple phrases with double consonants.

No		Word	English	Hmong example	English transliterated
1	bh*	bhoo	*shake*	Bhoo hwj txob.	Shake black peppers.
2	bl*	blaum	*sticky*	Ib tais mov *blaum.*	*One bowl rice* ***sticky.***
3	ch	chais	*peel*	Koj *chais* lub txiv.	*You* ***peel*** *the fruit.*
4	dh	dhia	*jump*	Kuv *dhia* tsis siab.	*I* ***jump*** *not high.*
5	gh*	ghaus	*crooked*	Txoj kev *ghaus* heev.	*The road is too* ***crooked.***
6	hl	hlub	*love*	Koj *hlub* kuv heev.	*You* ***love*** *me much.*
7	hm	Hmoob	*Hmong*	Koj yog *Hmoob.*	*You are* ***Hmong.***
8	hn	hnub	*sun, day*	*Hnub* twg koj tuaj?	*What* ***day*** *you come?*
9	jh*	jhai	*fear, afraid*	Koj *jhais* tsov dhau.	*You* ***fear*** *tiger much.*
10	kh	khau	*shoe*	Yog kuv nkawm *khau.*	*It is my pair* ***shoes.***
11	ml	mluav	*dent, as dented in*	Koj tsoo thiaj *mluav.*	*You hit to* ***dent*** *it.*
12	nc	nce	*climb*	Koj *nce* tus ntaiv.	*You* ***climb*** *a ladder.*
13	nk	nkaum	*hide, stay*	Kuv *nkaum* hauv tsev.	*I* ***stay*** *inside house.*
14	np	npua	*pig*	Koj pom tus *npua.*	*You see a* ***pig.***
15	nq	nqos	*to swallow*	Koj *nqos* lub noob.	*You* ***swallow*** *the seed.*
16	nr	nres	*stop, pause*	Koj *nres* nov tso.	*You* ***stop*** *here first.*
17	nt	ntub	*wet*	Nag *ntub* koj tag.	*Rain* ***wet*** *you all.*
18	ny	nyob	*stay, live*	Koj *nyob* nov los?	*You* ***live*** *here hah?*
19	ph	phom	*gun*	Koj puas muaj *phom*?	*You do have* ***guns****?*
20	pl	plas	*owl*	*Plas* pw nruab hnub.	***Owls*** *sleep during days.*
21	qh	qhia	*tell, inform*	Thov koj *qhia* kuv.	*Please you* ***tell*** *me.*
22	rh	rho	*pull, like pulling weed*	Pab *rho* cov nyom.	*Help* ***pull*** *the grass.*
23	th	thiab	*and*	Koj *thiab* kuv mus pw.	*You* ***and*** *I go sleep.*
24	ts	tsov	*tiger*	Kuv pom ib tus *tsov.*	*I see one* ***tiger.***
25	tx	txaus	*enough*	Koj noj *txaus* lawm	*You eat* ***enough*** *already.*
26	xy	xyuas	*visit, see*	Koj tuaj *xyuas* kuv.	*You come* ***visit*** *me.*

* Some people use "**b**" in place of "**np**", bl = npl, nplh = bh, "**gh**" in place of "**nkh**", "**jh**" in place of "**ntsh**." These "b, bh, bl, blh, g, gh, j, and jh" are more popular among young people.

Yog li, koj yuav tau xyaum kom koj paub cov ntawv txiv – consonants, ntawv niam – vowels, *uas kuv nyiam hu ua* ***ntawv suab***, thiab cov cim – tones. To help you learn these double consonants, let's take a look at some simple phrases from a normal conversation.

Basic greeting and conversation between *Nraug Zaj* and *Nkauj Paj.*

Nraug Zaj	Nkauj Paj
Nyob zoo ohs Paj.	Nyob zoo ohs Zaj.
Koj tuaj ua si thiab los?	Aws, kuv tuaj ncig ua si thiab los mas.
Ua ab tsi lawm xwb ohs Paj?	Tseem niaj hnub ua hauj lwm thiab xwb.
Kuv los tib yam thiab.	Zoo los mas, Zaj. Rau siab ua hauj lwm es yus thiaj li muaj nyiaj los siv ohs.
Yeej yog li los mas.	Mus zoo koj ohs.

Practice Reading

No.	Hmong	English
1.	Kuv **xav** haus dej.	I **would like** to drink water.
2.	Koj yog **leej twg**?	**Who** are you?
3.	Lo lus no **nyeem** li cas?	How do you **read** this word?
4.	Thiab **sau** li cas?	And how to **write**?
5.	Koj sau rau **kuv.**	You write for **me.**
6.	Koj puas **paub** lus Hmoob?	Do you **know** Hmong?
7.	Kuv paub **me me** xwb.	I know **very little** only.
8.	Hais lus **Askiv** xwb.	Speak **English** only.
9.	Ua tsaug **ntau.**	Thank you **much.**
10.	Ib yam pes tsawg?	How much is each item?
11.	Koj **muag** pes tsawg?	You **sell** for how much?
12.	Ob **duas** xwb ohs.	Two **dollars** only.

Hmong = English
xav = would like to
leej twg = who
li cas = how
pes tsawg = how much
ntau = much, a lot
npaum cas = how much
twg = which, what, where

Odds but Useful

No	Hmong	English	Remark
1.	Koj muaj pes tsawg xyoo?	You have how many years?	Transliterated!
		How old are you?	***Proper English***
2.	Koj lub npe hu li cas?	Your a name call what?	Transliterated
		What is your name?	***Proper English***
3.	Koj yuav mus qhov twg?	You will go where?	Transliterated
		Where are you going?	***Proper English***
4.	Koj mus kev tsis ncaj li.	You go road not straight.	Transliterated
		You do not walk straight.	***Proper English***
5.	Koj los pab kuv.	You come help me.	
		You come to help me.	

Triple Consonants

The triple consonants are nothing more than taking the double consonants and add the third phonetical consonant to the end. For this reason, I will not provide my "*zoo nraug*" – handsome, picture with the ugly tongue any more. However, I want you to truly understand its phonics methodology. Therefore, let's decipher the Hmong word "**hm**os." In the slowest utterance, you must follow these steps:

1. Close your mouth
2. Exhale through ***your nose*** to aspirate the "**h**" about 30% then
3. Uttering the **mos.** The equivalent English phonics is "hmm***aw***." Don't say this word like "ha maw", but instead like "hmm maw."

Now let's look at the word "**Hml***os*", and the English phonics is "**hml***aw.*" Now how do we pronounce this word? Well, try uttering the, "hmm **law**" as fast as you can and that is the correct pronunciation.

1. Close your mouth
2. Exhale through ***your nose*** to aspirate the "**h**" about 30% then
3. Uttering the "**mos**" and then
4. Utter the "**los**". In other words, *English phonics*, say "hmm **maw law**" as *one utterance*.

The word "**hmlos**" is considered a *nasal-aspirated* word. Meaning the air escapes 30% through your nose, and 70% through your mouth. On the other hand, the "h" suffix consonants are considered the *mouth-aspirated* consonants, i.e., **k***h* like the word **key** which has a *puffing sound* through the mouth.

To help you understand what I am talking about, let us look at two wave graphs I recorded below. The top graph is the word "**Moob**", and the bottom graph is the word "**Hmoob**."

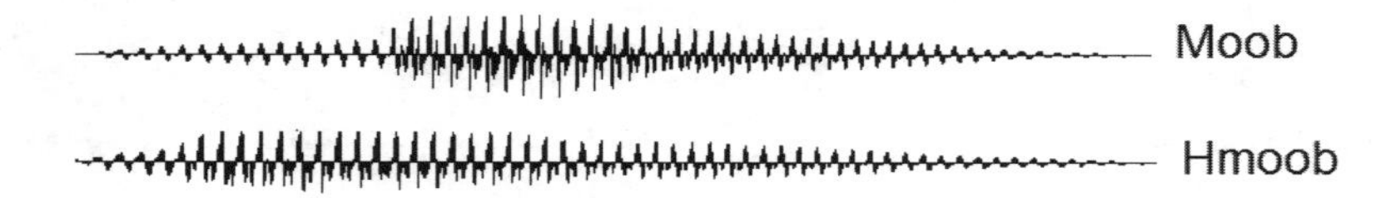

As you can see, the sound file of the word "**Moob**" started with a more gradual and *unaspirated* "M + ***oob***", and the word "**Hmoob**" started out with a puffing, *nasal-aspirated*, "**H** + *moob*." This is how the native Hmong speakers hear and able to detect – as good as a computer **:)**
Next, we will analyze the differences between the words "**nab**" and "**hnab**" sounds. These two words are very similar in phonics and the only difference is the *aspirated* "**h**". Don't worry too much if you can't hear the difference at first; however, once you know the difference, your ears will hear their differences, too. In other words, *until you believe or know, you won't perceive – hear.* At first, the Hmong word "**nab**" might even sound like "**nah**" in English, but it is not. It has a **higher pitch** that is similar to the pitch of the syllable "**YO**-" of the word "YO-yo", and "**nab**" means *a snake*, and **hnab** means *a bag*. For now, just believe me that the English phonics "**nah**" has a different meaning than the phonics "**hmm** nah" in Hmong, s*nake* and *bag*, respectively.

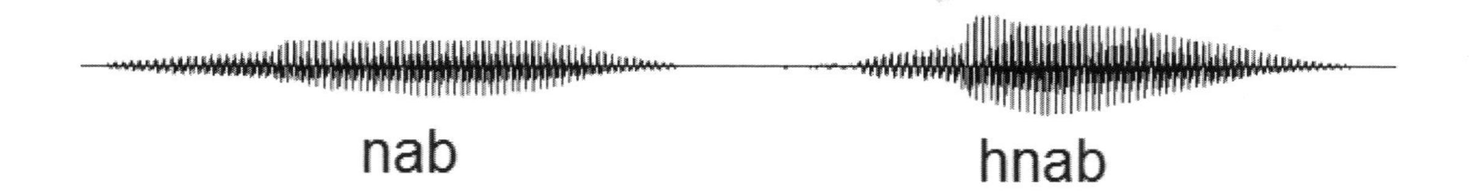

The graph above was a single recording wave file of the words "**nab**" and "**hnab.**" So, seeing is believing right? Great! The graph on the left is obviously different than the one on the right, but there is a pattern that is very similar, and I want you to see it better than most native Hmong speakers. Why? Because we have the best master – *the sound recorder*! Grasshopper, the graphs look like a pair of eyes, the smaller eye on the left is winking at you, and the one on the right is staring at you with dual waves. No, that is not what I am talking about! What I am trying to make you see is the graph on the right, *the inner and lower graph*, is similar to the graph on the left. So then, the outer and taller lines on the right graph is the *aspirated "H"* which was missing from the left word "**nab**."

Grasshopper, don't you be overly concerned about **nab** and **hnab** because these are no different than the phonics and words of the English, **dad** and **dat** to the native Hmong speakers. Once you have finished reading this book, you will be able to detect them all.

Next, we will examine the sound graph of the words "bos" and "bhos" like English words "baw" and "b**h**aw", aw as in l**aw**. The word "b*h*os" has an "h" suffix – *mouth-aspirated.*

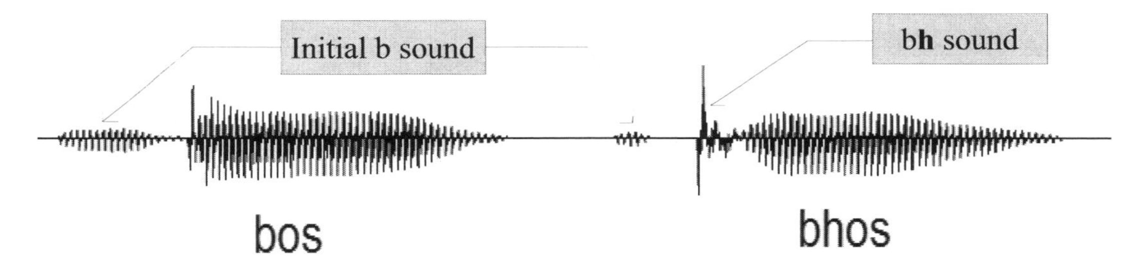

Again, both graphs don't look much different except for the word "b**h**os" has a spike "h", puffing, right after the "b", and both started out with a smaller wave – "**b**". Huh... I feel like I am teaching you about wavenology rather than Hmong phonology here, but I believe in the old saying, "*A picture is worth more than 1,000 words.*" so I hope it is helpful to you. Another reason I want to show you these graphs is to earn your trust because unless you believe you can learn, you can't really succeed or be willing to immerse yourself into learning. And I absolutely believe you can learn the Hmong language.

Again, please play with your own pronunciation by recording your own voice because hearing your own voice from a computer is different than hearing from your mouth. So my suggestion for you is to go get a reasonable mic and start recording your own voice so you can hear as a listener. By listening to your own voice, and comparing them to the audio on my website, you should be able to tell whether the sounds are similar to each other or not.

Triple Consonants

There are fifteen triple consonants, and I will show you phonetically how the third consonant is being added to the end of each of the double consonants you have already learned. One thing to remember is that you must pronounce each consonant in the Hmong phonics way, i.e., "**hos** + **mos** + **los**" = **hmlos**. If not, none of these will make sense to you. The Hmong "os" sounds exactly as the English word "**awe**" or as ***aw*** in the word l**aw**.

No	How to combine	Consonant	Word example	English Meaning
1	bl + *h*	bl*h**	blhaib/npl*h*aib	*ring, like a diamond ring.*
2	**h** + ml	**h**ml	hmlos	*dented in.*
3	**h** + ny	**h**ny	hnyav	*heavy, like too much weight.*
4	nc + *h*	**n**c*h*	ncho	*smoke, like the smoke from a fire.*
5	nk + *h*	**n**k*h*	nkhaus	*crooked, curve – not straight.*
6	np + *h (bh**)*	**n**p*h*	nphau	*to flip or tip over.*
7	np + *l (bl**)*	**n**pl	nplua	*slippery*
8	nq + *h*	**n**q*h*	nqhuab	*dry, like a drying pond.*
9	nr + *h*	**n**r*h*	nrhoob	*stocking*
10	nt + *h*	**n**t*h*	nthe	*to yell*
11	n + ts *(like jaw)*	**n**ts	ntsaum	*ants.* ***nts*** *as in* **jam**
12	n + tx	**n**tx	ntxub	*to hate*
13	pl + *h*	pl*h*	plhu	*face, the face of person.*
14	ts + *h*	ts*h*	tshiab	*new, as not old*
15	tx + *h*	txh	txhiab	*thousand*

* Some people use "blh" in place of the "nplh", "j" in place of "nts."

** Some people use the "b" in place of the "np"

Again, you can memorize these consonants, but my recommendation for you is to know how each of the consonants sounds like, and when combined with others, you can still pronounce them in a phonetical way. This phonology is similar to English, i.e., **s** + **p** + **l** = **spl** for the word **spl**it, and **s** + **h** + **r** = **shr** for the word **shr**ink etc... Eventually, you will recognize every word, and this will come when you have earned your Hmong tongue. Just remind yourself that you are a new born child, and it normally takes at least two to three years for most children to speak decent. So don't be too harsh on yourself. Just learn what you like first. If there are certain areas you don't quite understand, go back and read the same section several times, and try to read my mind and it might come to you. Many times we create our own failures because this is like cutting down a fruit tree before it ever has a chance to bloom and give us fruits. However, people are different than trees because each of us has our own limits and knowledge. Some people learn things fast but forget easy; others learn things slow but remember for life.

More Detailed of the Triple Consonants

No	Combine	Consonant	How to pronounce
1	bl + *h*	bl*h***	The "bl" is exactly like the English "bl" as in **bl**ock. The "h" suffix is the ***mouth-aspirated*** or puffing sound after the "bl."
2	***h*** + ml	**h***ml*	This one has the ***nasal-aspirated*** "h" so this means you will be puffing through your nose prior to uttering the "ml."
3	***h*** + ny	**h***ny*	This is similar to the **hml** consonant above. Try aspirating through your nose to form the "h" prior to uttering the "ny."
4	nc + ***h***	nc*h*	Utter the "**nc**" then finish it with the ***mouth-aspirated*** "h"
5	nk + ***h*** *(gh**)*	nk*h*	Utter the "**nk**" then finish it with the ***mouth-aspirated*** "h"
6	np + ***h*** *(bh**)*	np*h*	Utter the "**np**" then finish it with the ***mouth-aspirated*** "h"
7	np + ***l*** *(bl**)*	***npl***	Say this consonant as the English **bl** as in **bl**ock
8	nq + ***h***	nq*h*	Utter the "nq" then finish it with the ***mouth-aspirated*** "h"
9	nr + ***h***	nr*h*	Utter the "nr" then finish it with the ***mouth-aspirated*** "h"
10	nt + ***h***	nt*h*	Utter the "nt" then finish it with the ***mouth-aspirated*** "h"
11	n + ***ts*** *(j**)*	***nts***	Say this consonant as the English **J** as in **J**aw.
12	n + ***tx***	***ntx***	*See image below.*
13	pl + ***h***	pl*h*	Utter the "pl" then finish it with the ***mouth-aspirated*** "h"
14	ts + ***h***	ts*h*	Utter the "ts" then finish it with the ***mouth-aspirated*** "h"
15	tx + ***h***	tx*h*	Utter the "tx" then finish it with the ***mouth-aspirated*** "h"

** Some people use **j** in place of "*nts*", **bl** in place of "*npl*", and **gh** in place of "*nkh.*"
Notice that most of these triple consonants have the *"**h**" suffix – mouth-aspirated.*

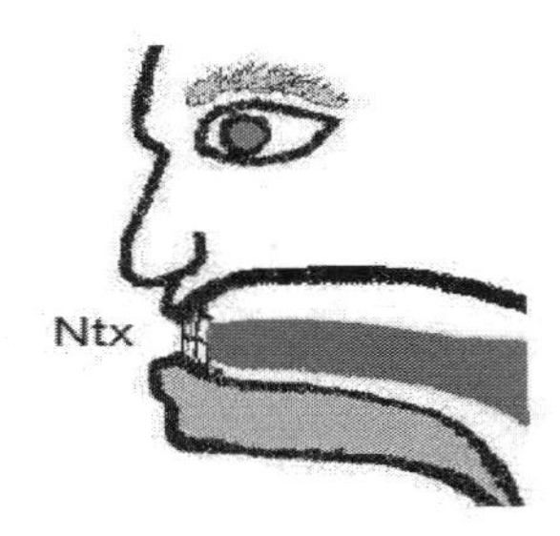

To say this "ntx", pronounced "ntxos", you need to start the Hmong consonant "nos" first. Once you have your mouth in the "nos" position, you are now ready to add the "txos" so the result is "ntxos." If this does not work for you, try saying the "ntos + xos" = ntxos. Realistically, the "n" is the base and the rest are being phonetically added to it.

For English phonetic this would be similar to the "**n + t + s**", as in the English word "a**nts** or a**ntz**." So if we create a new word "a*ntsaw*" and mute the **a**, the "*ntsaw*" would have a similar phonics like the Hmong word "ntxos."

Triple Consonants

Consonant	Word	Picture	Example & Practice Reading
Blh* *blhos*	blh + *aib* Blh*aib*	**Blh**aib / Ring	You have a <u>gold</u> **ring**. *Koj muaj ib lub* ***blhaib*** *<u>kub</u>.* *Nej puas* ***muag*** *blhaib kub?* *Do you* ***sell*** *gold rings?*
Hml *hmlos*	hml + *os* Hml*os*	**Hml**os / Dent	**Dent** Like a dented or sunk in surface. You **dented** the kettle. *Koj tsoo lub fwj kais* ***hmlos.*** hmlos hmluav hmliam hmlub hmlab hmleem hmliav hmlom.
Hny *hnyos*	hny + *av* Hny*av*	**Hny**av / Heavy	<u>This</u> **rock** is very heavy. *Lub* ***pob zeb*** *<u>no</u> hnyav heev.* hnyav hnyuv hnyeb hnyob hnyuj hnya hnyooj hnyeem. *Hnya means squint* *Hnyuv means intestine.*

- Some people use "blh" in place of the "nplh" like "blhaib" instead of "nplhaib."

<u>Practice Reading</u>

Yog koj kawm los txog nov ces koj keej heev li lawm nawb. Kuv yuav tsis qhia txog kev nyeem, tabsis piav txog peb lo lus saum toj xwb. Lub *blhaib* lossis *nplhaib* ces yog lub *ring*. Lub blhaib nyob siab lossis saum toj ntawm lub fwj kais uas mluav ib sab. Lub nram qab kawg ces yog lub *pob zeb* loj thiab hnyav heev. Tus poj niam no yuav nqa tsis tau vim lub pob zeb hnyav heev li. Nyob rau hauv nruab nrab ces yog lub fwj kais uas *hmlos* ib sab lawm. Sab uas hmlos yog sab xis, *the right side*.

Koj paub nyeem ntawv Hmoob zoo lawm. *You know how to read Hmong well already.* Yog li, *therefore*, thov qhuas koj, *want to congratulate you.* Yog koj muaj sij hawm, *if you have time,* thov koj sau ntawv tuaj qhia kuv paub, *please write to let me know.* Nyob zoo koj. *Goodbye to you.*

Triple Consonants

Consonant	Word	Picture	Example & Practice Reading
Nch *nchos*	nch + o Nch*o*	**Nch**o pa / Smoke	**Smoke** – like the black smoke from a fire that just get started. The fire <u>emits</u> some black **smoke**. *Lub cub tawg <u>ncho</u> ib cov **pa** dub.* Peb hnov lawv hais lus nchav heev. Nchaiv Phaj yog ib lub npe. Koj mus kev nchuj nchias.
Nkh *nkhos*	nkh + *aus* Nkh*aus*	**Nkh**aus / Curve	This road is too **curvy**. *Txoj kev no **nkhaus** heev.* Txoj kev nkhaus tsis muaj neeg xav taug. Taws nkhaus tsiv rauv; neeg laus tsiv tu. ***Tus neeg siab nkhaus** ces yog **a crooked person.***
Nph *nphos*	nph + *oo* Nph*oo*	**Nph**oo / Shake	**Shake** black peppers <u>on</u> my pho. ***Nphoo** hwj txob <u>rau</u> kuv tais fawm.* Peb taug txoj kev nkhaus mus pom ib lub cub tawg ncho pa dub nciab puag tim roob tuaj. Lub roob pob nphau nphwv los npog lub pas dej.

Practice Reading

Peb taug ib txoj kev nkhaus nkhaus mus pw tom hav zoo. Thaum mus txog ces peb mus rauv ib lub cub tawg, **fire place**, uas peb siv los ua mov thiab ci nqaij. Thaum peb pib noj su ces peb mam li nco tias peb tsis tau rau jev, **salt**. Yog li, peb thiaj li mam siv hwj jev los nphoo rau ua ntej peb noj.

Muaj ib cov neeg lawv nyiam siv tus **J** los hloov tus "***nts***" uas yog **have the same phonics**. Tsis paub tias Hmoob yuav siv tus twg tiag, tabsis kuv yog tus sau ces kuv yuav tau qhia rau nej cov kawm kom nej pom los nej thiaj li paub. Ib txhia neeg lawv kuj siv tus **B** los hloov tus "***np***", thiab tus **G** los hloov tus "***nk***" vim cov ntawv no, yog hais raws suab Askiv ces *they have the same phonics or pronunciation.* Rau kuv, kuv nyiam siv cov ntawv tshiab, **b**, **j**, and **g** because they are much shorter.

Triple Consonants

Consonant	Word	Picture	Example & Practice Reading
Npl *nplos*	npl + *ooj* Npl*ooj* *(blong)*	**Npl**ooj / Leaf	The insect carries a **leaf**. *Tus kab kwv daim **nplooj**.* Lub caij ntuj qhua ces ua rau ntoo zeeg nplooj tag, tabsis lub caij ntuj nag ces blooj ho rov hlav puv roob. Ib nplooj siab ces yog *a leaf of heart* – a piece of heart that is.
Nqh *nqhos*	nqh + *uab* Nqhua*b*	**Nqh**uab / Dried up	**Dried up** Like a dried up pond. The fish died because the pond **dried up**. *Cov ntses tuag vim lub pas dej **nqhuab**. Tsis los nag ces tej pas dej nqhuab tag. Did not rain so the ponds all dried up.*
Nrh *nrhos*	nrh + *au* Nrh*au*	**Nrh**au cag / Root	**Root** Like *growing* roots. This bamboo is **rooting**. *Yav xyoob no **nrhau cag**.* Txiav xyoob los tsau dej kom nws *nrhau cag* lawm ces koj mam li coj mus cog thiaj li ciaj nawb.

Practice Reading

Ib lub teb chaws twg ces yeej muaj ib daim av. Nyob rau hauv lub teb chaws ces tseem muaj dej, xyoob thiab ntau hom ntoo. Tsis tag li, neeg tseem siv av los cog qoob loo, xws li pob kw, nplej, dib thiab taub tej. Thaum lub caij ntuj qhua ces nws sov thiab tshav kub heev. Yog li, tej pas dej me thiaj li lau thiab nqhuab tag. Lub caij ntuj no nws ua rau tej nroj tsuag tuag thiab pib zeeg nplooj zom zaws.
Tabsis lub caij ntuj nag rov tawm tuaj ces kuj ua rau tej xyoob thiab ntoo rov nrhau cag, *growing roots*, thiab hlav nplooj zom zaws. Lo lus "zom zaws" means everywhere, *as blooming everywhere*.

Triple Consonants

Consonant	Word	Picture	Example & Practice Reading
Nth *nthos*	nth + *uav* Nth*uav*	**Nth**uav / Open	**Open** Like a flower that is **opening** or blooming. The red flower **opens** very pretty. *Lub paj liab* ***nthuav*** *zoo nkauj heev. Koj nthe nrov dhau. You yell too loud.* *Koj* ***nthee*** *qe means you* ***fry*** *eggs.*
Nts *ntsos*	nts + *es* Nts*es* *(jay)*	**Nts**es / Fish	In the ocean there are many kinds of **fish**. *Hauv dej hiav txwv muaj ntau hom* ***ntses****. Neeg ntse hais lus tob; neeg ruam hais lus chob.* *Ntsia* ***kuv*** *= watch* ***me****.* *Ntsaum = ants* ***Ntseeg*** *kuv =* ***believe*** *me.*
Ntx *ntxos*	ntx + *uam* Ntx*uam*	**Ntx**uam / Fan	**Fan** Like a small hand fan. People use **fans** to cool them off. *Neeg siv* ***ntxuam*** *los ua kom lawv txias. Ntxias means to entice.* ***Ntxeev*** *means* ***turn*** *or* ***flip*** *over.*

Practice Reading

Lub caij ntuj nag ces tej nag ua rau tej paj ntoos tawg nthuav zoo nkauj thiab ja iab nyob puv roob thiab puv hav. Tej hav dej los loj thiab ntws huv si ua rau tej mi jes zoo siab zoo jws npaum li muaj ib lub ntuj *tshiab (chia)* tawm tuaj. Tabsis txog kiag rau lub caij ntuj so ces hnub los kub, huab cua los sov~ kawg li. Yog li, neeg thiaj tsim tej kiv cua, *fans*, thiab *ntxuam* los siv rau lub caij ntuj so no. Yog koj xav noj nqaij *ntses* ces koj yuav tau hais li nram qab no: *Koj puas* ***muag*** *nqaij ntses?* Asking for a specific kind of fish. *Koj puas muaj cov ntses tilapia?* Kuv muaj los mas. Ib tug pes tsawg ohs? Rau duas xwb ohs. ***Asking for flowers.*** *Koj muaj pes tsawg hom paj ohs?* Kuv muaj ntau hom nawb. *I have many kinds*. Koj xav yuav hom paj twg? *What kind do you like to buy?* Kuv xav yuav hom hu ua ***lily*** no. Suab Hmoob yog "lib lim" no. Muaj thiab los mas. Ib lub paj yog peb duas xwb. ***Asking for rice.*** Nej puas *muag* mov (cooked rice)? Kuv muaj mov txua thiab mov nplaum. *I have the non-sticky and sticky kinds.* Kuv yuav **tsib duas** cov mov nplaum. *I want to buy* ***five dollars*** *of the sticky rice.* Ua tsaug ntau nawb. *Thank you very much.*

Triple Consonants

Consonant	Word	Picture	Example & Practice Reading
Plh *plhos*	plh + *uab* Plh*aub* *(plow)*	**Plh**aub Qes / Eggshell	**Shell, eggshell** Like the shell of an egg. Two **eggshells**. *Ob daim **plhaub qes**.* *Dib lub plhu daj heev.* *Dee's face is very pale.*
Tsh *tshos*	tsh + *eb* Tsh*eb* *(ch**ay**) as in d**ay***	**Tsh**eb / Car	I have a yellow **car**. *Kuv muaj ib lub **tsheb** daj.* *Koj muaj ib lub tsheb tshiab.* *You have one new car.* *Kuv tshaib means I am hungry.* *Koj tshem means you remove.*
Txh *txhos*	txh + *aum* Txh*aum*	**Txh**aum / File	**File** Like a metal file. People use **files** to file other metals. *Neeg siv **txhaum** los txhaum lwm yam hlau. Txhua = every* ***Txhua yam** means **everything**.* *Txhaum also means **wrong**.*

Txhaum is a metal file mainly use for filing other metal and wood surfaces. Another term which is very close to this tool is called "*txhuam*" and it is a device or tool Hmong use for peeling the dried corn seeds from the corncob. Additionally, this word "txhuam" can be a verb for "txhuam" pob kws. *Ref: From my mother Ntxhi Tsab Xyooj.*

Practice Reading

Hais txog peb yam duab uas muaj nyob rau saum toj ces neeg siv li nram qab no. Cov qe yog ib yam uas tib neeg nyiam noj tshaj. Ib txhia neeg lawv muab hau kom siav, tabsis ib txhia neeg lawv nyiam muab kib xyaw mov. Tsis tag li, qe kuj muaj ntau hom xws li qe qaib zoo txawv qe os. Daim duab nruab nrab ces yog ib lub tsheb *tsuas*, color, daj. Kuv hu color ua "tsuas" as **stain** in English. Peb nyiam caij tsheb mus kav khw (shopping). Daim duab hauv qab lossis kawg nkaus ces yog rab txhaum, *a metal file*. Rab txhaum yog ib rab uas neeg siv los txhaum (to file) lwm yam hlau uas xeb, *rusted*, kom du thiab tshiab tuaj. Tabsis rab txhaum no tsis muaj tus ko, *handle*, lawm nawb. Thiab rab "txhaum" mas txawv rab txhuam. Rab txhuam yog ib daim ntoo muaj ib tus ntsia lossis hniav uas neeg siv los txhuam cov ntsiav pob kws tawm ntawm tus *txha pob kws*, the cob or corncob.

The Triple Consonants with Pictures

Quadruple Consonants

These quadruple consonants are easy to learn because you already have learned the three triple consonants along with many of the *mouth-aspirated* "**h**" consonants. Again, make sure you really puff to a point that you *can hear the "h" sound clearly.*

No	How to combine	Consonant	Word example	English meaning
1	npl + ***h***	nplh*	nplh*aib* or *blhaib*	*Ring, like a diamond ring.*
2	nts + ***h***	ntsh*	ntsh*ai* or *jhai*	*Afraid, fear, scare*
3	ntx + ***h***	ntxh	ntxh*w*	*Elephant*

* Some people use "**blh**" to replace the "***nplh***", and "**jh**" to replace the "***ntsh***."

The consonant "**nplh**" can be pronounced as "**blh**" with the mouth-aspirated "h". Say this consonant like this: *blos + hos = blhos or Nplos + hos = nplhos.*

The consonant "**ntsh**" is easy, too. The "**nts**" is pronounced as the English "**jaw.**" Therefore, the "ntsh" is like "jos + hos = *jhos*" or "ntsos + hos = *ntshos.*" Again, make sure you utter the "jhos" in one utterance. This is easy. Try to say my name with a big cough – **Jh**ay! And this word has the same phonics like the Hmong word "**ntsh**ej or **jh**ej." Therefore, **nts**os + **h**os = **ntsh**os.

The last consonant "**ntxh**" is for the King of the jungle, **ntxhw** – the elephants. And I think you deserve to have a picture to help you out here.

How to pronounce the "ntxh" consonant

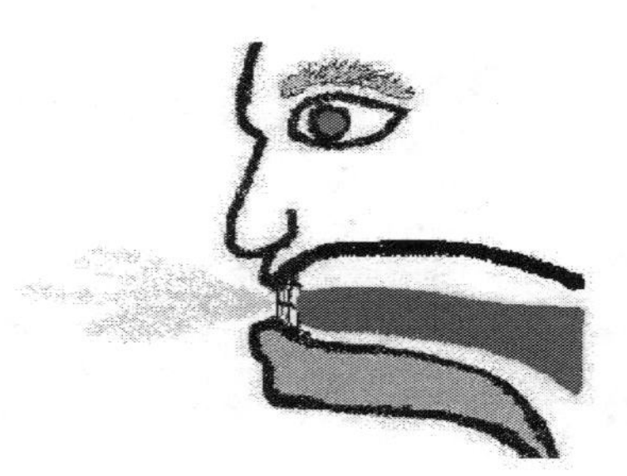

This consonant is a phonetic combination of the "nos + tos = ntos". Then "ntos + xos = ntxos", and then the "ntxos + *hos* = ntxhos." To say this consonant right, you do as follows:

1. Bite your teeth together like the image shown above.
2. Place the tip of your tongue by forming the "**nos**" like the picture above. Make sure you press your tongue evenly behind *both teeth* so you have enough force to puff out the "**h**" sound.
3. Now say the "**ntxhos**" by puffing air simultaneously with the "**ntxos**" and you have it.

See that was **ea**sy! By the way, how many tones did you hear when I said the English word "**ea**sy?" Two, very good, and here they are: **Ea**^{b}-sy$_{\mathbf{m}}$

Quadruple Consonants with Pictures

Consonant	Word	Picture	Example & Practice Reading
Npl*h* *nplhos*	nplh + *aib* Nplh*aib*	**Nplh**aib / Ring	Ring Like a diamond ring. You have a <u>gold</u> **ring**. *Koj muaj ib lub* ***nplhaib*** *<u>kub</u>.*
Nt*sh* *ntshos*	ntsh + *iab* Ntsh*iab*	**Ntsh**iab / Clear	Clear Like a ***clear*** and ***clean*** bottle of water. This is a **clear** bottle of water. *Nov yog ib fwj dej* ***ntshiab.*** *Kuv* ***ntshai*** *means I am* ***afraid****.* ***Ntshaw*** *means* ***desire to****.*
Nt*xh* *ntxhos*	ntxh + *w* Ntxh*w*	**Ntxh***w* / Elephant	People use **elephants** to <u>pull</u> logs. *Neeg siv* ***ntxhw*** *los <u>cab</u> cav.* *Ntxhais pab ntxhua khaub ncaws.* *Daughters help wash clothes.* *Tub kam ntxuav tais thiab diav.* *Sons agree to wash bowls and spoons.* ***Ntxhe*** *means* ***echo****.*

Practice Reading

Zoo siab heev uas koj tau kawm thiab mloog kuv tej lus qhuab qhia nawb. Kuv nrog koj zoo siab thiab kuv ntseeg tias koj yuav muaj peev xwm los hais, sau thiab paub txog lus Hmoob zoo lawm yav pem suab. Yog koj kawm thiab nyeem los txog qhov no, ces koj yeej paub lus Hmoob zoo kawg li lawm. Ntxiv mus ces tsuas yog kawm cov lus tshiab, *new vocabulary*, thiab kev siv lawm xwb.

Kuv nrog koj zoo siab heev. *I am very happy for you.*

A big congratulations to you my tenacious and sagacious Grasshopper. You have now learned all the Hmong consonants. However, this is just the beginning of your Hmong learning journey, and without practicing, your mouth and tongue will naturally go back to where they are used to – your native language. Therefore, you must incorporate these new tongue movements into your daily life if you want to speak Hmong well. And remember, the only limit to learning is the limit you put on yourself – not your tongue nor your ability. Just remember, you are a musical instrument where you can choose to play only one kind of music or blend it with a lot of others, and each type of melody creates a different mood and activates different hearing nerves not only in our heart but in our soul.

Consonants, Vowels and Tones Chart

Single	poly-consonants
B*	b***h*** bl bl***h***
C	c***h***
D	d***h***
F	
G*	g***h***
H	**h***l* **h***m* **h***ml* **h***n* **h***ny*
J*	j***h***
K	k***h***
L	
M	m*l*
N	n*c* nc***h*** n*k* nk***h*** n*p* np***h*** np*l* npl***h*** n*q* nq***h*** n*r* nr***h*** n*t* nt***h*** nt*s* nts***h*** nt*x* ntx***h*** n*y*
P	p***h*** p*l* pl***h***
Q	q***h***
R	r***h***
S	
T	t***h*** t*s* ts***h*** t*x* tx***h***
V	
X	x*y*, x*z*[1]
Y	
Z	

* Some people use a "B" in place of "**np**", "G" in place of "**nk**", and "J" in place of "**nts**."

H prefix means *nasal-aspirated**, i.e., **h***m*, **h***n*.
H suffix means *mouth-aspirated*, i.e., c***h***, d***h***, k***h***.
* Except for the "***HL***" consonant.

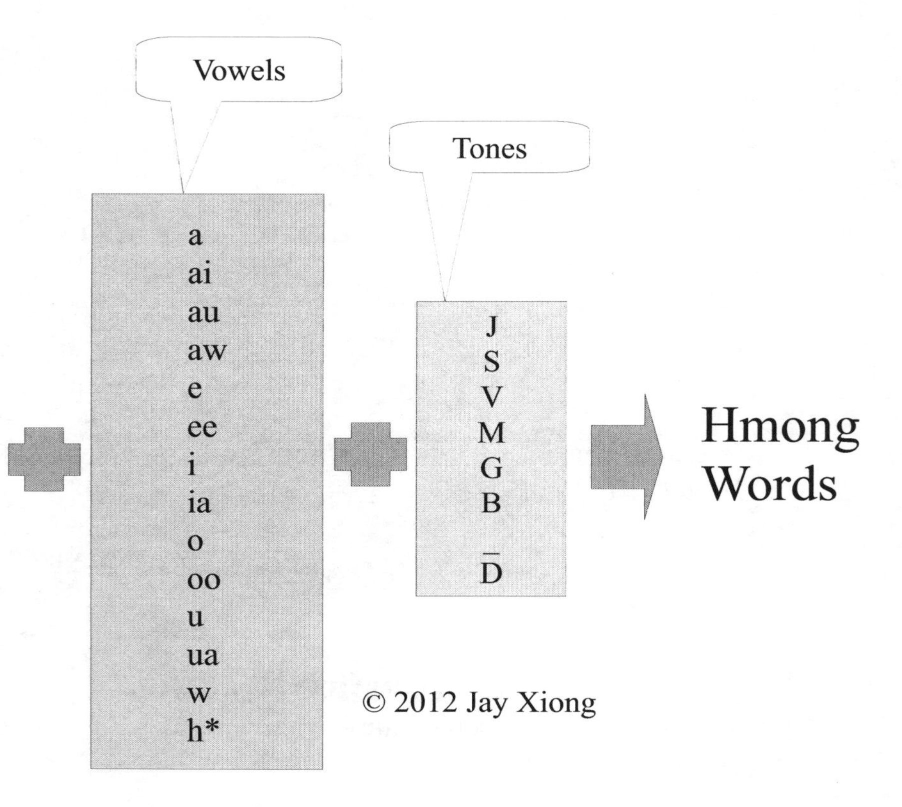

These are all the words combination in the Hmong language so if you can read any of these consonants, vowels, and tones, you should not have any problems reading and writing Hmong.

* h is also a silent vowel used for words such as ohs, ohm, ahm. This is a new vowel that I invented.

[1] New consonant for English "**z**" as in the word "**z**ip"

Consonants, Vowels and Tones Chart Exercise

Please have your students write down the double, triple, quadruple consonants, vowels and tones. Or you might want to read from the previous page and have your students write them in the appropriate place.

Single	poly-consonants
B	
C	
D	
F	
G	
H	
J	
K	
L	
M	
N	
P	
Q	
R	
S	
T	
V	
X	
Y	
Z	

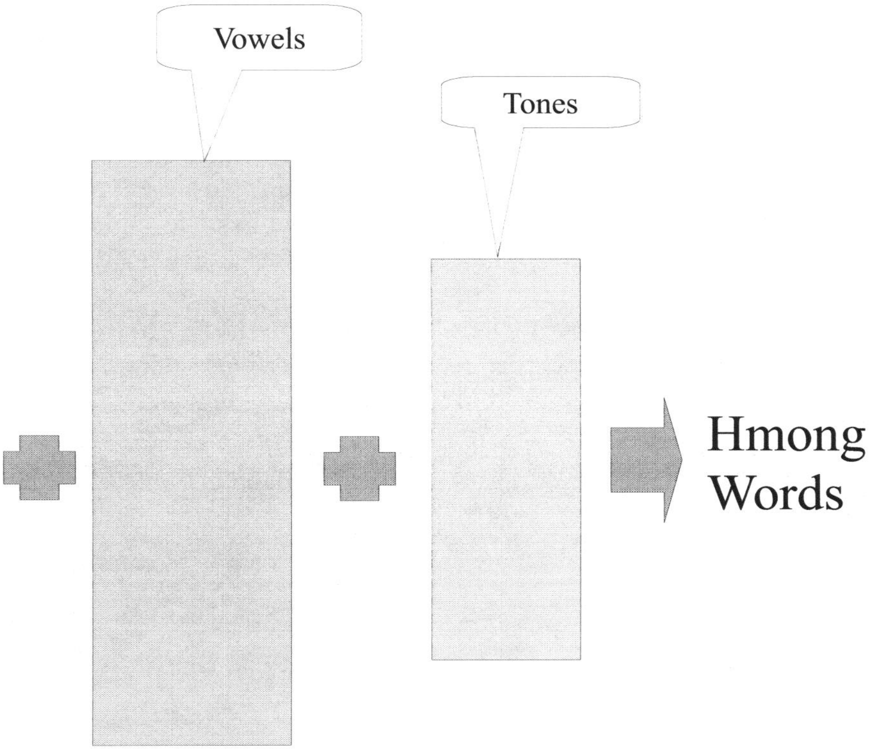

Vowels

Tones

Hmong Words

Pronouns

Hmong pronouns are similar to English; however, unlike English, there are no objective nor possessive pronoun forms – *just subjective pronouns*. For English, the first "person" pronoun has four forms (I, me, my, mine), but Hmong has only one form – **kuv**. So let's look at the difference between the *first* and *second* pronouns between these two languages.

	Subjective	Objective	Possessive	Possessive
1st person - English	I	Me	My	Mine
Hmong	***Kuv***	***Kuv***	***Kuv***	***Kuv***
2nd person - English	You	You	Your	Yours – *one person only*
Hmong	***Koj***	***Koj***	***Koj***	***Koj***

Notice that the English *first person pronoun* has four different forms, **I, me, my** and **mine**. However, the Hmong form has only one form called "**kuv**." Likewise, the English *second person* pronoun has three different forms, **you**, **your** and **yours** while the Hmong has one form called "**koj**."

So what does this mean to English speakers? Well, let me answer you with this question. Would you rather learn four different forms to mean "You" or just one? In other words, "I, me, my, mine" are all referring to the same person, "I", that is! Therefore, the single form is simple and it is more consistent with all other nouns, i.e., cow, fish, river etc... What I am trying to say here is that some languages only have one form for each pronoun, and the Hmong language is one of them. For example:

No	Hmong	English transliterated	Proper English
1	Kuv *nyiam* koj.	I *like* you.	I *like* you.
2	Koj *nyiam* kuv.	You *like* I.	You *like* me.
3	Koj *nyiam* koj.	You *like* you.	You *like* yourself. (*koj tus kheej*)
4	Kuv *lub tsev liab.*	I a house red.	My *red house.*
5	*Nov yog* kuv li.	This is I thing.	*This is* mine.

Number 1 is syntactically the same for both Hmong and English.
Number 2 is different and the difference is the word "me" in English.
Number 3 is not proper in English because of *you* – not *yourself* – got it?
Number 4 is different between "*Kuv*" and "*My.*"
Number 5 is different between "*Kuv*" and "*mine.*"

If you are confused, just remember that only "*Koj thiab Kuv*", "You and I." Of course, the proper order of where to place pronouns is still very much the same for both languages – subjective pronouns are always at the beginning of a sentence and possessive pronouns are at the end. If either a ***noun*** or a ***classifier*** is placed right after a pronoun, then that pronoun is most likely a *possessive pronoun*, for example: Kuv ***lub*** tsev = ***my*** *house*. Koj tsev neeg = ***your*** *family.* Kuv niam mus tsev lawm means ***my*** mother went home already etc... And *koj hu kuv* means *you call me*.

With that being said, here are some Hmonglish, English but speak like the Hmong way, for example:

No	English	Remarks
1	I like you.	**I** is a *subjective* pronoun and **like** is a verb, and **you**, in this position is at the end of the sentence so it is an *objective* pronoun. Now if you reverse this sentence around, it would look like the example number 2 below.
2	You like I.	This is strange for English speakers but the "I" here should stay the same like the pronoun "you" above, and this is how the Hmong language works. In other words, any pronouns that you place after the verb *like* is being liked by the pronoun in front of that verb. For example: ***I** like **you** and **you** like **I**. And not "**you** like **me**" which is the proper English.* ***Kuv** nyiam **koj** thiab **koj** nyiam **kuv**.*

Again, the order or position of where the pronoun is being placed is very similar in both languages. For example: **Kuv** hlub **kuv** niam vim *nws* hlub **kuv** heev.
I love **my** mother because *she* loves **me** a lot.

As you already know, **you, your, yours** are still referring to the same person – **you**. At a first glance, the Hmong way seems strange, but I can assure you that once you know the Hmong language, you will be able to speak it consistently well without carrying too many exceptions and extra words.

No	Hmong	English	Hmong Example	English transliterated
1	kuv	I, my, mine, me.	Kuv kawm lus Hmoob.	***I** learn language Hmong.*
2	phau ntawv	A book.	Phau ntawv no yog **kuv li**. Kuv li = mine. Kuv = I or me.	*This book here is **I thing**.*
3	rau	To	Muab rau **kuv.**	*Give to **I.**Give to me.*
4	qauv siv	Usage example.	Qauv **siv** phau ntawv no.	*Example **use** a book this.*
5	no	This	Phau ntawv **no** yog kuv li.	*The book **here** is I thing.*
6	yog	Is or belong to	Phau ntawv no **yog** kuv li.	*The book here **is** I thing.*
7	li	A possessive word.	Phau ntawv no yog kuv **li.**	*This book here is I **thing**.*
8	thiab	And, too, also	Koj **thiab** kuv. Kuv **mus** thiab.	*You **and** I. I **go** too.*

The purpose of these little exercises is to familiarize you with the similarity of the two languages even though the Hmong word stays the same, but pragmatically the word moves to its proper positions similar to English. So when you try to understand the English on the last column, you won't because it does not make English grammatical sense. However, when you read the Hmong column, it makes sense to the native Hmong speakers. The word "**li**", pronounced "lee" is a possessive word or form, and it is generally placed after the pronouns to signify its ownership. For example, "Phau ntawv no **yog** leej twg li?" means "*This book here **belongs** to whom?*" Qhov nyiaj no yog ***Paj li***. This money here is **Paj's**. Phau ntawv nov yog ***koj li***. This book is **yours**. Lub tsheb no yog ***peb li***. This car is **ours**.

So far we have covered only two pronouns: **You** and **I** or ***Koj*** *thiab* ***Kuv.*** Now we are ready to learn the rest of the pronouns.

No	English	Hmong	English objective and possessive pronouns		
1	I	Kuv	*my*	*me*	*mine*
2	You	Koj – one person	*your*	*yours*	
3	You	Neb – two persons (*you two*)			
4	You	Nej – more than two persons	*your*	*yours*	
5	They	Nkawv – exactly two persons			
6	They	Lawv – more than two persons	*their*	*them*	*theirs*
7	We	Wb – two persons (*we two)*			
8	We	Peb – more than two persons	*our*	*ours*	
9	He	Nws	*his*	*him*	
10	She	Nws	*her*	*hers*	
11	It	Nws	*its*		

Even though Hmong has only one pronoun for each form or person, the order of placement is similar to English in many ways. For example:

Hmong	English
Muab rau *kuv.*	Give to *me.*
Xa rau *koj.*	Send to *you.*
Koj pab *kuv.*	You help *me.*
Kuv lub tsev.	*My* house.
Kuv niam.	*My* mother.
Kuv zoo siab.	*I* am happy.

Once again, the English pronouns change from subjective to possessive and objective, but the Hmong pronouns remain the same through out. However, when the Hmong use pronouns as possessive pronouns, they will generally end the possessive pronouns with either the object names or their classifiers, For example:

English	Hmong	
This book is *mine.* This is my *book.*	Phau ntawv no yog **kuv *phau*** *or* Phau ntawv no yog **kuv *li.*** Nov yog **kuv** *phau ntawv.* Or *phau ntawv no yog kuv* ***li.*** The word ***li*** is a general term used mostly in place of the object and in this case is "phau" – a booklike object. For example, *Nov yog kuv li.* For the most part, Hmong generally place the classifier at the end of a sentence to indicate the ownership of an object. For example:	
	Lub	**Li**
This car is ***mine.***	*Lub tsheb no yog kuv* ***lub.***	*Lub tsheb no yog kuv* ***li.***
This knife is ***mine.***	*Rab riam no yog kuv* ***rab.***	*Rab riam no yog kuv* ***li.***
This house is ***yours.***	*Lub tsev no yog koj* ***lub.***	*Lub tsev no yog koj* ***li.***

English			Hmong		
Pronoun	Verb	Past tense	Pronoun	Verb	Past tense
You	go →	went.	Koj	mus →	mus.
I	*go* →	*went.*	*Kuv*	*mus*	*mus.*
We	go →	went.	Peb	mus	mus.
She	*goes* →	*went.*	*Nws*	*mus*	*mus.*

Hmong verbs **stay** the same.

Practice

Please fill in the Hmong equivalent pronouns on the right of each English pronoun.

English	Hmong	English	Hmong	English	Hmong
You	*koj*	He		You two	
I		She		We two	
We		Us		Our	
They		Them		His	

No	Hmong	English	Translate into Hmong
1	*kuv*	I go home.	Kuv _____ tsev.
2	*koj*	You come here.	K______ _______ nov.
3	*peb*	We like you.	P______ nyiam ______.
4	*nej*	You drink water.	N___ h____ d____.
5	*neb*	You help me.	N_____ pab ______.
6	*lawv*	They call us.	L ____ ____ p____.
7	*peb*	We call you.	P______ ______ k_____.
8	*koj*	You eat rice.	K______ ______ mov.
9	*nws*	He likes you.	Nws ______ k______.

Below are more examples.

No	Hmong	English	Hmong	English
1	Kuv *mus* tsev.	I *go* home.	Koj *haus* dej.	*You **drink** water.*
2	Koj *mus* tsev.	You *go* home. (*one person*)	Nej *pab* kuv.	*You **help** me.*
3	Nej *mus* tsev.	You *go* home. (*you all*)	Koj *los* nov.	*You **come** here.*
4	Peb *mus* tsev.	We *go* home. (*we all*)	Wb mus *noj mov.*	*We go **eat rice.***
5	Lawv *mus* tsev.	They *go* home.	Nej los *noj mov.*	*You come **eat rice.***
6	Nws *mus* tsev.	He/she ***goes*** home.	Nws *paub* koj.	*He/she **knows** you.*
7	Paj *mus* tsev.	Paj ***goes*** home.	Koj hais **ab tsi**?	*You say **what?***

Notice that the verb "**go**" in English changes to "goes" for the pronouns "he, she and it", but the verb "**mus**" of the Hmong stays the same. Also, in Hmong, there is no pronoun for he or she. Instead Hmong uses the word "**nws**", and it is analogous to the English word "**it**." Additionally, the Hmong word "**noj mov**" means "**eat rice**", but under most general use, it means "**eat meal**." For example: *Los nrog peb noj mov ohs* means *come eat with us*. However, "noj nqaij" means "eat meat" and "noj zaub" means "eat vegetables." Therefore, the Hmong words "**noj mov**" means "**eating**" in general.

Sometimes the Hmong people use the pronoun "**nws**" to represent the mentioned pronoun that is in the same sentence as to not keep repeating that same pronoun, and it is less direct as well. For example:

***Koj** ua neeg siab ncaj nawb es **nws** thiaj li tsis txom nyem mog.*
Nws tsis txhob ua neeg phem mog. This is talking indirectly to the second pronoun, *koj.*

Below are Hmong verbs and words that are similar to the English "-ing, -ed" verbs:

No	Hmong	English
1	*Koj mus tsev lawm.*	You *went* home already.
2	*Koj mus tsev.*	You *go* home.
3	*Koj mus tsev.*	You *are going* home.
4	*Koj twb mus tsev.*	You *have gone* home.
5	*Koj twb mus tsev lawm.*	You *had gone* home already.
6	*Koj tab tom noj.*	*You are eating*. Tab tom means "*in the process*" of.
7	*Koj sau **tau** ntau phau ntawv.*	You *have written* many books.
8	*Kuv nyiam koj.*	I *like* you.
9	*Peb twb noj hmo lawm.*	We *ate* dinner already.
10	*Kuv twb noj mov tag lawm.*	I ate *already.*
11	*Vim li cas koj tsis tau ua?*	*Why* you have not done?
12	*Rau qhov kuv tseem kawm ntawv.*	*Because* I am still studying.
13	*Koj **muag** qaib.*	You **sell** chickens.
14	*Peb ua teb.*	We do farming or *we farm.*
15	*Koj mus qhov twg?*	You are going *where?*
16	*Peb mus taj laj xwb.*	We go shopping only. *Taj laj* is a Lao word.
17	*Koj puas **muaj** mov?*	Do you *have* rice?
18	*Ib **phaj** pes tsawg?*	A **plate** is *how much*?
19	*Rau duas ohs.*	Six dollars.
20	*Ua tsaug nawb.*	Thank you.
21	*Tsis ua li cas.*	Not a problem.
22	*Mus zoo.*	Goodbye.

The word "**twb**" means "*already*" in English, and the word "**tab tom**" means "*in the process of.*" So then if you say, "Kuv ***tab tom*** noj mov." This means "I am *eating now*" or "I am *still eating.*" Another word the Hmong people use frequently is the word "**tseem**", and it means "*still.*" For example: *Kuv **tseem** noj mov* means "*I am **still eating.***" And *kuv **tseem** tab tom noj mov* means *I am still in the process of eating*. The word "**tab tom**" is like "*in the process of*", and "**tseem**" means ***still***.

Let's recap the Hmong pronouns one more time.

No	Hmong	English
1	Kuv	**I**, my, me, mine.
2	Koj	**You**, your, yours – singular or for one person only.
3	Lawv	**They**, their, theirs, them – for more than two persons only.
4	Neb	**You** (two persons) – you two.
5	Nej	**You** (more than two persons) – you all.
6	Nkawv	The **two of them** as a third person.
7	Nyias	**One** as *one* should be happy with himself or herself – onself.
8	Nws	He/she/it.
9	Peb	**We**, our, ours, us – more than two persons only.
10	Wb	**We** (two persons)
11	Yus	**One** as oneself
12	Luag	**Others**, like other people or person. This can be singular or plural.
13	Yawg	**He** or that **man**. Tus yawg hnav lub ris liab. The **man** wears the red pants.
14	Pog	**She** or that **woman**. Tus pog uas laus tshaj. The **woman** that is oldest.

Don't worry about **my**, **mine** and **me** at this point because we will be learning the differences plentifully later on. For now, all you need to understand is that "**koj**" means "**you**", and "**kuv**" means "**I**" and the rest, i.e., my, me, mine are going bye-bye.

Let's look at some more examples

No	Hmong	English transliterated	Proper English Translation
1	Koj **ntseeg** kuv.	*You **believe** I.*	You believe *me.*
2	Cia **kuv** qhia koj.	*Let **I** tell you.*	Let *me* tell you.
3	Phau ntawv no yog kuv li.	*This book is I thing.*	This book is *mine.*
4	Koj muaj pes tsawg **xyoo**?	*You have how many **years**?*	*How old* are you?
5	Koj muab **rau** kuv.	*You give **to** I.*	You give to *me.*

Strange? No, only your eyes and ears. If you were taught to speak like the Hmong way, you wouldn't even notice the strangeness at all. For most people, different means strange. In other words when we say, "Joe gives to John, You give to I, and I give to Joe" are understandable already. Now to call this right and wrong or *proper grammar* is another story. For instance, the pronoun "you" can be used as both nominative (*subject*) and objective which is similar to the Hmong pronoun "kuv"; however, for the pronoun "**I**" it changes to "**me**" for objective, for example: **I** give to **you**, and **you** give to **me**.

Verbs and Adverbs

Verbs are the action of any language, and it gives specific instructions. Unlike English, Hmong verbs don't change and do not have "-ed, -ing and -s" such as English words "wanted, wanting and wants." **Hmong verbs don't change except for times, locations, and pronouns.**

Verbs

No	Hmong	English transliterated
1	Kuv **nyiam** koj.	*I **like** you.*
2	Koj **paub** kuv.	*You **know** me.*
3	Kuv **paub** koj.	*I **know** you.*
4	Koj **muaj** nyiaj.	*You **have** money.*
5	Kuv **haus** dej.	*I **drink** water.*
6	Koj **pab** kuv.	*You **help** me.*
7	Kuv **mus** tsev.	*I **go** home.*
8	Koj **los** nov.	*You **come** here.*

As you can see, these verbs are very similar in both languages.

Present Tense			Past Tense		
1	He **likes** me.	Nws ***nyiam*** kuv.	4	He **liked** me.	Nws ***nyiam*** kuv.
2	You **like** me.	Koj ***nyiam*** kuv.	5	You **liked** me.	Koj ***nyiam*** kuv.
3	They **like** me.	Lawv ***nyiam*** kuv.	6	They **liked** me.	Lawv ***nyiam*** kuv.

Adverbs

Hmong adverbs are similar to English; however, the order might be different. Generally, adverbs are placed ***after the verbs***, i.e., Kuv *hlub* koj ***heev*** means I *love* you ***much.*** Here are some examples:

No	Hmong	English	Proper English
1	Kuv *nyiam* koj **heev.**	I *like* you **much.**	I like you **a lot.**
2	Koj **maj mam** *mus* kev.	You **slowly** *walk*.	You walk **slowly.**
3	Koj *muaj* nyiaj **ntau.**	You *have* money **much.**	You have **a lot** *of* money.
4	Kuv pab koj **heev.**	I help you **much.**	I help you **a lot.**
5	Kuv nyiam koj **dhau.**	I like you **much.**	I like you **a lot.**
6	Kuv nyiam koj **heev dhau.**	I like you **very much.**	I like you **very much.**
7	Koj ***kav tsij*** kawm lus Hmoob.	You *keep on* learning Hmong.	kav tsij = *keep on, continue on*

See more examples of adverbs on page 82.

Past Tense Verbs

No	English	Hmong
1	*Yesterday* I **ate** lunch.	*Nag hmo* kuv **noj** su.
2	I **came** to see you *before*.	Kuv **tuaj** saib koj *puag ta*.
3	Yesterday we **saw** you.	Nag hmo peb **pom** koj.
4	I **cut** the grass yesterday.	Kuv **txiav** nyom nag hmo.
5	He **wanted** to sleep.	Nws **xav** pw.
6	She **cooked** dinner.	Nws **ua** hmo.

Nag hmo = yesterday. *Lawm* and *twb* means *done* or in the *past*.

Present Tense Verbs

No	English	Hmong
1	Today I **eat** lunch.	Hnub no kuv **noj** su.
2	I **come** to see you today.	Kuv **tuaj** saib koj hnub no.
3	Today we **see** you.	Hnub no peb **pom** koj.
4	I **cut** the grass today.	Kuv **txiav** nyom hnub no.
5	He **wants** to sleep.	Nws **xav** pw.
6	She **cooks** dinner.	Nws **ua** hmo.

Hnub no = today, but realistically it means as follows: *Hnub = day, no = this or here* in Hmong.

Future Tense Verbs

No	English	Hmong
1	Tomorrow I *will* **eat** lunch.	Tag kis kuv *yuav* **noj** su.
2	I *will* **come** to see you tomorrow.	Kuv *yuav* **tuaj** saib koj tag kis.
3	Tomorrow we *will* **see** you.	Tag kis peb *yuav* **pom** koj.
4	I *will* **cut** the grass tomorrow.	Kuv *yuav* **txiav** nyom tag kis.
5	He *will* ***want*** to sleep.	Nws *yuav* **xav** pw.
6	She *will* ***cook*** dinner.	Nws *yuav* ***ua*** hmo.

Tag kis = tomorrow, *yuav* = will. *Mam li* also means will, i.e., kuv *mam li* mus = I *will* go.

As you can see from the above examples, both languages are very similar except for the verbs of the English past tense, i.e., **ate, saw, wanted** etc...

More Examples

No	Hmong	English
1	Kuv ***noj*** kuv pluas su.	I ***ate*** my lunch.
2	Kuv ***noj*** kuv pluas su.	I ***eat*** my lunch.
3	Kuv ***yuav noj*** kuv pluas su.	I ***will eat*** my lunch.
4	Koj ***hu*** kuv nag hmo.	You ***called*** me last night.
5	Koj ***hu*** kuv thaum koj mus txog tsev.	You ***call*** me when you get home.
6	Nws ***noj*** ntau heev.	He ***eats*** too much.
7	Lawv ***noj*** ntau heev.	They ***eat*** too much.
8	Nws *tab tom* ***haus*** dej.	He ***is drinking*** water now.

Perhaps you may not quite understand and/or like how the Hmong syntax works, but let's compare to some of the English ways that I think are somewhat similar to the Hmong construct. For example:

No	Hmong	English
1	Kuv ***txiav*** kuv cov nyom nag hmo.	I ***cut*** my grass yesterday.
2	Kuv ***txiav*** kuv cov nyom hnub no.	I ***cut*** my grass today.
3	Kuv *yuav* ***txiav*** kuv cov nyom tag kis.	I *will* ***cut*** my grass tomorrow.

As you can see, Hmong verbs work exactly like this English verb "**cut**" without ever changing. So how do you know when certain action was done?

Well, a typical question most people want to know is as follows:

1. Who?
2. Does what?
3. Where?
4. When? Yesterday means in the past so we don't need to use a past tense verb. Doing so it is like having two negatives or past tense words. So yesterday I eat is as logical as yesterday I cut.
5. How many or how much? Numbers already tell you how many, i.e., 5 **book** not 5 **books.** And the word "**books**" is as good as the word "**deer**" because you still don't know how many.

And when we can answer these questions then we should not need to change the verbs, for example:

Do to **did** and **done**
Eat to **ate** and **eaten**
Walk to **walk*ed***

Well, I believe you have learned enough about some differences between these two languages. If you are still confused, ***it is not the Hmong syntax it is you and*** *my bad* ***English :)***

Grammar and Syntax

Before we dive into grammar, let's review the keys I used in my **Lus Hmoob Txhais** dictionary:

No	English	Abbreviation	Hmong	Luv
1	pronoun	*pro*	tswv	*t*
2	adverb	*adv*	piav ua	*pu*
3	verb	*v*	ua	*u*
4	conjunction	*conj*	txuas	*tx*
5	adjective	*adj*	piav yam (piav txog)	*p*
6	noun	*n*	yam	*y*
7	interjection	*interj or int*	nthe	*nth*
8	preposition	*prep*	rau	*r*
9	classifier	*cl. or cla.*	hom	*h*
10	article	*art*	[number] + *classifier, i.e.,* ***ib lub***	

First, let's define what the word "**grammar**" means. Grammar, to me, is a method of conveying instructions in the most succinct way whether it be *verbal* or *written* form. In linguistic term it is called syntax, and syntax is the **rule** of how a language is constructed in the proper order. This is where computer *syntax comes from* – the proper and order of commands that makes sense to computers.

Huh, that is more than you care to know. In its simplest term, grammar means **syntax or rule**. With that being said, each language has its own rule; however, most languages do have similar construct such as *subject-verb-object.* Here are some examples of both English and Hmong syntax:

	Pronoun	Verb	Article	Adjective	Object		Adverb
English ⇒	I	like	a	red	car		a lot

	Pronoun	Verb	Quantity	Classifier	Object	Adjective	Adverb
Hmong ⇒	Kuv	nyiam	ib	lub	tsheb	liab	heev.

Here is the translation breakdown of the above sentences:

***I** = Kuv, **like** = nyiam, **a** = ib lub, **red** = liab, **car** = tsheb, **a lot** = heev.*

A lot, much, very = ***heev.*** *However, English articles,* **a, an** *and* **the**, ***are not*** *equal to Hmong* ***classifiers***.

Koj = ***You, your, yours***. **Koj** niam hu li cas? *What is* ***your*** *mother's name?*

Kuv = **I, my, me, mine**. **Kuv** txiv hu ua Txoov Neeb. ***My*** *father's name is Chong Neng.*

Kuv muab nov rau ***koj*** *= I give this to* ***you****. Koj* ***xa*** *rau* ***kuv*** *= You* ***send*** *to* ***me***.

I like **four** red cars a lot = Kuv nyiam **plaub** *lub* tsheb liab heev.

I like **many** red cars a lot = Kuv nyiam **ntau** *lub* tsheb liab heev.

I ***like the*** red car *only* = Kuv ***nyiam lub*** tsheb liab *xwb.* → No numbers specified here. ***A specific car.***

More Grammar

Let's look at the basic **subject-verb-object** construct.

No	Subject	Verb	Object	Equivalent transliterated
1.	Kuv	*mus*	tsev.	I *go* home.
2.	Koj	*noj*	mov.	You *eat* rice.
3.	Peb	*los*	tsev.	We *come* home.
4.	Koj	*hais*	kuv.	You *talk about* me. You *mention* me.
5.	Dev	*haus*	dej.	Dog *drinks* water.
6.	Nab	*tom*	nas.	Snake *bites* squirrel.

The above sentences are very general and without any classifiers. So let's add some classifiers to the first three sentences.

No	Subject	Verb	**Classifier**	Object	English Translation
1.	Kuv	mus	**lub**	tsev.	I go to a house.
2.	Koj	noj	**tais**	mov.	You eat a bowl of rice.
3.	Peb	los	**lub**	tsev.	We come to a house.

Now let's add adjectives to the above examples.

No	Subject	Verb	Classifier	Object	**Adjective**	English Translation
1.	Kuv	mus	lub	tsev	**loj.**	I go to a **big** house.
2.	Koj	noj	tais	mov	**nplaum.**	You eat a bowl of **sticky** rice.
3.	Peb	los	lub	tsev	**me.**	We come to a **small** house.

For more general sentence constructs, most complete sentences will have the following syntax:

No	**Subject** +	**verb** +	**qty** +	**classifier** +	**object** +	**adj**	**English**
1.	Koj	noj	peb	tais	mov	txua.	You eat three bowls of non-sticky rice.
2.	Koj	haus	tsib	fwj	cawv	dawb.	You drink five bottles of white wine.
3.	Koj	noj	ntau	daim	nqaij	qaib.	You eat many pieces of chickens.

Simple phrase

No	Pronoun	Verb	English
1.	Kuv	kam.	*I allow.*
2,	Kuv	paub.	*I know.*
3.	Kuv	hnov.	*I hear.*
4.	Kuv	nyiam.	*I like.*

Kuv kam koj mus tsev = *I allow you to go home.* Kuv hnov nws hais lus = *I hear him talk.*
Kuv paub nws zoo = *I know him well.* Nws nyiam noj mov = *He likes to eat* or eat rice.

Simple Phrase with "tsis"

No	Pronoun	Tsis	Verb	English transliterated	Proper English
1.	Kuv	***tsis***	kam.	I ***not*** allow.	I ***do not*** allow.
2.	Kuv	***tsis***	paub.	I ***not*** know.	I ***do not*** know.
3.	Kuv	***tsis***	hnov.	I ***not*** hear.	I ***do not*** hear.
4.	Kuv	***tsis***	nyiam.	I ***not*** like.	I ***do not*** like.

Perhaps the Hmong word "**tsis**" is analogous to the English word "don't" or "*dis*" as in **dis**allow.

No	Pronoun	Tsis	Verb	Verb	English	Proper English
1.	Kuv	***tsis***	kam	mus.	I ***not*** allow go.	*I **don't** want to go.*
2.	Kuv	***tsis***	paub	hais.	I ***not*** know say.	*I **don't** know how to say.*
3.	Kuv	***tsis***	hnov	cem.	I ***not*** hear yell.	*I **didn't** hear yell.*
4.	Kuv	***tsis***	nyiam	ua.	I ***not*** like do.	*I **don't** like to do.*

No	Pronoun	Tsis	Verb	Verb	Verb	English	Proper English
1.	Kuv	***tsis***	kam	mus	pab.	I *not* allow go help.	*I don't want to go help.*
2.	Kuv	***tsis***	paub	hais	zoo.	I *not* know say good.	*I don't know how to say good.*
3.	Kuv	***tsis***	hnov	cem	phem.	I *not* hear yell bad.	*I did not hear bad yell.*
4.	Kuv	***tsis***	nyiam	ua	dog dig.	I *not* like do so so.	*I don't like to do so so.*

Future Tense

No	Pronoun	Yuav	Verb	English
1.	Koj	***yuav***	kam.	You *will* allow *or let.*
2.	Koj	***yuav***	paub.	You *will* know.
3.	Koj	***yuav***	hnov.	You *will* hear.
4.	Koj	***yuav***	nyiam.	You *will* like.

Future Tense with "tsis"

No	Pronoun	Yuav	*Tsis*	Verb	English
1.	Koj	yuav	***tsis***	kam.	You will *not* allow.
2.	Koj	yuav	***tsis***	paub.	You will *not* know.
3.	Koj	yuav	***tsis***	hnov.	You will *not* hear.
4.	Koj	yuav	***tsis***	nyiam.	You will *not* like.

Other words and phrases that Hmong like to use.

No	**Hmong**	**English**
1.	Kuv *tsis* **lam** hais lus.	I *don't* just talk. Lam means not for real or without best effort.
2.	Kuv *tsis* **tshua** nyiam ua.	I *don't* really like to do.
3.	Koj **lam** *taus* **lam** hais.	You just say *without thinking, to ramble.*
4.	Kuv **xub** noj.	I ***first*** eat or I eat ***first.***
5.	Koj noj **tom qab** kuv.	You eat ***after*** me.
6.	Koj noj **ua ntej** kuv.	You eat ***before*** me.
7.	Koj yog tus **kawg.**	You are the ***last*** one.

Interrogative Sentence

No	Subject	+ verb	+ classifier	+ noun	Where, when, who, what, whom
1.	Koj	+ *mus*	+ leej	+ **twg**?	You ***go*** *to whom?*
2.	Koj	+ *yuav*	+ txoj	+ **twg**?	You ***buy*** *which one?*
3.	Koj	+ *noj*	+ lub	+ **twg**?	You ***eat*** *which one?*

No	Subject	+ verb	+ verb	+ verb	+ object	English
1.	Koj	+ ***puas***	+ *xav*	+ *mus*	+ tsev?	*Would you like to go* home?
2.	Koj	+ ***puas***	+ *xav*	+ *yuav*	+ mov?	*Would you like to buy* rice?
3.	Koj	+ ***puas***	+ *xav*	+ *noj*	+ mov?	*Would you like to eat* rice?

Puas = would and xav = like. Mov means cooked rice.

Unlike English, Hmong can place the adverb or questioning words either at the front or at the end of a sentence. So any time you see the interrogative or questioning words, i.e., *twg, ab tsi, puas*, then you know it is an interrogative sentence. However, let's standardize it by always putting them at the end!

No	Hmong	English transliterated
1.	Koj mus tsev hnub ***twg***?	You go home ***what*** day?
2.	Hnub ***twg*** koj mus tsev?	***What*** day you go home?
3.	Koj xav kom kuv pab ***ab tsi****?*	You would like me to help **what**?
4.	Koj xav kom kuv pab koj *li cas*?	You want me to help you **how**?
5.	Koj ***puas xav*** pab tiag maj?	You **would like** to help for real?

However, the following construct is not **too** common:

No	Uncommon Hmong	Proper Hmong	English
1.	*Ab tsi* koj noj?	Koj noj *ab tsi?*	*What* are you eating?
2.	*Leej twg* yog koj?	Koj yog *leej twg?*	*Who* are you?
3.	*Qhov twg* koj mus?	Koj mus *qhov twg?*	*Where* are you going?
4.	*Qhov twg* yog koj li?	Koj li yog *qhov twg*?	Which one is yours?

One thing to keep in mind is that there were very few written Hmong scripts, and so to say that certain syntax is correct and/or incorrect is going to be a tough debate. However, most people would agree that the logical way is the way how most native speakers use their language. Additionally, I believe you will learn Hmong the most by providing the literal, *transliterated*, translations. Otherwise, it would be something like the following:

Hmong	English
Koj muaj pes tsawg xyoo?	*How old are you?*

These two phrases have similar meanings, but word for word they are not the same. So the proper translation for the Hmong line is: *You are/have how many years?* And the proper translation for the English line is: *Pes tsawg laus yog koj or* ***koj laus pes tsawg?*** So as a beginner, you want to know the direct meaning and translation of each word from both languages, and when you are good, you will be able to translate *better* base on content rather than transliterated translations, for example: **Koj mus qhov twg → Where are you going**?

Let's just speak freely like a real Hmong speaker:

Nyob zoo. Zoo siab uas kuv tau tuaj ntsib nej hnub no. Tsis muaj ib yam uas yuav ua rau kuv zoo siab tshaj qhov tau tuaj pom nej sawv daws li no. Kuv xav tias ntshe tiam no peb yuav tsis muaj txoj hmoo rov los sib pom li no lawm tiag. Tab sis ua tsaug rau Tswv Ntuj vim nws tseem hlub peb txhua leej, thiab tsom kwm peb zoo heev; yog li, peb thiaj li muaj txoj hmoo zoo los sib jib dua. Ua tsaug Tswv Ntuj.
Hello. Happy that I have come to meet you today. There is nothing that would make me more happy than coming here and seeing all of you like this. I thought that perhaps in this lifetime we would not have the fortune to see each other like this again. But thanks to God because he still loves everyone, and looks upon us very good; therefore, we then have this good fortune to meet again. Thank you God.

To fully comprehend Hmong grammar, it will take more than just these few pages, but I certainly hope you have learned enough to start speaking like *most two year old children*.

I believe there are three types of conversation constructs

1. Asking questions, what, where, when, who, and how etc...
2. Answering the questions
3. General conversation

So let's recite some of the common Hmong questioning words. These words become more like nouns. For example: You go ***where***. You go ***when*** etc...

Twg?	Which What Who When	Tus **twg**? ***Which*** *one?* Leej **twg**? ***What*** *person or* ***which*** *person or plainly "**who**?"* Hnub **twg**? ***What*** *day or* ***which*** *day?* **Thaum** twg? *At* ***when*** *or just plainly "**when**?"* **Tiam** twg? *Which* ***generation*** *or what* ***generation?*** **Tav twg** nws mam los tsev? ***When*** *is he coming home?*
Ab tsi? Dab tsi?	What Why	**Ab tsi** nyob ntawv? ***What*** *is over there?* Koj noj **ab tsi**? *You eat* ***what****?* Koj tuaj **ab tsi**? *You come for* ***what****?* Koj mus **ab tsi**? *You go* ***for what?*** *Mus qhov twg = go where.*
Ua cas? Ua li cas?	Why	**Ua cas** koj tsis qhia peb? ***Why*** *you did not tell us?* **Ua li cas** koj ho tsis pab? ***Why*** *didn't you help?*
Pes tsawg? Npaum *li cas*?	How much? How many?	Koj muaj **pes tsawg** tus me nyuam? *You have* ***how many*** *kids?* Koj xav yuav **npaum li cas**? ***How much*** *do you want to buy?* Koj muaj **pes tsawg** lub tsev? *You have* ***how many*** *houses?* Koj hlub kuv **npaum li cas**? *You love me* ***how much****?*
Vim *li cas?* Tim *li cas?* Yog *li cas?*	Why Why Why	**Vim li cas** koj tsis qhia kuv? ***Why*** *didn't you tell me?* **Tim li cas** koj ho mus? ***Why*** *did you go?* **Yog li cas** koj ua li? ***Why*** *did you do that?*

Puas?	Do Are Would	Koj **puas** nyiam kuv? ***Do*** *you like me?* Koj **puas** mus tsev? ***Are*** *you going home?* *Koj **puas** tshaib plab? **Are** you hungry?* *Koj **puas** xav noj?* ***Would*** *you like to eat?* Puas as a verb means broken *or damaged.* Lub tsheb puas lawm.
Xav	Would Would like	Kuv ***xav mus*** tsev. *I **would like** to go home.* Kuv ***xav*** *mus* pw. *I **like** to* go *sleep.* Kuv ***xav*** *noj* mov. *I would like to eat.* *Xav also means think, i.e., cia kuv xav means let me think.*

As you can see from the these examples, Hmong generally will put the pronouns first, the doer, followed by the verbs and then the questioning words to construct a question or an interrogative sentence, for example: Koj mus *qhov twg*? = You go *where*?

Answering Questions

Rau qhov Vim tias Twb yog	Because	**Vim li cas** koj tsis qhia kuv? **Rau qhov** kuv tsis paub. ***Because*** *I don't know.* **Ua cas** koj tsis tuaj? ***Vim tias*** *kuv tsis xyeej.* ***Because*** *I am not available.* **Ua cas** koj mus tsev? ***Twb yog*** *kuv muaj hauj lwm.* ***Because*** *I have work.*

Practice

Please fill in the missing Hmong words on the left that are equivalent to the English on the right.

No	Hmong	English	
1	Koj ________ xav noj?	**Would** you like to eat?	*puas*
2	Nej ________ paub nws zoo?	**Do** you know him well?	*puas*
3	Koj ________ mus qhov twg?	Where **would** you like to go?	*xav*
4	Koj ________ mus qhov twg?	**Are** you going anywhere?	*puas*
5	____ _____ koj tsis hu kuv?	**Why** didn't you call me?	*Ua cas*
6	______ yog koj chim?	**Are** you mad?	*puas*
7	Koj muaj nyiaj ________ ______?	**How much** money do you have?	*pes tsawg*
8	Koj yog leej _____?	**Who** are you?	*twg*
9	Koj _____ kam pab kuv?	**Can** you help me?	*puas*
10	Koj xav noj ________ _____?	**What** do you like to eat?	*ab tsi*
11	____ ____ ua rau koj chim?	**What** made you angry?	*ab tsi*
12	Koj chim rau leej ________?	**Who** are you upset with?	*twg*
13	Hnub _______ koj mus tsev?	**What** day are you going home?	*twg*
14	Nej ________ muag ntses?	**Do** you sell fish?	*puas*
15	Leej _________ hu koj?	**Who** called you?	*twg*

Common Hmong Verbs

Using Hmong verbs is easy, use any pronouns, *koj, kuv, peb* plus any *verbs, i.e.,* ***kuv*** *mus tsev.*

No	Hmong	English	*Hmong Example*	No	Hmong	English	*Hmong Example*
1	ua**	*do*	*Koj **ua** mov.*	28	mob	*hurt*	*Nws **mob** tes.*
2	noj	*eat*	*Koj **noj** mov.*	29	txiav	*cut*	*Kuv **txiav** tus pas.*
3	haus	*drink*	*Kuv **haus** dej.*	30	xaws	*sew*	*Nws **xaws** lub ris.*
4	mus	*go*	*Wb **mus** tsev.*	31	ntub	*wet*	*Los nag **ntub** peb.*
5	pw	*sleep*	*Nej mus **pw.***	32	tsav	*drive*	*Peb **tsav** tsheb mus tsev.*
6	zaum	*sit*	*Wb **zaum** nov.*	33	yuav	*buy*	*Koj **yuav** mov rau peb noj.*
7	sawv	*stand*	*Nws **sawv** nov.*	34	quaj	*cry*	*Tus ab me **quaj** heev.*
8	los	*come*	*Nej **los** ntawm no.*	35	luag	*smile*	*Nws **luag** rau koj.*
9	zoo	*good**	*Koj **zoo** dua nws.*	36	chim	*mad**	*Peb **chim** rau nws.*
10	phem	*bad**	*Nws **phem** heev.*	37	qaub	*pull down*	*Kuv qaub tsob ntoo.*
11	ceev	*fast**	*Koj **ceev** dhau.*	38	yeem	*agree*	*Kuv **yeem** ua li nws hais.*
12	qeeb	*slow**	*Nws **qeeb** dhau.*	39	pub	*give*	*Lawv **pub** mov rau peb noj.*
13	hlub	*love*	*Kuv **hlub** koj.*	40	muab	*take*	*Nws **muab** lawv rab pas.*
14	nyiam	*like*	*Nej **nyiam** peb.*	41	nqa	*bring*	*Koj **nqa** rab rauj tuaj pab.*
15	ntxub	*hate*	*Neeg **ntxub** dab.*	42	dag	*lie, trick*	*Nws **dag** peb xwb.*
16	me	*small**	*Koj **me** dua nws.*	43	nyiag	*steal*	*Nws **nyiag** lawv nyiaj.*
17	loj	*big**	*Nws **loj** dua koj.*	44	pom	*see*	*Leej twg **pom** nws ua?*
18	tuag	*die*	*Tus tsov **tuag.***	45	tsoo	*crash*	*Lub tsheb **tsoo** tus ntoo.*
19	ciaj	*live*	*Nws **ciaj** rov los.*	46	ntaus	*hit*	*Nws **ntaus** tus dev.*
20	huv	*clean*	*Khob dej **huv.***	47	liam	*accuse*	*Lawv **liam** peb xwb.*
21	hais	*talk*	*Koj **hais** lus zoo.*	48	khiav	*run*	*Peb **khiav** mus ua si.*
22	hem	*scare*	*Dab **hem** peb.*	49	poob	*fall*	*Lawg **poob** los raug peb.*
23	pab	*help*	*Nej **pab** peb ua.*	50	kub	*burn*	*Dej **kub** nws tes.*
24	hu	*call*	*Koj **hu** rau kuv.*	51	ziab	*dry, tan*	*Nws pw **ziab** tshav.*
25	teb	*answer*	*Koj tsis **teb** kuv.*	52	no	*cold**	*Hmo ntuj **no** heev.*
26	sau	*write*	*Kuv **sau** lus Askiv.*	53	sov	*hot*	*Peb **sov** heev li.*
27	so	*rest*	*Peb **so** nov tso.*	54	tuav	*hold*	*Kuv **tuav** nws tes mus kev.*

* Adjectives in English can be used as *verbs* and *adjectives* in Hmong.

** **ua** means to work, to cook, to do, and to "be" etc...

More Hmong Verbs

No	Hmong	English	Hmong	English
1	nov qab	*forget*	cheb	*to sweep*
2	txaj muaj	*shy*	chim	*being mad, angry, upset*
3	txhawj	*worry, concern*	thuam	*to disparage, belittle, criticize*
4	txawj	*know how*	lees	*to admit, confess*
5	nco	*to think of*	nplua	*to fine (as a fee), slippery*
6	laub, hliv	*to pour*	nyiam	*like*
7	yuam	*to force*	tub sab	*to steal*
8	yuav	*to buy, purchase*	dhuav	*being tired of*
9	thov	*to beg*	qias	*being filthy*
10	tho	*to drill (a hole, for example)*	tsuas	*to produce a stain.*
11	ev	*to carry on the back*	tsuag	*being saltless, tasteless. No flavor.*
12	thauj	*to take, carry (in your car)*	daw	*salty, too much of.*
13	txawb	*1. to throw. 2. to put*	poog	*to join, to live with, mix with*
14	txhawb	*to support*	poob	*drop, fail, fall*
15	txo	*1. to put down. 2. to cut*	thim	*to back off, to return or refund.*
16	txias	*cold*	them	*to pay, reimburse*
17	deev	*to have sexual intercourse*	txhem	*to trim, to rid off unwanted portions*
18	xeeb (tub)	*being pregnant*	tsw	*having an odor or smell*
19	plam	*disconnect, break*	tsav	*to drive*
20	pluam	*being separated, disjointed*	txhuam	*to scratch or rub against*
21	tu	*break, as broken*	txhaum	*to file, like using a metal file*
22	to	*having a hole, punctured*	rhais	*to hang, to place*
23	tog	*to sink (in water)*	rhiab	*afraid, ticklish*
24	tov	*to mix, there*	ntshai	*to fear, scare*
25	toob	*to trick, to scam*	rub	*to pull*
26	ntes	*to arrest, capture*	kov	*to touch*
27	tom	*to bite*	thawb	*to push*
28	cheem	*to stop, prevent*	khawb	*to scratch*

The Hmong word "tuaj" means *to go* to other people's *place* or *home.*

The Hmong word "**los**" means *to return to* one's own home, i.e., *Kuv twb **los** tsev lawm.*

For example: **Koj los nov** means ***you come here***. **Koj los tsev** means ***you come home***. The word "tuaj" also means "come" but from their own place, i.e., **koj** *tuaj* **saib kuv**. **Nej** *tuaj* **pab peb** ltn...

Again, it might seem weird when you are comparing Hmong grammar to English because you are used to English and not Hmong. I truly believe most words can be directly translated, but some words, if you can describe or define it then you are very good. For example, "*Koj siab zoo" = "You are kind.*"

Let's look at some examples in more details:

No	Hmong	English	Remarks
1	Kuv **no**. Koj sov. Koj pw. Koj paub. Koj muaj. Koj los. Koj mus.	I *am* **cold**. You are hot. You sleep. You know. You have. You come. You go.	The missing word is "**am**", but when you look at the Hmong phrase, you understand that ***I am cold.*** In other words, the way the Hmong language is spoken is as if there **is no** "***to be***" verb. This is the reason why some foreigners speak as follows: **I bad.** Means ***I am bad.*** **You no good.** Means ***you are no good.*** **We very happy.** Means ***we are very happy.***
2	Hnub no **tshav ntuj**.	Today *is* **sunny**.	Today = Hnub no, and the verb "**is**" is missing in the Hmong. Sunny got translated into: **Tshav** means *sunny* and **ntuj** means *world.* Therefore, ***sunny** world* is equivalent to "*is sunny.*"
3	Koj **siab**.	You *are* **tall**.	You = koj, and ***siab*** means ***is tall***.
4	Koj **nrawm** *heev.*	You are *very* **fast**.	You = koj and **is fast** = **nrawm**, and heev = very.

I believe that, for the most part, human languages are very similar but 25 – 30 % are very distinctive or unique, and these you can only provide a summary or descriptive translation. This then is why I came up with the following metaphor:

A person without his native language is like a fruit without its native juice.

We are all human beings, like apple and pear trees, living and growing up in the same land, but yet distinctively we produce our own juice, and speak our own language. The real question human beings must ask themselves is: *Do we want to make all different kinds of fruits to produce the same juice?* Perhaps not! Even computer programming languages we still have more than one language when we are programming within the same computer operating system. This then proves that each language has its own unique way of searching and retrieving information whether it be computers or humans. Here is another quote of mine about knowing another language:

Knowing another language is like knowing a different cooking recipe.

One of the most common Hmong dish is called the "***zaub tsuag***." ***Zaub*** means vegetables and ***tsuag*** means "*no flavor*" and just *plain water* use for boiling the vegetables.

Perhaps you already know that the Latin-based language is widely known and popularly used throughout the world. However, the confusion is the fact that the writing might look the same but it has different meanings for different language. For example, the English word "**zoo**" means *a place where people keep many wild animals*, but the same spelling in Hmong "**zoo**", pronounce **zhong**, means *good or well*. However, humans can learn many languages and even more computer languages, too. For example, I know Laos, Hmong and English, and five different computer programming languages. Our brain and memory have very little limits when it comes to learning. The only limits is our age and times because we can not learn everything fast enough within our lifetime.

Now back to Hmong verbs. Verbs are the main elements that connect and keep things in motion. Therefore, we must know a lot of verbs if we want to communicate effectively. If all fail, don't forget to use your *hands* and *body language* because that works just about anywhere in the world, too.

No	Hmong	*Hmong Example*	English	No	Hmong	*Hmong Example*	English
1	ntshaw	*Kuv ntshaw ib lub tsev tshiab thiab loj.*	longing for or desire to have	13	tsuav	*Koj pab* ***tsuav*** *cov zaub los kib.*	chop
2	ntsuas	*Koj ntsuas kom yog.*	measure	14	ntxuav	*Koj pab* ***ntxuav*** *tais.*	wash
3	tau	*Wb tau mus thiab mas.*	had, did	15	saib	*Nws* ***saib*** *peb noj.*	watch
4	xa	*Koj xa duab tuaj nawb.*	send	16	cem	*Lawv* ***cem*** *nws phem*	yell
5	txais	*Peb txais tau lawm ohs.*	receive, get	17	thawb	*Koj* ***thawb*** *kuv ntog.*	push
6	txiav	*Nws txiav txoj hlua.*	cut, chop	18	ntog	*Nws* ***ntog*** *vim yog koj thawb.*	fall
7	hloov	*Peb hloov lub chaw.*	replace, change	19	pw	*Peb* ***pw*** *ib hmos.*	sleep
8	phais	*Tus kws kho mob phais nws lub plawv.*	operate, cut (*incision*)	20	sawv	*Nej* ***sawv*** *los noj mov.*	wake up
9	zoo	*Nws zoo lawm ohs.*	heal, well	21	haus	*Peb* ***haus*** *dej xwb.*	drink
10	lwj	*Lub dib lwj tag lawm.*	rot	22	tsoo	*Nws* ***tsoo*** *lub tsheb.*	crash
11	do	*Koj pab do lauj kaub zaub.*	stir	23	kho	*Peb* ***kho*** *lub tsheb.*	fix
12	kiv	*Lub log tsheb kiv ceev.*	spin	24	co	*Koj* ***co*** *tsob ntoo.*	shake

Negatives in the Hmong is very simple, and it is equivalent to the English "**no** or **not**", and somewhat it is similar to the English "**dis-**" verb prefix, i.e. **dis**like, **dis**agree, **dis**approve etc... For example:

No	Hmong	English	*Transliterated English*
1	Kuv ***tsis*** nyiam koj.	I *don't* like you.	*I* ***no*** *like you. Or I not like you.*
2	Kuv ***tsis*** *tau* pom koj.	I *have not* seen you.	*I* ***no*** *see you. Or I not see you.*
3	Peb ***tsis*** hnov nej hu.	We *did not* hear you call.	*We* ***no*** *hear you call. Or I not hear you call.*

The following Hmong ***words*** are considered ***negatives*** when used in front or before verbs.

No	Hmong	English	*Hmong example. English*
1	tsis	not or no	Peb ***tsis*** mus nawb. *We don't go okay.*
2	tsis *txhob*	do not, are not	Peb ***tsis txhob*** mus nawb. *We don't go okay.*
3	txhob*	not or no. This word "**txhob**" is being used interchangeably with the word "**tsis**" as well as after the word "**tsis**", i.e., *tsis txhob* mus = don't go.	Peb ***txhob*** mus nawb. *We don't go okay.* A another word that is similar to "**txhob**" is ***txhawb*** *and it means to support or to encourage.*
4	thab	not or no	Kuv ***thab*** nyiam. I *don't* like.

The word "tsis" means "not" and the word "txhob" means "to encourage or urge" to do more. So personally, I think the proper grammar is only use the word "tsis" and not "tsis txhob" or "txhob." The words "*tsis txhob*" means "*not to urge* or *not to encourage*." The word "thab" also means *to bother.*

Here are some examples of the negative words mentioned above.

No	Hmong	English
1	Koj *tsis* paub hais lus Askiv.	You *don't* know how to speak English.
2	Koj *tsis* ua li peb hais.	You *did not* do according to what we said.
3	Koj *tsis txhob* mus.	You *do not* go.
4	Peb *txhob* cem lawv.	We *do not* yell at them. We do not badmouth them.
5	Koj *tsis txhob* noj.	You *do not* eat. You should not eat.
6	Koj *txhob* noj.	You *do not* eat. But it is more like *"you not eat."*
7	Kuv *thab* nyiam mus.	I *don't* like to go.

* Like I said before, the Hmong word "tsis" is equivalent to the following English negative forms:

Tsis = *not, no, do/does not.* For example: Kuv tsis nyiam pw = I don't like to sleep.
Tsis = *are/is not.* For example: Kuv tsis yog tus neeg phem = I am not a bad person.
Tsis = *have/has not.* For example: Kuv tsis tau mus = I have not gone.
Tsis = *will/would not etc...* For example: Tag kis kuv tsis mus = Tomorrow I will not go.

Hmong Adverbs

Perhaps you already know that most highly educated people do talk differently than the less uneducated ones – more succinct words with a lot of *adverbs* and *colorful adjectives*.

Hmong Verb	Meaning	Changing to Adverb	English Adverb
Maj	*Hurry*	Maj ***nroos***	Hurried***ly,*** *hastily.*
Tshiab	*New*	Tshiab ***khiv***	New***ly***
Rua	*Open*	Rua ***plias***	Open***ly***
Nruj	*Tight*	Nruj ***nreem***	Tight***ly***

No	Hmong	English	Hmong example	English transliterated
		Below are some Hmong adverbs		
1	*maj mam*	slowly	*Koj* ***maj mam*** *noj.*	You *slowly eat.*
2	*nrawm nroos*	hastily	*Nws mus kev* ***nrawm nroos.***	He walks *hastily.*
3	*txhob txwm*	purposely	*Koj* ***txhob txwm*** *dag.*	You *purposely* lie.
4	*tab meeg*	openly	*Koj* ***tab meeg*** *hais.*	You *openly* say.
5	*nyuam qhuav*	just (like just go)	*Koj* ***nyuam qhuav*** *mus.*	You *just* went.
6	*dhau*	much or a lot	*Koj nyiam kuv* ***dhau.***	You like me *much.*
7	*heev*	very, serious	*Koj phem* ***heev.***	You are *very* bad.
8	*khov kho*	solidly, sturdy	*Nws ua tau* ***khov kho.***	He built it *solidly.*
9	*yog li*	therefore	*Yog li, peb yuav ua li cas?*	Therefore, what should we do?
10	*txawm**	even though	*Txawm koj mus los kuv nyob.*	Even you go I still stay.

* Mostly, Hmong use this word with other words, i.e., "*txawm* ***tias****, txawm* ***yog****, txawm* ***ho***" etc...

Actually, there is not much of a difference between Hmong and English when it comes to adverbs. However, the order or position is very important. For example:

Nws phem heev is not the same as **nws *heev* phem**, and this is not any different than English.
For example: **He is very bad** is not the same as **he is bad *very***.

For some adverbs, you can place them anywhere and it still makes sense. However, for some, they are in a specific order, and this is true for both languages. Again, each language has its own syntax or grammar, and you will learn them once you know enough words and verbs to put them into phrases and sentences. Like I said in the beginning, the first thing to master is the ability to read and understand some of the basic words, i.e., pronouns, verbs and a few lovely words that you like the most. For example:

No	Pronoun +	Verb +	Object =	Sentence	English transliterated
1.	Kuv	mus	tsev. =	*Kuv mus tsev.*	*I go home.*
2.	Koj	noj	mov. =	*Koj noj mov.*	*You eat rice or you eat.*
3.	Nej	pub	tsov. =	*Nej pub tsov.*	*You feed tiger.*
4.	Peb	tsav	tsheb. =	*Peb tsav tsheb.*	*We drive car.*
5.	Nas	tom	tes. =	*Nas tom tes.*	*Squirrel bites hand.*
6.	Lawv	dag	peb. =	*Lawv dag peb.*	*They trick us. They lied to us.*
7.	Koj	muaj	nyiaj. =	*Koj muaj nyiaj.*	*You have money.*

Now looking at the Hmong and English syntax, both are very similar. Properly, the things that were *missing are the articles* in the English. However, the Hmong examples are very acceptable and proper but not some of the English sentences, i.e., *we drive cars* or *we drive a car* would be more correct. Just remember, *you, he, and I* **drive** car. No "-s" for *drives* and *cars*, and "**lub** tsheb" is analogous to the English "**a** car" or "**the** car." For example, *lub* tsheb *liab = the red* car, and *lub* tsheb = *a* car.

Adjectives, Conjunctions and Prepositions

Adjectives play an important role in our daily conversations because it adds colors and characteristics to objects; therefore, without adjectives objects would be formless and colorless.

No	Hmong	English	No	Hmong	English	No	Hmong	English
1	zoo	good	24	phem	*bad*	45	muag	*soft, tender*
2	loj	*big*	25	me	*small*	46	tawv	*hard, tough*
3	ntev	*long*	26	luv	*short*	47	ruaj	*sturdy, solid*
4	deb	*far*	27	ze	*near*	48	nkees	*tired*
5	siab	*tall*	28	qes	*short*	49	qub	*old*
6	dawb	*white*	29	dub	*black*	50	tshiab	*new*
7	tob	*deep*	30	ntiav	*shallow*	51	nplaum	*sticky*
8	dav	*wide*	31	maj	*hurry*	52	no	*cold*
9	nqaim	*narrow*	32	qeeb	*slow*	53	txoom	*wrinkle*
10	chim	*mad*	33	zoo siab	*happy*	54	xos liam	*dirty, filthy*
11	*ncaj*	*straight*	34	hluas	*young*	55	huv	*clean*
12	rog	*fat*	35	yuag	*skinny*	56	liab	*red*
13	zoo *nkauj*	*pretty*	36	dab tuag	*ugly*	57	ntsuab	*green*
14	pluag	*poor*	37	nplua nuj	*rich*	58	daj	*yellow*
15	zoo *nraug*	*handsome*	38	txaj muag	*shy*	59	tseeb	*real, true*
16	cuaj khaum	*stingy*	39	chim	*upset, mad*	60	cuav	*dag, fake*
17	huv	*clean*	40	qias	*dirty*	61	kheej	*round*
18	tshav *ntuj*	*sunny*	41	pos huab	*cloudy*	62	pluav	*flat, dented*
19	laus	*old*	42	siav	*cooked, ripe*	63	tiav	*complete, done*
20	sov	*warm*	43	kub	*hot, gold*	64	ntsim	*spicy, hot*
21	tub *nkeeg*	*lazy*	44	nquag	*ambitious*	65	qhuav	*dry*
22	nrov	*loud*	45	ceev	*fast*	66	ntub	*wet*
23	kim	*expensive*	46	pheej yig	*cheap*	67	tiaj	*even , flat*

Keep in mind that most Hmong adjectives can also be used as verbs. For example: ***Koj siab dua kuv*** means *you are taller than me.* ***Kuv no heev*** *means I am very cold.*
The words "**zoo nkauj**" means "*pretty girl*", and "**zoo nraug**" means "*pretty guy.*" These are close to the English words "**pretty girl**" and "**handsome guy**." The word "**siab ncaj**" means "*heart straight*" which means not *wicked* or not *crooked* then – honest, candid, and sincere that is.

Here are some adjective examples

No	Hmong	Hmong Example	English	Equivalent English
1	phem	*Peb muaj ib lub tsheb **phem.***	bad	*We have a **bad** car.*
2	me	*Nws nyiam lub tsev **me.***	small	*She likes a **small** house.*
3	luv	*Koj cov plaub hau **luv.***	short	*Your hair is **short.***
4	ze	*Koj nyob **ze** heev.*	near/close	*You live very **near** (or close).*
5	qes	*Tsob ntoo **qes.***	short	*A **short** tree.*
6	dub	*Peb muaj ib tus nees **dub.***	black	*We have a **black** horse.*
7	ntiav	*Lub pas dej **ntiav** heev.*	shallow	*The pond is very **shallow.***
8	laus	*Koj muaj ib daim teb **laus.***	old	*You have an **old** farm.*
9	qeeb	*Koj khiav **qeeb** dua kuv.*	slow	*You run more **slow** than me.*
10	zoo siab	*Neeg **zoo siab** hais lus mos.*	happy	*Happy people talk soft (friendly).*
11	siab phem	*Neeg **siab phem** hais lus phem.*	wicked	***Wicked** people talk bad.*
12	yuag	*Tus nyuj **yuag** mus kev qeeb.*	skinny	*A **skinny** cow walks slow.*
13	dab tuag	*Nws **dab tuag** dhau.*	ugly	*It is very **ugly.***
14	nplua nuj	*Tsawg leej neeg **nplua nuj.***	rich	*A few people are **rich.***
15	xos liam	*Nws lub tsev **xos liam** heev.*	dirty	*His house is very **dirty.***
16	npag	*Lawv yog neeg **npag.***	chubby	*They are **chubby** people.*
17	nka tawv	*Koj **nka tawv** dhau.*	slender	*You are very **slender** (skinny).*
18	pos huab	*Hnub no **pos huab** heev.*	cloudy	*Today is very **cloudy.***
19	hluas	*Koj **hluas** tshaj kuv.*	young	*You are more **young** than me.*
20	no	*Kuv **no** heev.*	cold	*I am very **cold.***
21	siav	*Kuv nyiam noj nqaij **siav** xwb.*	cooked	*I like to eat **cooked** meat only.*
22	nyoos	*Koj puas nyiam noj nqaij **nyoos**?*	raw	*Do you like to eat **raw** meat?*
23	qub	*Kuv muaj ib lub tsev **qub**.*	old	*I have one **old** house.*
24	tshiab	*Koj muaj ib lub tsheb **tshiab**.*	new	*You have one **new** car.*
25	txawv	***Txawv** neeg ces **txawv** siab.*	different	***Different** person has **different** heart.*
26	tib yam	*Kuv nyiam koj tib yam.*	same	*I like you the **same.***
27	tsau	*Kuv noj **tsau** lawm.*	full	*I eat **full** already. → am full.*
28	tshaib	*Tus neeg **tshaib** noj mov ntau.*	hungry	*A **hungry** person eats a lot.*
29	txaj muag	*Koj yog ib tus neeg **txaj muag**.*	shy	*You are a **shy** person.*

More Adjective Examples

No	Hmong	Hmong Example	English	Equivalent English
1	zoo	*Peb muaj ib lub tsheb **zoo.***	good	*We have a **good** car.*
2	loj	*Nws nyiam lub tsev **loj.***	big	*He/she likes a **big** house.*
3	ntev	*Koj cov plaub hau **ntev.***	long	*Your hair is **long.***
4	deb	*Koj nyob **deb** heev.*	far	*You live very **far.***
5	siab	*Tsob ntoo **siab.***	tall	*A **tall** tree.*
6	dawb	*Peb muaj ib tus nees **dawb.***	white	*We have a **white** horse.*
7	tob	*Tus dej hiav txwv **tob** heev.*	deep	*The ocean is very **deep.***
8	loj	*Koj muaj ib daim teb **loj.***	large	*You have a **large** farm.*
9	ceev	*Koj khiav **ceev dua** kuv.*	fast	*You run more **fast** than me.*
10	chim	*Koj **chim** rau kuv.*	mad	*You are **mad** at me.*
11	siab ncaj	*Neeg **siab ncaj** hais lus zoo.*	honest	***Honest** people talk nice.*
12	rog	*Tus nyuj **rog** mus kev qeeb.*	fat	*A **fat** cow walks slow.*
13	zoo nkauj	*Nws **zoo nkauj.***	pretty	*She is **pretty.***
14	pluag	*Coob leej neeg **pluag.***	poor	*Many people are **poor.***
15	zoo nraug	*Nws **zoo nraug** heev.*	handsome	*He is very **handsome.***
16	cuaj khaum	*Lawv yog neeg **cuaj khaum.***	stingy	*They are **stingy** people.*
17	huv	*Lub tsev **huv.***	clean	*A **clean** house.*
18	tshav ntuj	*Hnub no **tshav ntuj** heev.*	sunny	*Today is very **sunny.***
19	laus	*Kuv **laus** tshaj koj.*	old	*I am more **old** than you.*
20	sov	*Kuv nyiam haus dej **sov.***	warm	*I like to drink **warm** water.*

Again, don't be confused with some English adjectives that are being used as verbs in Hmong. Otherwise, you will be comparing apples to oranges. Just like the English word "cook" is being used as both a *verb* and a *noun*, i.e., You *cook* dinner and you are the *cook*, and that is how the Hmong language works. **I *am fat*** would be translated into Hmong as"***Kuv rog***" because there isn't a "**to be**" verb in Hmong. For the closest to the "**to be**" verb would be the Hmong word "**yog**" but you can't use it like English. For example, you can't say, "**Koj yog *rog***" because that would mean "You are *the fat*." However, it is okay to say something like this: **Koj *yog* ib tus neeg *rog***. Meaning ***you are a fat person.***

Again, keep in mind that the examples above are the equivalent translations only, and some of these words do have multiple meanings for both English and Hmong. I still remember when we just came to the United States and some people would translate the Hmong line, "Koj *daj ntseg*" to English as, "You *yellow ears*." Koj = you, daj = yellow, and ntseg = ears. Therefore, the translation was a perfect and best direct translation, but **it is improper English**. The proper English is, "*You are pale.*"

Conjunctions

No	Hmong	English	Example
1	thiab	and	*Koj **thiab** kuv.* You ***and*** me. Kuv thiab koj. *I and you.*
2	ces	then	*Yog kuv qhia koj **ces** lawv yuav chim. If I tell you **then** they will be mad.*
3	los	or	*Koj **los** kuv mus ua.* You **or** I go do.
3	los sis	and/or	*Koj **lossis** kuv mam li mus ua.* You **and/or** I will go do.
4	tab sis tiam sis	but	*Nws tuaj txog lawm, **tabsis** nws nkees heev.* He has arrived, **but** he is very tired.
5	rau qhov vim vim tias vim yog	because	*Kuv tsis tuaj saib nej **vim tias** kuv tsis muaj nyiaj.* I did not come to visit you **because** I did not have money. *Kuv tsis paub **vim yog** tsis muaj neeg qhia kuv.* I did not know ***because*** no one told me.
6	twb vim twb yog	because	*Kuv tsis tuaj **twb yog** kuv tsis muaj tsheb.* I did not come **because** I did not have a car.
7	yeeb vim	because	*Kuv tsis tuaj **yeeb vim** yog kuv tsis paub.* I did not come **because** I did not know.

Prepositions

No	Hmong	Hmong Example	English	Example
1	ntawm	Lub tsev ***ntawm*** lub pas dej.	*at, by*	*The house **at** the pond.*
2	hauv	Nws nyob ***hauv*** tsev.	*inside*	*He is **inside** the house.*
3	nrauv/nraum	Nws nyob ***nraum*** zoov.	*outside*	*He is **outside** the house.*
4	sauv/saum	Tso rau ***saum*** lub rooj.	*above, on*	*Put **on** the table.*
5	hauv qab	Tso rau ***hauv qab*** lub rooj.	*below/under*	*Put **under** the table.*
6	dhau	Nws nyob ***dhau*** lub roob.	*over, past*	*He lives **over** the mountain.*
7	ze	Peb nyob ***ze*** koj.	*near, close to*	*We live **near** you.*
8	nram/nrav	Lawv nyob ***nram*** tus dej.	*by, down by*	*They live down **by** the river.*
9	ua ntej	Hu kuv ***ua ntej*** thaum tav su.	*before, in front*	*Call me **before** noon.*
10	pem/pev	Nws nyob ***pem*** lub roob.	*up, up by*	*He lives up by the mountain.*
11	hauv	Muab nws tso ***hauv*** lub thawv.	*in, inside*	*Put it **in** the box.*
12	nruab nrab	Peb nyob ***nruab nrab*** ntawm nej.	*between, middle*	*We live **between** you.*

For the most part, Hmong prepositions are very similar to English. These are just a few prepositions to help you understand and see the similarity between Hmong and English.

Past, Present and Future Tenses

One of the reasons why I believe the Hmong language is easy to learn is the fact that verbs stay the same regardless of the past, present or future use. More importantly, there is no participle form either. Now you might be wondering how can a person know when certain action was done. Well, to answer your question, let's answer you with this question, "When did you **cut** your grass?"

The answer might be something like, "I ***cut*** my grass ***yesterday***." So if you don't have any problems with this very verb, "cut", you will do even better with the Hmong verbs because there are no "*do, did, done, doing and does*" to mean the same verb – do.

No	Hmong	English	Remarks
1	Kuv **mus** tsev.	*I **go** home.*	General present tense.
2	*Nag hmo* kuv **haus** dej.	*Last night I **drank** water.*	Past tense. **Last night** means in the past.
3	Nws tab tom **noj** mov.	*He/she is eating.*	Similar to: ***He still eats.***
4	Tag kis peb **mus** tsev.	*Tomorrow we **go** home.*	**Tomorrow** is in the future.
5	Hnub no peb **tuaj.**	*Today we **come.***	
6	Lwm xyoo peb **mam** *mus.*	*Next year we **will** go.*	

As you can see, if a sentence is without a specific time, i.e., yesterday or tomorrow, being referenced then the sentence is considered a present tense. And if you already referenced a specific time, i.e., yesterday, then you don't have to change the verb from **do** to **did**. Otherwise that is a double past tense sentence which is similar to, "I *did ate* my lunch."

No	Hmong	English	Remarks
1	Nag hmo kuv **pw.**	*Yesterday I **slept.***	*Yesterday* is the past. *Slept* is a past tense of sleep. So then this is like ***double past tense*** – like I **did went**, for example.
2	Nag hmo kuv **txiav** nyom.	*Yesterday I **cut** the grass.*	Here the verb **cut** does not change. So how do we know when? *Yesterday!*
3	Kuv **noj mov** tag lawm.	*I **ate** already.*	Already means in the past or has been done.
4	Tag kis, kuv **yuav mus** tsev.	*Tomorrow I **will go** home.*	The word **yuav** is equivalent to the English word ***will** or **shall**, and **mus** = **go.***

The Hmong word "**noj mov**" means "**to eat**" or eat food in general. However, the Hmong word "**noj**" also means "**eat**" in English, too. For example: Koj **noj** ab tsi? Means you **eat** what? So if someone is asking you to eat with them, he might say something like this: ***Nrog kuv noj mov ohs*** and it means ***eat with me***. However, "noj su" means "eat lunch", and "noj hmo" means "eat dinner." So when people ask you, "*Koj puas tau **noj mov**?*" It means "*Have you **ate*** or *did you **eat yet**?*" The key or questioning word here is "**puas**", i.e., *puas* paub, *puas* mus, *puas* yog etc...

More Hmong Verbs

No	Hmong	English	No	Hmong	English	No	Hmong	English
1	mus	*go*	30	kib	*fry*	59	haum	*fit*
2	los	*come*	31	faib	*divide*	60	hem	*to scare someone*
3	haus	*drink*	32	pib	*begin*	61	txua	*carve, make, create*
4	ntxub	*hate*	33	hlais	*cut*	62	hle	*take off*
5	pab	*help*	34	ntxiv	*add, again*	63	hloov	*change, replace*
6	hlub	*love*	35	hla	*skip*	64	cia	*let, allow*
7	pw	*sleep, lie down*	36	tsuab	*grab*	65	tsuav	*chop*
8	pom	*see*	37	tsuas	*stain*	66	fiav	*to swing*
9	pub	*give free to*	38	tsum	*stop*	67	tsuj	*to step on*
10	txhawj	*concern*	39	tsaug zog	*sleep*	68	suav	*count, also Chinese*
11	qhib	*open*	40	rho	*subtract*	69	zaum	*sit*
12	kaw	*close*	41	khiav	*run*	70	mus *kev*	*walk*
13	nta	*turn on*	42	huam	*multiply*	71	quaj	*cry*
14	muag	*sell*	43	qw	*yell*	72	ntub	*wet*
15	yuav	*buy*	44	ntog	*fall*	73	ntiav	*to pay someone*
16	ntaus	*hit*	45	tshuab	*blow air*	74	tseg	*to save, to stop*
17	dhia	*jump*	46	ntshai	*fear*	75	tshaib	*hungry*
18	thaiv	*block*	47	ntiab	*evict*	76	luag	*laugh*
19	tso	*let, release*	48	chim	*mad*	77	*tsau*	*full, satiated*
20	tig	*turn*	49	piav	*explain*	78	ntxo	*bite*
21	tev	*peel*	50	caum	*chase*	79	ntxuav	*wash*
22	tua	*kill, shut*	51	khawb	*scratch*	80	khuam	*stuck*
23	tuav	*hold*	52	khi	*tie*	81	khib	*envy*
24	tuam	*kick*	53	kho	*fix*	82	khob	*knock*
25	txav	*move*	54	poob	*fall*	83	foom	*curse*
26	sim	*try*	55	puag	*hug*	84	puas	*damage*
27	ntes	*arrest*	56	cem	*scold*	85	cav	*argue*
28	ntseeg	*believe*	57	coj	*take*	86	cog	*plant*
29	tswj	*manage*	58	cuam	*throw*	87	nqhis	*thirst, being thirsty*

Some of the verbs in Hmong may not have the equivalent English ***verbs***. For example, the Hmong verb "**zoo**" means **good** or **well** as well as "is/are good", too. For example: Koj **zoo** means "*You **are good.***"

No	Hmong	English Past	Present Singular/plural	Past / present participle – *gerund*
1	noj	*ate*	**eats/eat**	*eaten, eating*
2	sau	*wrote*	**writes/write**	*written, writing*
3	mus	*went*	**goes/go**	*gone, going*
4	hais	*said*	**says/say**	*said, saying*
5	txiav	*cut*	**cuts/cut**	*cut, cutting*

Words that Indicate Future Tenses

No	Hmong	English
1	mam or mam li	*will, shall*
2	yuav, yuav tsum	*will, shall, should*
3	lwm (hnub, zaus, xyoo ltn...)	*next (day, time, year etc...), other time*
4	tag kis, nag kis	*tomorrow, day after tomorrow*
5	ib (chim, tsam, ntsis, pliag ltn...)	*a or one (moment, short time etc...), later on.*

These are just a few, and any words that refer to the future would definitely be a future tense.

Future Tense Examples

No	Hmong	English
1	Kuv ***mam*** ua...	*I **will** do...*
2	Kuv ***mam li*** ua nawb.	*I **will** do okay.*
3	Koj ***yuav*** mus pw los?	*You **will** go to sleep?*
4	Lwm zaus kuv ***yuav*** pab koj.	*Next time I **will** help you.*
5	Tag kis peb ***mam li*** mus tsev.	*Tomorrow we **will** go home.*
6	Ib chim wb ***mam li*** mus tsev	*Later on we **will** go home.*
7	Thaum twg koj ***yuav*** tuaj saib peb?	*When **will** you come to visit us?*
8	Thaum twg koj ***mam li*** tuaj?	*When **are** you coming?*
9	Thaum twg wb ***mam li*** mus?	*When **are** we going?*
10	***Lwm xyoo*** kuv mam li tuaj saib koj.	***Next year** I will come to visit you.*

Numbers and Their Spellings

Numbers are the same, 1,2,3 to 10 etc..., but just different pronunciation. This is because the Hmong written language was created based on the Latin alphabets. The word for "number" in Hmong is "**zauv**", but I prefer to call it "**suav**" for counting instead.

Number	Hmong	English	Hmong Example	English
0	voj	*zero*	*Lub voj ces yog lub qhoov qhuav.*	*A zero is an empty circle.*
1	ib	*one*	*Koj muaj **ib** lub tsev.*	*You have **one** house.*
2	ob	*two*	*Koj muaj **ob** tus me nyuam.*	*You have **two** children.*
3	peb	*three*	*Koj muaj **peb** lub tsheb.*	*You have **three** cars.*
4	plaub	*four*	*Peb pom **plaub** tus kauv.*	*We see **four** deer.*
5	tsib	*five*	*Koj muaj **tsib** xyoos.*	*You are **five** years old.*
6	rau	*six*	*Ib tais fawm yog **rau** duas.*	*One bowl of noodle is **six** dollars.*
7	xya	*seven*	*Lawv muaj **xya** leej tub.*	*They have **seven** sons.*
8	yim	*eight*	*Huab Tais muaj **yim** leej ntxhais.*	*King has **eight** daughters.*
9	cuaj	*nine*	*Koj muaj **cuaj** tsob ntoo.*	*You have **nine** trees.*
10	kaum	*ten*	*Ib tus neeg muaj **kaum** tus ntiv tes.*	*A person has **ten** fingers.*

Number	Hmong	English	*I wish English would be this way*
10	kaum	*ten*	*ten*
11	kaum *ib*	*eleven*	*ten-one*
12	kaum *ob*	*twelve*	*ten-two*
13	kaum *peb*	*thirteen*	*ten-three*
14	kaum *plaub*	*fourteen*	*ten-four*
15	kaum *tsib*	*fifteen*	*ten-five*
16	kaum *rau*	*sixteen*	*ten-six*
17	kaum *xya*	*seventeen*	*ten-seven*
18	kaum *yim*	*eighteen*	*ten-eight*
19	kaum *cuaj*	*nineteen*	*ten-nine*
20	nees nkaum*	*twenty**	*twoty, twoty-one, twoty-nine etc...*

- I don't know where the Hmong word "**nees nkaum**" came from because it does not come from ***ib*** txog ***kaum***. Likewise, the English word "**twenty**" is also a mystery to me because it does not appear anywhere between ***one*** and ***ten***. Therefore, Hmong should change the word "**nees nkaum**" to be "***ob caum***" instead, and I like ***twoty*** instead of ***twenty*** for English, too.

Number	Hmong	English	No	Hmong	English
20	**nees nkaum**	***twenty***	50	**tsib caug**	***fifty***
21	nees nkaum *ib*	*twenty-one*	51	tsib caug *ib*	*fifty-one*
22	nees nkaum *ob*	*twenty-two*	52	tsib caug *ob*	*fifty-two*
23	nees nkaum *peb*	*twenty-three*	53	tsib caug *peb*	*fifty-three*
24	nees nkaum *plaub*	*twenty-four*	54	tsib caug *plaub*	*fifty-four*
25	nees nkaum *tsib*	*twenty-five*	55	tsib caug *tsib*	*fifty-five*
26	nees nkaum *rau*	*twenty-six*	56	tsib caug *rau*	*fifty-six*
27	nees nkaum *xya*	*twenty-seven*	57	tsib caug *xya*	*fifty-seven*
28	nees nkaum *yim*	*twenty-eight*	58	tsib caug *yim*	*fifty-eight*
29	nees nkaum *cuaj*	*twenty-nine*	59	tsib caug *cuaj*	*fifty-nine*
30	**peb caug**	***thirty***	60	***rau caum***	***sixty***
31	peb caug *ib*	*thirty-one*	61	rau caum *ib*	*sixty-one*
32	peb caug *ob*	*thirty-two*	62	rau caum *ob*	*sixty-two*
33	peb caug *peb*	*thirty-three*	63	rau caum *peb*	*sixty-three*
34	peb caug *plaub*	*thirty-four*	64	rau caum *plaub*	*sixty-four*
35	peb caug *tsib*	*thirty-five*	65	rau caum *tsib*	*sixty-five*
36	peb caug *rau*	*thirty-six*	66	rau caum *rau*	*sixty-six*
37	peb caug *xya*	*thirty-seven*	67	rau caum *xya*	*sixty-seven*
38	peb caug *yim*	*thirty-eight*	68	rau caum *yim*	*sixty-eight*
39	peb caug *cuaj*	*thirty-nine*	69	rau caum *cuaj*	*sixty-nine*
40	**plaub caug**	***forty***	70	**xya caum**	***seventy***
41	plaub caug *ib*	*forty-one*	71	xya caum *ib*	*seventy-one*
42	plaub caug *ob*	*forty-two*	72	xya caum *ob*	*seventy-two*
43	plaub caug *peb*	*forty-three*	73	xya caum *peb*	*seventy-three*
44	plaub caug *plaub*	*forty-four*	74	xya caum *plaub*	*seventy-four*
45	plaub caug *tsib*	*forty-five*	75	xya caum *tsib*	*seventy-five*
46	plaub caug *rau*	*forty-six*	76	xya caum *rau*	*seventy-six*
47	plaub caug *xya*	*forty-seven*	77	xya caum *xya*	*seventy-seven*
48	plaub caug *yim*	*forty-eight*	78	xya caum *yim*	*seventy-eight*
49	plaub caug *cuaj*	*forty-nine*	79	xya caum *cuaj*	*seventy-nine*

Number	Hmong	English	No	Hmong	English
80	**yim caum**	***eighty***	91	cuaj caum *ib*	*ninety-one*
81	yim caum *ib*	*eighty-one*	92	cuaj caum *ob*	*ninety-two*
82	yim caum *ob*	*eighty-two*	93	cuaj caum *peb*	*ninety-three*
83	yim caum *peb*	*eighty-three*	94	cuaj caum *plaub*	*ninety-four*
84	yim caum *plaub*	*eighty-four*	95	cuaj caum *tsib*	*ninety-five*
85	yim caum *tsib*	*eighty-five*	96	cuaj caum *rau*	*ninety-six*
86	yim caum *rau*	*eighty-six*	97	cuaj caum *xya*	*ninety-seven*
87	yim caum *xya*	*eighty-seven*	98	cuaj caum *yim*	*ninety-eight*
88	yim caum *yim*	*eighty-eight*	99	cuaj caum *cuaj*	*ninety-nine*
89	yim caum *cuaj*	*eighty-nine*	**100**	***ib puas***	***one hundred***
90	**cuaj caum**	***ninety***	**1000**	***ib txhiab***	***one thousand***

The reason I think Hmong should change the word "**nees nkaum**" to "**ob caum**" is because "ob" means "2" and "*caum* or *caug*" means *tens*. Therefore, *ob caug*, *peb caug*, *plaub caug* are more logical. Again, the term **caum** means tens, and **pua** means hundreds and **txhiab** means thousands. Another term Hmong use to refer to 10,000 is called "**vam**", such as the saying, "*txhiab niaj pua vam.*"
So the word, "**pua vam**" means 100 of 10,000 or *one million*. Another term some Hmong people use for million is called "plhom"; however, this word might have been created recently only. Just like the terms I invented called nphom* means billion, rhom* means trillion and zom* means zillion.

Frankly, I don't believe Hmong people have terms for anything greater than the word "txhiab" because we never have to count anything that large. So to express in one million one would say "**ib txhiab txhiab**" meaning 1000 times 1000 which it comes after the **cuaj pua cuaj caum cuaj txhiab** or 999,000. Therefore, to reach a million, one can say "1000 * 1000 = 1,000,000, and one billion it would be **ib txhiab** huam **ib txhiab txhiab** or 1000 * 1000,000 = 1,000,000,000 etc...

No	Hmong	English	Number ranges
1	caum, *caug*	tens	10 to 99
2	pua, *puas*	hundreds	100 to 999
3	txhiab	thousands	1000 to 9999
4	vam	10 thousands	10 000
5	100 vam	100 * 10,000	1 000 000
6	1000 vam	1000 * 10,000	10 000 000

* Term I invented when I wrote the Hmong Dictionary called "Lus Hmoob Txhais" back in 2005, page 591, with the ISBN of **0-9726964-1-5.**

Word Meanings and Numbers

caum = 10, pua = 100, txhiab = 1000

1	kaum	10 = one tens
2	nees nkaum	20, but I think this should be "***ob caug***" as below instead.
3	**ob + caum**	2 + tens = 20 – *my invention only*
4	peb + caum	3 + tens = 30
5	plaub + caum	4 + tens = 40
6	tsib + caum	5 + tens = 50
7	rau + caum	6 + tens = 60
8	xya + caum	7 + tens = 70
9	yim + caum	8 + tens = 80
10	cuaj + caum	9 + tens = 90
11	pua	hundreds. Ces ib puas txog cuaj pua
12	txhiab	thousands. Ces ib txhiab txog cuaj txhiab

English	Hmong
add (+)	ntxiv
subtract (-)	rho
divide (/)	faib
multiply (x)	huam
percent (%)	feem

No	Hmong	Hmong	English	English		Number
1	xya	*caum*	seven	*tens*	7 + 0	70
2	xya	*pua*	seven	*hundreds*	7 + 00	700
3	xya	*txhiab*	seven	*thousands*	7 + 000	7 000
4	xya caum	*txhiab*	seventy	*thousands*	70 + 000	70 000
5	xya pua	*txhiab*	seven hundred	*thousands*	700 + 000	700 000
6	xya txhiab	*txhiab*	seven	*millions*	7 000 + 000	7000 000
7	xya txhiab txhiab	*txhiab*	seven	*billions*		7000 000 000

Of course, it is difficult to count numbers this way, but since we don't have any other words to express millions and billions in Hmong, it might be good to understand how the primitive counting system works. So when a person says, "***kuv muaj ob caum txhiab***, what does it mean?" It means he has 20,000. *Rau caum* txhiab = 60,000, and *cuaj txhiab* txhiab = **9,000**,*000*.
If you are still confused, don't worry! If you happen to have this much money, someone will be more than happy to help you count them correctly.

For now, just remember the basics – **caum** means *tens*, **pua** means *hundreds* and **txhiab** means *thousands*. So knowing **ib** txog **cuaj**, *one* to *nine*, you can count in Hmong with no problems. Just watch out for the weird number **nees nkaum** (twenty) because this word means "*a horse is hiding.*" Personally, I like my way of counting – **ob caug** instead. So ya, please help spread the new word "ob caug" instead of that *hiding horse.* **:)**

Practice Reading Hmong with Numbers

Kev suav nyob rau hauv lus Hmoob mas yooj~ yim xwb. Koj pib **ib, ob, peb, plaub, tsib, rau, xya, yim, cuaj,** ces **kaum** xwb. Dhau kiag **kaum** ces rov hais **ib** txog **cuaj** li no: "**kaum ib**, **kaum ob**, **kaum peb** txog **kaum cuaj**" xwb los mas. Thaum koj suav mus txog **kaum cuaj** ces siv lo lus *tshiab* kuv qhia, "**ob caug**" xwb. Dhau plaws *ob caug* ces yog **ob caug ib**, **ob caug ob, ob caug peb** txog **ob caug cuaj** ces xaus kiag rau **peb caug**. Ces rov pib kiag **peb caug ib**, **peb caug ob, peb caug peb** txog kiag rau **pe<u>b</u> cau*g* cuaj** ces **plau<u>b</u> cau*g*, tsi<u>b</u> cau*g*, rau cau*m*, xya cau*m*, yim cau*m*, cua*j* cau*m*** mus txog ntua **ib puas** xwb tiag – *one hundred*. Notice the tone changed from "caug" to "cau**m**" after tsi**b** caug – 50. This is because the *preceding* words (rau, xya, yim and cuaj) have changed from the "**b**" – *high pitch* to other lower pitches. However, you can still use the "**caum**" if you like.

Hais txog ntawv suav (*numbers*) Hmoob ces yeej tsis nyuaj vim Hmoob cov lus mas nws xwm yeem heev – *consistent*. Koj sau raws li lub suab hais kiag xwb. Xws li **ob** xyoos ces yog **two** years, kaum ob xyoos ces yog 12 years, thiab 213 ces yog **ob puas** *kaum peb* xwb which is 200-10-3 xwb. Dhau li ces yog txhiab lawm. Xyoo *ob txhiab kaum peb* ces yog year 2013. Ib lub hlis twg muaj *peb caug* hnub ces txhais tias each month has **30** days. Ib hnub muaj *ob caug plaub* teev ces txhais tias a day has 24 hours. Hais txog kev ua (do) ***lej*** – a Lao term, koj muab *kaum* <u>rho</u> *ob* ces tshuav *yim* (10-2 = 8). *Ob caug tsib* <u>rho</u> *tsib* ces tshuav *ob caug* xwb (25 – 5 = 20). 25 + 5 ces muaj *peb caug*. *Kaum* <u>ntxiv</u> *kaum* ces muaj *ob caug* xwb (10 + 10 = 20). **Ntxiv** ces yog *addition* hos **rho** ces yog *subtraction*. **Ib puas** <u>faib</u> rau **ob** ces yog ***tsib caug*** xwb (100 / 2 = 50). Hos *ib puas* <u>huam</u> *ob* ces yog *ob puas* xwb (100 x 2 = 200). Yog koj kawm tau **ib** mus txog rau **kaum**, **pua**, thiab **txhiab** lawm ces koj yeej hais thiab sau tau cov ntawv suav Hmoob no lawm los mas. Xws li: *Ib txhiab ib puas kaum peb* ces yog **1113** xwb.

Nej ho puas nyiam muab sau ua li nram no maj? **Ib txhiab ib** ces muab sau ua **ib-txhiab-ib** no naj? Raws li kuv xav mas tsis txhob muab sau muaj **kab txuas, –**, li vim peb cov lus Hmoob mas tsis yog sau li ntawv. Qhov tseeb tiag nws yog los ntawm kab lus es tsis yog los ntawm kab sau. Xws li thaum yus hnov ib tus neeg hais tias, "**ib txhiab ib**" ces yus twb paub tias yog "**1001**" lawm. Hos thaum yus pom lwm tus neeg sau, "**ib txhiab ib**" los yus yeej paub tias yog "**1001**" lawm ces tsis tas yuav muab sau ua,"**ib-txhiab-ib**" li.

Nov yog kuv li kev xav xwb; yog li, nej leej twg ho nyiam los ho siv mus. Tsis nyiam los sau thiab siv li nej nyiam xwb. Qhov tseeb tiag yog yus tho tau txoj kev zoo thiab ncaj ces yus tsis thov kom neeg taug los neeg yuav taug, tabsis yog yus tho tau txoj kev nkhaus ces txawm thov los neeg yeej tsis lawv yus qab li thiab nawb.

1,500 ces yog sau ua lus hais tias, "***ib txhiab tsib puas***." 405 ces sau tias, "***plaub puas tsib***." 450 ces sau tias, "***plaub puas tsib caug.***" Qhov kuv xav kom hloov ces yog tus "**nees nkaum**" xwb. Yog li, tus suav **23** ces cia muab sau tias, "***ob caug peb***" es kom nws zoo xwm yeem li tus suav 33, 43, uas yog "***peb caug peb***, thiab ***plaub caug peb***" ltn... Yog nej tsis nyiam tus "*ob caug*" ces nej siv lo lus qub tias, "*neeg nkaum peb*" uas zoo nkaus li tus "*nees nkaum peb*" kom peb tsis pom nws xwb. Sau ntawv suav Hmoob tsis nyuaj vim peb tsis muaj cov suav rov qab li Askiv, ***sixteen, seventeen*** uas yog zoo li *6 tens* and *7 tens* because "*teen*" means in the tens. Yog li, *kaum rau*, *kaum xya*, *ob caug*, *ob caug rau*, *peb caug, peb caug xya, plaub caug, plaub caug cuaj* txog rau ***pua*** ces ***txhiab*** xwb. Yog li, kuv thiaj li tsis tham ntau txog kev *sau thiab suav* vim kuv ntseeg tias nej yeej paub zoo lawm. Qhov nej xav tau yog kev sau tias 1 = ***ib***, 2 = ***ob***, thiab ***kaum*** yog 10, ***puas*** *yog* 100, thiab ***txhiab*** yog 1000 ltn... xwb. Ib txhia Hmoob kuj siv lo lus "***phav***" uas yog lus Nplog thiab txhais tias yog "***txhiab***", xws li: ***Koj muaj tsib phav*** ces txhais tias ***koj muaj tsib txhiab*** no thiab.

Some Differences between Hmong and English

Before we jump into more advanced learning, let me share with you some of the differences between Hmong and English. I already mentioned this earlier, but knowing more is better than less.

Verbs

Verbs in the Hmong language do not have *past tense*, i.e., **did**, **went** etc..., and does not have "**-ed**" after the verbs, i.e., **wanted**. Furthermore, there are no present participle, "**-ing**" and verbs stay the same regardless when you use them and there is only one verb form for both singular and plural. Meaning there are no such thing like the English verbs "**are, is, do, does, and -s**", and there is no "**to**" after verbs such as "like **to**, want **to,** learn **to**" etc... For example:

No	Hmong	English transliterated	Proper English
1	Kuv nyiam ***noj.***	I like ***eat.***	I like ***to*** eat.
2	Kuv xyaum ***tsav*** tsheb.	I learn ***drive*** car.	I learn ***to*** drive **a** car.
3	Kuv ***xav*** pw.	I ***want*** sleep.	I want ***to*** sleep.
4	Koj ***tshuav*** ab tsi?	You ***have*** what ***left***?	What do you **have left**?

Nouns, Singular and Plural

Unlike English, Hmong does not have plural nouns, no "-s" after the nouns, i.e., cow**s**, and no words such as "**men, ladies**" but only words like **deer** and **fish.** In other words, it does not matter *one deer* or *many deer* there is no "**s**" period. For example:

No	Hmong	English	Remarks
1	Kuv muaj **tsib** tus nyuj.	*I have **five** cows.*	**Five** indicates more than one.
2	Lawv muaj **ntau** lub tsev.	*They have **many** houses.*	**Many** indicates more than one.
3	Koj muaj **ib** *tug* me nyuam.	*You have **one** child.*	No **a** or **the** (article) in Hmong, but lots of *classifiers.*
4	Wb muaj **plaub** tus me nyuam.	*We have **four** children.*	**Four** indicates more than one.
5	Kuv pom **coob** tus mos lwj.	*I saw **many** deer.*	**Many** deer and ***not deers.***

Hmong language is not alone when it comes to having no plural forms, Thai, Laos and other monosyllabic Asian languages don't have plural forms either. These languages use numbers to indicate the quantities instead of adding the "s" to the nouns.

Adjectives

Adjectives are colorful in all human languages, but the order of coloring varies. For English, adjectives **go before the** nouns or objectives, but for Hmong most **adjectives go after the** objectives or nouns.

No	Hmong	English
1	Peb nyiam lub *tsev* ***loj*** thiab ***dav.***	We like a ***big*** and ***spacious*** *house.*
2	Lawv muaj ib lub *tsheb* **liab**.	They have a ***red*** *car.*
3	Koj yog ib tus *neeg* ***zoo.***	You are a ***good*** *person.*

Classifiers

Not like English, Hmong does not have articles, "**a**, **an** and **the**", but have many **classifiers**. A **classifier** *is a word or morpheme that corresponds to a semantic class of nouns or objects.* Perhaps the best way to help you understand Hmong classifiers is to borrow a quote from the world famous Martial Artist, **Bruce Lee**:

"Empty your mind, be formless, shapeless – like water. Now you put water into a cup, it becomes the cup, you put water into a bottle, it becomes the bottle, you put it in a teapot, it becomes the teapot. Now water can flow or it can crash. Be water, my friend."

Similarly to Bruce Lee's line, when you put rice into a spoon, it becomes *a spoon of rice* – **ib diav mov**. When you put rice into a bowl, it becomes *a bowl of rice* – **ib tais mov**. So it begins from a single grain, **lub**, to whatever containing the items, i.e., ***tsu, tais, phaj,*** *steamer, bowl, plate respectively.* Generally, you must use a classifier when you specify a *number* or *quantifying* the objects.

Generally, the Hmong "ib" is analogous to the English "one, a, an, and the", for example: Ib tus nyuj = a cow. Ib lub tsev = a house. Ib tus neeg = one person etc...

No	Hmong	English	Transliterated English
1	Koj muaj **kaum** *rab* diav.	*You have ten spoons.*	*you have ten a spoon.*
2	Nej **plaub** *tus* nyuaj.	*Your four cows.*	*you four a cows.*
3	Nej muaj **tsib** *lub* tais?	*You have five bowls.*	*you have five a bowl.*
4	Lawv muag **rau** *lub* tsev.	*They sell six houses.*	*they sell six a house.*
5	**Coob** *leej* neeg tuaj saib peb.	***Many*** *people come to see us.*	*many a person come see us.*
6	Koj muaj diav ntau heev.	*You have very many spoons.*	*you have spoon many.*

What is really missing in the Hmong is the English word " **of** ", for example:
A cup **of** water = ib khob dej. One plate **of** rice = Ib phaj mov. Here is another example:

No	Hmong	English
1	Kuv muaj ib ***pab*** nyuj.	I have one ***herd*** of cows. And "pab nyuj = herd cows."

Here is a breakdown of the above two sentences:

No	Hmong	English
1	Kuv	I
2	muaj	have
3	ib	one
4	pab	herd
5		**of** (*no equivalent in Hmong*). Perhaps the closest would be "***hom***"
6	nyuj	cows

A classifier is a word defining or describing the type of objects in its current environment. For example, **pab** means **herd** in this case. It is incorrect in this example to omit the word "herd" because it is classifying the environment of the "cows." Therefore, the English "***noun of***" is analogous to the Hmong classifiers, for example, ***group*** *of,* ***piece*** *of, and* ***box*** *of etc...*
pab ***daim*** ***thawv*** *→ in Hmong respectively.*

So the only word that was missing in the Hmong sentence above is the word "**of**", and perhaps for a *classified reason*, got it? Let's look at more examples:

No	Hmong	**Englis**h transliterated	Better English
1	Kuv muaj **ib** *pab* nyuj.	I have **one** *herd* cow.	I have **a** *herd* ***of*** cows.
2	Kuv muaj **ib** *tug* nyuj.	I have **one** cow.	I have **one** cow.
3	Kuv muaj **coob** *tug* nyuj.	I have **many** a cow.	I have **many** cows.
4	Kuv muaj **ib** *tiaj* nyuj.	I have **one** *field* cow.	I have **a** *field* of cows.
5	Kuv muaj **ib** *vaj* txiv ntoo.	I have **one** *fence* fruit trees.	I have an enclosed fence **of** fruit trees.

What might be confusing to English speakers is perhaps the missing word "**of**" after words such as herd, flock, group etc... For example, a group ***of*** people = *ib pab neeg.* A bus *full* ***of*** people = *ib tsheb neeg.* Number 4 is different and it used the "tiaj" which is equivalent to a field that is full of cows. In other words, the "field" defines or classifying the environment of the cows that I have. For example: I have a truck ***of*** cows; I have a house ***of*** people; I have a box ***of*** papers. But these would be translated into ***English-Hmong*** as follows:

English: *I have one truck cows. I have one house people. I have one box papers.*
Hmong: *Kuv muaj ib tsheb nyuj. Kuv muaj ib tsev neeg. Kuv muaj ib thawv ntawv*

No	Classifier	Equivalent English Word Classification
1	tsob	plants, trees and things that grow from the ground
2	res	bunch or a stem *of flowers*
3	rab*	items with short length and/or **tools with handles.**
4	tus, tug*	humans, animals, and/or parts of such entities.
5	leeg, leej	human, person
6	pab	group, herd, flock, team, school (*of fish, for example*)
7	pawg	group but more for a *pile-like, flock, school* entities, i.e., ib *pawg* neeg
8	lub	plate, house, building, heart, egg, country, boat – round-like entities
9	phau	book
10	daim	piece, land, leaf, blanket, farm, field, sheet. Objects with flat surface.
11	txoj	rope-like items, road, path, way, line etc...
12	ntiv	digits, fingers, toes, tip. *Ib ntiv qhiav – a piece of ginger.*
13	txhais/sab	hand, foot, shoe. Generally means half or one side of. *Sab = half of, side of.*
14	koog	grove, cluster, tract, forest
15	sob	school (*of fish, for example*)
16	pob	bunch, clump, lump, bundle.

17	thooj	a piece round-like objects, ib thooj mov. Usually a smaller amount than "pob"
18	tauv	bunch (*of grapes or flowers, for example*)

I believe the classifiers "tus and rab" are being used interchangeably, and no one really had ever defined, that I know of, which one really should be used for what objects or entities. So I am going to attempt to make a recommendation here. I believe the classifier "**rab**" should *only be used* to refer to **tools with handles**. For example: *Rab riam, rab taus, rab hmuv ltn...*

The classifier "**tus**" should be used to refer to **entities such humans, animals and any other species, including parts from these entities,** i.e., *tus txha, tus ntiv tes, tus tw etc...*

No	Hmong	English
1	Nov *puas yog* koj ***rab*** riam?	Is this your knife?
2	Leej twg ***rab*** diav nov?	Whose spoon is this?
3	Koj puas pom kuv ***tus*** nees?	Do you see my horse?
4	Neeg muaj ntau ***tus*** txha.	Humans have many bones.
5	Koj yog kuv ***tus*** hlub.	You are my love.

General Interrogative Phrase

No	Hmong	English
1.	Koj puas **paub** lub zos no hu li cas?	Do you **know** the name of this city?
2.	*Koj **puas** kam peb mus ua si?*	***Do** you mind if we go play?*
3.	Koj puas **nco qab** thaum peb tuaj saib nej lawm?	Do you **remember** when we came to visit you?
4.	*Koj puas **tseem** hlub kuv thiab?*	*Do you **still** love me?*
5.	Koj puas **ntseeg** tias kuv niaj hnub xav txog koj?	Do you **believe** that I think of you every day?
6.	*Koj puas **hnov** tias lawv khiav lawm?*	*Did you **hear** that they moved?*
7.	Koj puas paub tias kuv **nyiam** koj heev?	Do you know that I **like** you a lot?
8.	*Koj puas xav kawm lus **Askiv**?*	*Do you want to learn **English**?*
9.	Koj puas paub **sau** ntawv Hmoob?	Do you know how to **write** Hmong?
10.	*Koj lub **npe** hu li cas?*	*What is your **name**?*
11.	**Koj** muaj pes tsawg xyoo?	How old are **you**?
12.	*Koj niam thiab txiv yog **leej twg**?*	***Who** are your parents?*
13.	Koj puas muaj **kwv tij** li thiab?	Do you have any **brothers**?
14.	*Hos **muam** ne, puas muaj li thiab?*	*And **sisters**, do you have any?*
15.	Koj puas **nkees**?	Are you **tired**?
16.	*Koj puas xav **haus** dej?*	*Do you want to **drink** water?*
17.	Koj puas **tshaib** plab?	Are you **hungry**?
18.	Wb **tsum** li no yom?	We **stop** here okay?
19.	*Koj puas **sab**?*	*Are you **tired**?*
20.	Koj puas yog ib tus neeg **ncaj ncees**?	Are you an **honest** person?
21.	*Kuv nug koj **chaw nyob** puas tau?*	*Can I ask for your **address**?*
22.	Koj nyob **hov deb** ntawm no nab?	**How far** do you live from here?
23.	*Koj puas kam **pab** kuv?*	*Can you **help** me?*

No	Hmong	English	No	Hmong	English
1	Koj puas **noj**?	Do you want to **eat**?	7	Koj puas xav **haus**?	Would you like to **drink**?
2	Koj puas **mus**?	Do you want to **go**?	8	Koj puas xav **nyob**?	Would you like to **stay**?
3	Koj puas **hnov**?	Do you **hear**?	9	Koj puas xav **pw**?	Would you like to **sleep**?
4	*Neeg* puas **nyiam**?	Do *people* **like**?	10	Koj puas xav **so**?	Would you like to **rest**?
5	Koj puas **hlub**?	Do you **love**?	11	Koj puas xav **paub**?	Would you like to **know**?
6	**Nws** *mob* qhov twg?	Where does **it** *hurt*?	12	Koj puas **nco qab**?	Do you **remember**?

Classifier Plus Verb

When you put a classifier in front of any verbs, that verb becomes the "**do-er**" or noun which is similar to English words ending with the "**-er**", i.e., sing**er**, do**er**, speak**er**, teach**er** etc...

No	Hmong	Transliterated English	Meaning
1	**Tus hais** lus mus twg lawm?	The one speaks go where?	Where is the say**er** or speak**er**?
2	**Tus ua** yog leeg twg?	The one does was who?	Who is the do**er**?
3	**Tus noj** yog kuv.	The one eats was me.	The eat**er** was me?
4	Leej twg yog **tus tub sab**?	Who is the one *steal*?	Who is the steal**er** or **thief**?
5	Koj puas yog tus ***hu nkauj***?	You are the one *sing*?	Are you the sing**er**?

As you can see, when you combine a classifier with any verbs, that verb becomes the noun – the ***doer.***

No	Hmong	Literal translation	English meaning
1	tus qhia	*the teach*	The teach***er***
2	tus kawm	*the learn*	The learn***er*** or student
3	tus yuav	*the buy*	The buy***er***
4	tus muag	*the sell*	The sell***er***
5	tus pab	*the help*	The help***er***
6	tus paub	*the know*	The person who knows, th know-***er***
7	tus ua noj	*the cook*	The ***cook***
8	tus ua	*the do*	The do**er**

This applies to plural classifiers such as "***pab, pawg, cov***" ltn... For example:
Nej cov qhia ntawv los nov. **You teachers** come here. **Nej cov ua** num los pab kuv. **You the doers** come help me. Generally, Hmong like to repeat the same verb when forming a noun or the "**doer**", for example: Tus ***qhia qhia*** ntawv puas nyob lawm? *Is the* ***teacher*** *still here?*
The English word "**cook**" is similar to how the Hmong language works. If you say, "**the** *cook*", cook is then a noun – **tus** *ua noj*. But if you say, "**I** *cook*", cook is a verb which is similar to "**kuv** *ua noj*." So the keyword is the *classifier*. If a verb is placed after a classifier, i.e., **tus** *qhia*, then that *verb* becomes a noun. In this example, "*tus qhia*" is equivalent to "*the teacher*", and "tus *kawm* = the *learner.*"

More of Different Classifiers

No	Hmong	Literal translation	Meaning
1	**Cov** qhia *qhia*	*The **folks** teach*	**Group of** teachers
2	**Pab** kawm *kawm*	*The **team** learn*	**Team of** learners
3	**Pawg** neeg yuav *yuav*	*The **group** buy*	**Group of** buyers

Okay, enough confusion here... Let's add a little life to the classifiers and verbs above so they can live. Actually, it is very simple once you stop comparing apples to oranges! For example:

Hmong	English
Peb kom **tus qhia** los *qhia* peb ib lwm ntxiv.	We ask the ***teacher*** to come *teach* us one more time.
Tus muag puas tseem nyob nov lawm?	Is the ***seller*** still here?
Tus ua noj yog leeg twg? tus ua noj = the cook	Who is the **cook**? ***Cook** here is a noun.*
Koj **ua** rau peb noj.	You **cook** for us to eat. ***Cook** here is a verb.*

Questioning Words

In the Hmong language, the question word is generally placed at the end of a sentence, For example:

No	Hmong	English transliterated
1	Koj mus ***qhov twg***?	You go ***where** or you go **which where**?*
2	Koj lub npe hu ***li cas***?	You name is called ***what***?
3	Nej nyob lub zos ***twg tuaj?***	You stay a city ***what come***?
4	Koj **tab tom** yuav mus ***qhov twg***?	You **right now** will go ***where***?
5	Koj puas paub?	Do you know? Puas yog? Is it correct?

Of course, the above translations are not correct in English but as a beginner, you want to see the closest word-for-word relation and translation first. Once you know more about both languages, you will be able to translate base on contents. Three words that Hmong love to use for short questioning are: "**Ab tsi**", "**hav"**, and "**ua cas**" and these words can be used without any other words, for example: ***Ab tsi? Hav?** = What? and **Ua cas?** = What happens or why?*

Let's look at the proper translation in both languages.

No	Hmong	English
1	**Koj** mus *qhov twg*?	*Where* are **you** going? Qhov twg = where.
2	**Koj** lub npe hu *li cas*?	*What* is **your** name? Hu li cas = what is called.
3	**Nej** nyob lub zos *twg tuaj*?	*What* city are **you** *from? Twg tuaj = where from.*
4	Koj muaj **pes tsawg xyoo**?	***How old*** are you? Pes tsawg xyoo = how many years?

The fundamental rule is the first pronoun is the one who is doing or performing the action. The second pronoun is the *objective* pronoun. So then, if I say, "*I like you*" it is very simply means you are being liked by me! Therefore, for Hmong syntax, You like *I* and I like you makes perfect sense like the Hmong line: Koj nyiam kuv thiab kuv nyiam koj; however, for English is: You like **me** and I like you.

Here are some more examples:

No	Hmong	English
1	Kuv *nyiam* koj.	I *like* you.
2	Koj ***raug*** kuv nyiam.	You *are **being*** **liked by** me.
3	Koj *nyiam* kuv.	You *like* me.
4	Kuv ***raug*** koj nyiam.	I *am **being*** **liked by** you.

The word "raug" has many meanings:
1. Hit like hitting a target.
2. Hit like physically hurting someone.
3. *Being verb by* like these examples.

However, very rare do Hmong speakers use the word "***raug***" or "***being** verb **by***" as in English. Why not just say what you mean and don't beat around the bush! Unlike English, interrogative sentences do not start with adverbs, i.e., ***Where** are you going?* Instead, Hmong syntax goes like: *You are going **where?*** So in the Hmong case, the word "**where**" acts as a **noun** instead. With this being said, you need to be careful not to translate English into Hmong as follows:

No	English	Hmong	Proper Hmong
1	**Where** are you going?	***Qhov twg** koj mus?*	*Koj mus **qhov twg**?*
2	**What** are you eating?	***Ab tsi** koj noj?*	*Koj noj **ab tsi**?*
3	**What** is your name?	***Ab tsi** yog koj npe?*	*Koj npe hu **li cas**?*

So what is the proper syntax for speaking Hmong? All you need to do is place the **questioning words**, such as **where, when, who,** and **what** at the end of your sentence with a question mark, and Hmong people will know. Here are some examples:

No	Hmong	**English** transliterated
1	Koj mus qhov ***twg?***	You go ***where?***
2	Koj hu ***li cas?***	You call ***what?*** The word "**li cas**" means "**what**"
3	Koj noj ***ab tsi?***	You eat ***what?***
4	Koj mus tsev thaum ***twg?***	You go home ***when?***
5	Koj mus lub tsev ***twg?***	You go to house ***which** or what?*

Like English, Hmong language has many exceptions. However, they are not as bad as English. Here are some questioning constructs that are similar to the English forms:

No	Hmong	English
1	***Thaum twg*** koj mus tsev?	***When*** do you go home?
2	***Leej twg*** hu koj?	***Who*** calls you?
3	***Hnub twg*** nej mam li tuaj?	***What day*** will you be coming?
4	***Tus twg*** yog koj poj niam?	***Which one*** is your wife?

The key questioning word is "twg", and it can be placed after any classifiers and nouns. For example:
Leej *twg*, hnub *twg*, cov *twg*, thaum *twg*, hom *twg*, tsob *twg*, txoj *twg*, and xyoo *twg* etc...

So overall, both English and Hmong languages are very similar in many ways. The hard part is learning enough words and immersing yourself enough into not only the language, but also into the culture, environment, and people so that you can actually see and hear from the native Hmong speakers. For now, I don't want to scare you too much because speaking Hmong is not that hard, but perfecting it as a second language you will need some real interaction with some native Hmong speakers and/or watch a lot of Hmong movies and Hmong karaoke. Don't be too harsh on yourself because some native Hmong speakers do not speak Hmong correctly either, *myself included.*

Furthermore, I truly believe that the Hmong spoken language itself is easy to learn, but the written Latin form is somewhat difficult due to the multiple consonants and the tone markers. This then makes each word very long and hard to remember and parse, i.e., **ntxh***uav*. The other problem is the monosyllabic language. For example:

No	Hmong	English
1	kwv	younger brothers. *Kwv ntxawg* means the very last and youngest brother.
2	tij, tij laug	older brothers. Tij is short version of "tij lauj."
3	kwv tij	relatives or brothers, mostly of the same last name.
4	txiv	1. father, male. 2. fruits. 3. to squeeze oneself into a tight place.
5	neej	life, family. For example: *Koj lub neej* means *your life.*
6	txiv neej	man, generally referring to a grown up and/or married male.
7	koj niam	A general term used for calling one's wife. Also means *your mother*, too.
8	koj txiv	A general term used for calling one's husband. Also means *your father*, too.

However, for Hmong-American, don't be too overly disappointed with the poly-consonants because the word "**ntxhw**" is actually much shorter than the English word "**elephant**."

The Hmong compound nouns are similar to some of the English words "**cow pony, fish tank, swimming pool**" etc... Some Hmong people like to hyphenate these compound nouns and some will just write them without any space nor hyphens. However, the preferred way is to separate them with space because the Hmong language is considered a mono syllabic language with **seven distinctive tones**. For tonal and monosyllabic language, it was suggested to keep each word, syllable, separated by one of the creators and founders of the Hmong Romanized Popular Alphabet (RPA), Frenchman Fr. Yves Bertrais July, 1930 – May, 2007. This monosyllabic writing system does not only exist in the Hmong language but also in Laos, Thai, and Vietnamese languages.

Most words in the Hmong language have *only one syllable* and each word has its own meaning, but when two or more words are combined together like the English compound words "**fish tank, swimming pool**" they have different meanings. However, there are very few words that have two or more syllables in the Hmong language, i.e., **tabtom, tabmeeg, pomxeeb, xosliam,** and these words perhaps should be written with a space between each syllable, i.e, **tab tom, tab meeg, pom xeeb, xos liam** etc... Just like the English word "***fish tank***" you must know both terms in order to understand its meaning. And the Hmong word such as "***kwv tij***" is the same thing – you have to know both "kwv" and "tij" to comprehend its meaning.

The last and a huge difference between Hmong and English is the Hmong ***open syllables*** *versus* English ***open*** and ***closed syllables***, i.e., **bye** and **mom**.

My opinion is that the Hmong language is about 90% monosyllabic and 100% tonal.

About the Hmong Mono Word Language

No	Hmong	English	No	Hmong	English
1.	Ib *txhais* tes.	*One **a** hand .*	6.	Sau.	*Write.*
2.	Ib *sab* tes.	*One **side** hand.*	7.	Sau *ntawv.*	*Write **letter.***
3.	Sab tes *xis.*	*Side hand **right.***	8.	Ua.	*Do or be.*
4.	Leej *twg.*	*Person **who.***	9.	Ua *ntej.*	*Do **before** or be **ahead.***
5.	Mus *kev.*	*Walk **way.***	10.	Tso zis.	***Release** urine.*

Some Hmong people like to combine words like “leej twg” to be “leejtwg”, and “sau ntawv” to be “sauntawv”, and “ua ntej” to be “uantej.” This type of words construction does not conform to what I believe is **mono**syllabic language. For example, “leej twg” are two words. “**leej**” means “**person**” and “**twg**” means “**who.**” Likewise, “**sau ntawv**” are two words. “**sau**” means “**write**” and “**ntawv**” means “**the script**” Last, “**tso zis**” are two words. “**tso**” means “**to release**” and “**zis**” means “**urine.**” So if one translates “**sauntawv**” to mean “**write**” then “*sau tus ntawv no kom zoo*” would have to be written like, “*sau**ntawv** tus **ntawv** no kom zoo.*”

English closed syllables vs Hmong open syllables

No English word with different ending letter.

1	mo***m***	mo***b***	mo***ss***	mo***p***	mo***d***

Each of the ending letters **m**, **b**, **s**, **p** and **d** above must be enunciated clearly in English, and this is a problem for most non-English speakers because they can't hear the difference between words such as “mo**b**” and “mo**p**.” And for English speakers, they do have problems with open syllables and tonal language such as Hmong because they are not trained to hear the different *ending tones*.

No Hmong word with different tone markers.

1	mua***j***	mua***s***	mua***m***	mua***g***	mua***b***

Each of the tone markers **j, s, m, g** and **b** above must be stressed with the correct pitch without closing your mouth. For example, “muab” has a phonics similar to the English word “**moua**” but with a high pitch similar to the “**YO**-” syllable of the word “**YO**-yo”, and “muam” has a low pitch similar to the “-yo” syllable. And the word “mua**b**” means *to give* and “mua**m**” means *sisters*.

The rule of thumb is to never close your mouth when speaking Hmong and you will be fine.

I hope you understand the illustration above because it is **very important** that you speak with tones correctly. For example, if you are trying to say the word “mua***g** – **to sell***” but instead you say it like “mua***s** – **to buy***”, without stressing the “**g**” tone, you would be *purchasing* instead of *selling*.

For this reason, many foreigners who came from a tonal language background generally will tend to speak English without closing their mouths and do not enunciate the ending letters clearly. The reason for that is because they are not comfortable with the new way of speaking – *fear of looking funny*. This very same reason applies to people who are learning Hmong as well. Nonetheless, you have to remind yourself that you rather look funny and pronounce it right than looking pretty and say the word wrong.

My suggestion for you to learn even better and faster is to have your teacher record the phonics of all the consonants, vowels and tones, and then try to mimic them. If you have computers and have access to the internet, you can go listen to these sounds at my website www.HmongDictionary.com

To improve your ability to read and write Hmong, you need to ***memorize – visually,*** three things:

1. Consonants – *the correct phonics of each letter, i.e.,* ***c, d, th*** *etc...*
2. Vowels – ***a, ai, aw*** etc...
3. Tones – ***j, s, v, m, g, b, _,*** *and* ***d.*** These are called "Cim" in Hmong.

And then, you must memorize all the **vitches**, my new term for you here. It means "***vowel + pitch***." For example, *eb, iam, awm, us, oob*. You should be able to pronounce these vitches easily. Then when you see words such as ***peb niam kawm lus*** ***Hmoob***, and it means "*Our mother learns Hmong*", you should be able to read each word quite well. And once you have mastered the vitches, you move on to the consonants, and then the whole word like you do in English.

Sweet Words

Sweet words are words that some people use at the end of a normal phrase or sentence, and it generally means friendly, polite or sweet. Here are some examples:

No	Word	Example
1	los	*Nej tuaj thiab* ***los****. Nws hais lus zoo heev* ***los.***
2	los mas	*Txhob ua li* ***los mas****. Peb hlub koj es peb thiaj li tuaj* ***los mas.***
3	ntag	*Nws tsis paub li* ***ntag****. Lawv ua li* ***ntag.***
4	ntag los	*Nws tsis paub li* ***ntag los****. Lawv ua li* ***ntag los.***
5	ohs*	*Koj lub npe hu li cas* ***ohs?*** *Koj yog xeem ab tsi* ***ohs?***
6	yom, yod	*Peb txhob mus* ***yod?*** *Lawv tsis kam ua li peb nyiam ne* ***yom.***
7	mog	*Kuv nyiam koj heev* ***mog****. Nej ua neeg zoo nawb* ***mog.***
8	nawb	*Koj txhob mus* ***nawb****. Lawv ua los puam chawj lawv* ***nawb mog.***
9	hos	*Peb tsis paub li* ***hos****. Twb yog nws ua kiag ntag* ***hos.***

* This is a new word I created.

This word "**ohs**" is not the same as the word "**os**" – sounds like **awe** in English, but the word , "**ohs**", I came up here is different. Again, you have to hear the actual sound from a Hmong speaker to understand what I am referring to here. The word "**os**" means **a duck** in Hmong, but the word "**ohs**" is mostly placed at the end of a sentence. This silent "h" also applies to not only the "**oh**" vowel, but also for the sound of the Hmong Leng's kwv txhiaj, for example, ca.... au**h**b.....a**h**m... luag leem tub o**h**m. The "h" after the "o" is a silent vowel pronounced in the back of your throat. Otherwise, the Hmong popular greeting, "Nyob zoo **os**" would translate into "hello duck" instead. To appreciate the new word "ohs", you have to phonetically sound the "*os + hos = ohs.*" It is not perfect but it is not *too ducky.*

The Blaming Game

Yes, Hmong are human and humans means taking credit for the good and blaming others for the bad. With that being said, the most popular word the Hmong people use to blame others is "**tim**", and it is analogous to the English "**because of**, **your fault**, **due to**" etc... For example:

Peb tuaj lig **vim yog *tim*** koj ntag**.** *We come late* because ***your fault.***
Peb tuaj lig **twb yog *tim*** koj ntag. *We come late **because of** you.*
Tim leej twg? ***Because of*** whom?

The Swear Words

True life does not exist without *love* and *hatred*, and that is just a part of human beings. Like a piece of magnet, it always has both positive and negative. So I have taught you the sweet words, the blaming game and you know what naturally comes afterward right? The yelling and swearing words. Therefore, I want to prepare you for not only the best but also be aware of some swear words some Hmong people like to use. With that said, Hmong generally use the following words when they are ***really angry***:

No	Hmong	English
1	Ntsej muag!	There is no English equivalent for this word, and it literally means a "face", and it can be directed to anyone, i.e., you, he, she etc... This "***ntsej muag***" can be used with any adjectives, i.e., *ruam, pluag* etc...
2	Tsov tom!	Tiger bites or kills. This term is more like for *cursing* someone so that tigers will bite or kill that person. However, some people like to use "***tsov tom***" to greet their *long time lost* friends, too.
3	tawg	A mean word, *slang*, for "***eat.***" Ua cas koj ***tawg*** ntau ua luaj? Why do you ***eat*** so much? Another slang word for "eat" is called "**laig**", too.

Here are some more examples

No	Hmong	English
1	Ntsej muag! Ua cas koj yuav *muaj plhus* ua luaj li naj?	You, why are you so arrogant?
2	Ntsej muag *ruam*, ua cas koj tsis paub ab tsi li?	You stupid face, why don't you know anything?
3	Tsov tom, uas cas koj ua li?	Tiger bites, why did you do that?
4	Tsov tom, tsov cab. Tsuv tum, tsuv hai – *Hmong Leng dialect.*	Tiger bites, tiger drags.

Mostly, Hmong use the word "**niag**" before these two words, for example:

Niag ntsej muag... Niag tsov tom ntawv... Niag ntsej muag siab phem... Niag tsov tom awh etc...

Now don't you go around and start swearing at people because if you get into trouble, don't blame me – blame yourself and your tongue, Grasshopper! I taught you these swear words in hope you would understand when someone swears at you and not the other way around. **:)** According to the old people, the line "***tiger bites***" was forbidden back in the old days when Hmong still lived in the jungle because if someone curses you like that, tigers might really kill you for real. Now you know the rest of the Hmong "***tiger bites***" story. And the term "***muaj plhus"*** means cocky, *show off* such as being *overly* assertive.

Repeating the Same Verb Means Greater or More

The Hmong language has a repeating use of the same verb to mean in **greater degree** or **more of** which is similar to English syntax "*very, very* good."

No	Hmong	English transliterated	Proper English
1	Kuv **nyiam *nyiam*** koj.	*I like like you.*	*I **like** you **much.***
2	Peb **xav *xav*** tuaj.	*I want want come.*	*I **much want** to come.*
3	Koj **muaj *muaj*** nyiaj.	*You have have money.*	*You **have a lot** of money.*

In a way, the first verb sort of tells you the type of verb, and the second same verb tells you that it is more or twice as much. This repeating syntax also exists in the Laos and Thai languages or perhaps most monosyllabic languages. **This repeating syntax can be more than twice, but it is uncommon.**

For this same word being used twice, I have come up with the character "~" to mean repeating again. So applying this repeating character to the above examples, they would look as follows:

No	Hmong	English
1	Kuv **nyiam~** koj.	*I like you much. Or I very like you.*
2	Peb **xav~** tuaj.	*We like to come very much.*
3	Koj **muaj~** nyiaj.	*You have a lot of money.*

This repeating character applies to verbs, adjectives, and adverbs. Therefore, instead of saying, "*Kuv nco koj heev kawg li*", it would be, "*Kuv **nco~** koj kawg li.*" And "*Kuv tsis **pom pom***" means "***I don't really see***" And "*Kuv tsis **care care***" means "*I don't **really care.***"

Now you know why some Hmong people translate the Hmong phrase, "*Kuv **nyiam nyiam** koj*" into English like "*I **like like** you" or Hmonglish, "Kuv tsis **care care** koj naj", and it means, "I don't really care about you."* Therefore, koj puas **xav~** kawm lus Hmoob means "*Do you really want to learn Hmong?*" In other words, the English word "***really***" is equivalent to the Hmong ***repeating*** word syntax. For example: *Nkees nkees* = ***really tired,*** *ntxub ntxub* = ***really hate,*** *xav xav* = ***really want*** *etc...*

Additionally, Hmong also like to use the word **"sis"** or **"sib"** in front of verbs (verb prefix) to indicate a reciprocal relationship or action.

No	Hmong	English
1	Lawv ***sib*** *hlub* heev.	*They love one another very much.*
2	Nej paub ***sib*** *pab* heev.	*You know how to help one another very much.*
3	Nkawv ***sib*** *ntaus.*	*The two people fight each other.*
4	Nkawv ***sib*** *yuav* tau 10 xyoo.	*They have been married for 10 years.*
5	Lawv paub ***sib*** *hlub* heev.	*They know how to love each other a lot.*
6	Wb ***sib*** *paub* tau ntau xyoo los lawm.	*We knew each other for many years already.*
7	Neb puas ***sib*** *paub*?	*Do you know each other?*

Hmong Common Nouns

No	Hmong	English	Hmong Example	English
1	av	*soil, dirt*	Cog zaub rau hauv **av.**	*Plant vegetables in the* ***soil.***
2	dej	*water*	Peb haus **dej** ntau heev.	*We drink a lot of* ***water.***
3	diav	*spoon*	Muab rab **diav** rau kuv.	*Give the* ***spoon*** *to me.*
4	dib	*cucumber*	Peb nyiam noj **dib** heev.	*We like to eat* ***cucumbers*** *a lot.*
5	fawm	*pho, noodle*	Nej puas muag **fawm**?	*Do you sell* ***pho****?*
6	kev	*way, road*	Peb mus txoj **kev** twg.	*What* ***road*** *are we taking?*
7	khau	*shoe*	Koj muaj ib nkawm **khau.**	*You have one pair of* ***shoes.***
8	khob	*cup*	Koj haus tag ib **khob** dej.	*You finished drinking a* ***cup*** *of water.*
9	kua txob	*peppers*	Tso plaub lub **kua txob.**	*Put in four* ***peppers****.*
10	lauj kaub	*pot*	Koj muaj ib lub **lauj kaub**.	*You have one* ***pot****.*
11	log cam	*cutting board*	Koj puas muaj **log cam**?	*Do you have a* ***cutting board****?*
12	mov	*rice (cooked)*	Nej puas muag **mov**?	*Do you sell* ***rice****?*
13	nqaij	*meat, flesh*	Tsov nyiam noj **nqaij.**	*Tigers like to eat* ***meat.***
14	ntawv	*script, letter*	Peb sau **ntawv** Askiv.	*We write English* ***letters.***
15	phaj	*plate*	Koj noj tas ib **phaj** mov.	*You finished eating a* ***plate*** *of rice.*
16	qaib	*chicken*	Koj nyiam noj nqaij **qaib** ci.	*You like to eat fried* ***chicken****.*
17	qav	*frog*	Nej puas muag nqaij **qav**?	*Do you sell* ***frog meat****?*
18	riam	*knife*	Hov rab **riam**.	*Sharpen the knife.*
19	ris	*pants*	Koj puas nyiam lub **ris**?	*Do you like the* ***pants?***
20	rooj	*table*	Nej muaj ntau lub **rooj.**	*You have many* ***tables.***
21	tais	*bowl*	Hais mov rau hauv lub **tais.**	*Put rice in the* ***bowl.***
22	tog	*chair*	Thov zaum lub **tog** no.	*Please sit on this* ***chair.***
23	tsev	*house, home*	Koj muaj tsib lub **tsev.**	*You have five* ***houses.***
24	tsheb	*car*	Kuv muaj ib lub **tsheb** xwb.	*I have one* ***car*** *only.*
25	tsho	*shirt*	Koj muaj ib lub **tsho** xiav?	*You have one blue* ***shirt.***
26	tshuab	*machine*	Lub **tshuab** khiav ceev.	*The* ***machine*** *runs fast.*
27	txaj	*bed*	Peb pw lub **txaj** twg?	*We sleep on which* ***bed****?*
28	txhuv	*rice – uncooked*	Nej puas muag **txhuv**?	*Do you sell* ***rice****? (uncooked)*
29	zaub	*vegetable*	Nej puas muaj **zaub**?	*Do you have* ***vegetables****?*

Hmong Common Nouns

No	Hmong	English	Hmong Example	English
30	cag	*root*	Ntoo muaj ntau tus **cag.**	*Trees have many **roots.***
31	cawv	*alcohol*	Kuv tsis nyiam haus **cawv.**	*I don't like to drink **alcohol.***
32	fwj	*bottle*	Peb muaj ib **fwj** cawv.	*We have one **bottle** of alcohol.*
33	hav zoov	*forest*	Lub zos no tsis muaj **hav zoov.**	*This city does not have **forest.***
34	hiav txwv	*ocean*	Peb mus ua si tom **hiav txwv.**	*We go play by the **ocean.***
35	huab	*cloud*	Hnub no tsis muaj **huab.**	*Today has no **cloud.***
36	huab cua	*weather*	Kuv nyiam **huab cua** zoo xwb.	*I like good **weather** only.*
37	laj kab	*fence*	Peb xov **laj kab.**	*We put up a **fence.***
38	liaj	*paddy field*	Neeg cog nplej hauv **liaj.**	*People plant rice in **paddy field.***
39	ntaub	*fabric*	Koj muaj ib daim **ntaub** liab.	*You have a red **fabric.***
40	ntawv	*paper*	Muab ib daim **ntawv** rau kuv.	*Give a piece of **paper** to me.*
41	ntoo	*tree*	Kuv muaj ntau tsob **ntoo.**	*I have many **trees.***
42	paj	*flower*	Nej cog **paj** ntau heev.	*You plant many **flowers.***
43	phuam	*towel*	Muab txoj **phuam** rau kuv.	*Give me the **towel**.*
44	pob kws	*corn*	Koj puas cog **pob kws**?	*Do you plant **corn**?*
45	pob zeb	*rock*	Peb pom ntau lub **pob zeb.**	*We see many **rocks.***
46	qhov rai	*window*	Tsev muaj ntau lub **qhov rai.**	*House has many **windows.***
47	qhov rooj	*door*	Lub tsev muaj ob lub **qhov rooj.**	*The house has two **doors.***
48	roob	*mountain*	Peb nce lub **roob** siab.	*We climb a high **mountain.***
49	taub	*pumpkin*	Peb cog **taub** los muag.	*We plant **pumpkins** to sell.*
50	taus	*ax or axe*	Siv **taus** los ntov ntoo.	*Use **ax** to cut trees.*
51	taw	*foot, feet*	Koj muaj ob txhais **taw.**	*You have two **feet.***
52	teb	*farm*	Peb muaj ib daim **teb.**	*We have one **farm.***
53	tes	*hand*	Mob kuv txhais **tes.**	*Hurt my **hand.***
54	tiab	*dress*	Poj niam nyiam hnav **tiab.**	*Women like to wear **dress.***
55	tshuaj	*medicine*	Siv **tshuaj** los kho mob.	*Use **medicine** to cure illness.*
56	tsiaj txhu	*animal*	Lawv tsis muaj **tsiaj txhu.**	*They don' have **animals.***
57	zis	*urine*	Kuv xav tau koj cov **zis.**	*I need to have your **urine**?*
58	zos	*city, village*	Peb nyob hauv lub **zos.**	*We live in a **city.***

Hmong Common Nouns

No	Hmong	English	Hmong Example	English
59	chiv	*fertilizer*	Rau **chiv** los pab cov zaub.	*Add **fertilizer** to help vegetables.*
60	chiv keeb	*beginning*	Thaum **chiv keeb**, neeg los qhov twg los?	*In the **beginning**, where did humans come from?*
61	choj	*bridge*	Peb tuam tus **choj** tshiab.	*We build a new **bridge.***
62	daus	*snow*	Peb tsis nyiam ***daus.***	*We don't like **snow.***
63	hli	*moon*	Lub **hli** ci thiab kheej heev.	*The **moon** is bright and very full.*
64	hlua	*rope*	Siv **hlua** los khi tus npua.	*Use **ropes** to tie the pig.*
65	*hluas* nkauj	*girlfriend*	Nws muaj ib tus *hluas* **nkauj.**	*He has a **girlfriend.***
66	*hluas* nraug	*boyfriend*	Nws muaj ib tus *hluas* **nraug.**	*She has a **boyfriend.***
67	hmo	*night*	**Hmo** *no* tsis muaj neeg li.	***Tonight** there are no people.*
68	hnub	*sun*	*Hnub no* lub **hnub** kub heev.	*Today the **sun** is very hot.*
69	hnub qub	*star*	Hmo ntuj peb pom **hnub qub.**	*At night we see **stars.***
70	hom	*kind, mark*	Lawv muaj ntau **hom** paj.	*They have many **kinds** of flowers.*
71	kev cai	*law, rule*	Lawv muaj ib txoj **kev cai** tshiab.	*They have a new **law.***
72	koob	*needle*	Siv **koob** los xaws khaub ncaws.	*Use **needles** to sew clothes.*
73	luam	*business*	Peb tsis paub ua **luam.**	*We don't know how to do **business.***
74	nkoj	*boat*	Peb siv lub **nkoj** mus nuv ntses.	*We use the **boat** to go fishing.*
75	nom	*official*	**Nom** tsim tau ib txoj cai tshiab.	*The **officials** enacted a new law.*
76	noob	*seed*	Peb muag **noob** paj.	*We sell flower **seeds.***
77	ntses	*fish*	Peb xav noj **ntses** kib.	*We would like to eat fried **fish.***
78	ntsev	*salt*	Noj **ntsev** ntau tsis zoo.	*Eat too much **salt** is not good.*
79	ntshav	*blood*	Neeg muaj **ntshav.**	*Humans have **blood.***
80	pas dej	*pond*	Peb muaj ib lub **pas dej** me.	*We have a small **pond.***
81	peev	*capital*	Nej nqes **peev** npaum li cas?	*How much **capital** did you invest?*
82	sawv ntxov	*morning*	Kuv mus tsev thaum **sawv ntxov.**	*I go home in the **morning.***
83	tav su	*noon*	Peb noj mov thaum **tav su.**	*We eat at **noon.***
84	taws	*firewood*	Nej puas muaj **taws?**	*Do you have **firewood?***
85	tsaus ntuj	*evening*	Thaum **tsaus ntuj** neeg los tsev.	*In the **evening** people come home.*
86	txiab	*scissors*	Siv **txiab** los txiav ntaub.	*Use **scissors** to cut fabrics.*

Hmong Common Nouns

No	Hmong	English	Hmong Example	English
87	dav hlau	*airplane*	Peb ya **dav hlau** tas hnub.	*We flew **airplane** all day.*
88	hlau	*metal*	Neeg siv **hlau** los ua tsheb.	*People use **metal** to build cars.*
89	hnab	*bag*	Peb muaj ib **hnab** txiv.	*We have a **bag** of fruits.*
90	hniav	*teeth, tooth*	Txhuam koj cov **hniav.**	*Brush your **teeth.***
91	kub	*gold*	Koj muaj ib lub blhaib **kub**.	*You have a **gold** ring.*
92	mom	*hat*	Peb yuav ntau lub **mom.**	*We buy many **hats.***
93	nkauj	*song*	Koj hu zaj **nkauj** zoo heev.	*You sing the **song** very good.*
94	nruas	*drum*	Nws paub ntaus **nruas.**	*He knows how to play **drum.***
95	nyiaj	*money*	Lawv muaj **nyiaj** ntau.	*They have a lot of **money.***
96	nyom	*grass*	Nyuj nyiam noj **nyom**.	*Cows like to eat **grass**.*
97	teb chaws	*country*	Hmoob tsis muaj **teb chaws.**	*Hmong does not have a **country.***
98	tooj	*copper*	Nej siv **tooj** los ua ab tsi?	*What do you **copper** for?*
99	tshis	*goat*	Nej puas muaj **tshis?**	*Do you have **goats?***
100	tsho	*shirt*	Kuv nyiam koj lub **tsho** dawb.	*I like your white **shirt**.*
101	tshob	*dipper*	Neeg siv **tshob** los *ce* dej.	*People use **dippers** to scoop water.*
102	tsua	*boulder*	Lub **tsua** loj heev.	*The **boulder** is very big.*
103	tsuag	*rat, mouse*	Peb pom ib tug **tsuag.**	*We see one **rat.***
104	tub rog	*soldier*	**Tub rog** tiv thaiv teb chaws.	***Soldiers** protect country.*
105	txhuas	*lead*	Nej siv **txhuas** los ua ab tsi?	*What do you use **lead** for?*
106	xeev	*state*	Koj nyob lub **xeev** twg tuaj?	*What **state** are you from?*
107	yawg	*grandpa*	Kuv **yawg** yog Vam Lis Xyooj	*My **grandpa** was Vang Lee Xiong.*
108	yeeb	*opium*	Neeg siv **yeeb** los ua tshuaj.	*People use **opium** for medicine.*
109	yij	*quail*	Neeg nyiam cuab **yij.**	*People like to trap **quails.***
110	yim	*family*	Hauv peb zos muaj 100 **yim.**	*In our town there are 100 **families.***
111	yoov	*fly*	Caij ntuj so muaj **yoov** heev.	*In summer there are many **flies.***
112	yus	*one, oneself*	**Yus** yuav tsum ua neeg zoo.	***One** ought to be a good person.*
113	zam	*attire, outfit*	Koj hnav tau lub **zam** zoo heev.	*You put on a very nice **attire.***
114	zib	*honey*	Dais nyiam noj **zib.**	*Bears like to eat **honey.***
115	zos	*city, village*	Peb lub **zos** muaj neeg coob.	*Our **city** has many people.*

Compound Words

Hmong like to use compound words and/or talking in pairs using words either antonym, synonym or words that are in the same environment. Below are some of the compound words.

No	Hmong	English transliterated
1	Tig mus, tig los.	*Turning back and forth. (turn go, turn come)*
2	Hais rov qab, rov quav.	*Saying back and forth about the same subject.*
3	Noj mus, noj los.	*Eating back and forth. (eat go, eat come)*
4	Hais zoo, hais phem.	*Saying good and bad. (say good, say bad)*
5	Neeg ntse, neeg ruam.	*The wise and the unwise. (person smart, person dumb)*
6	Tus muaj, tus pluag.	*The rich and the poor. (person rich, person poor)*
7	Nyob deb, nyob ze.	*From far and near. (live far, live near)*
8	Muaj vaj, muaj tse.	*Have a place and home. (have fence, have house)*
9	Muaj zoo kwv, zoo tij.	*Have good relatives, esp of the same last name.*
10	Tej neeg ncaj, neeg ncees.	*The good and honest people.*
11	Yus tej neej, tej tsa.	*One's relatives-in-law.*
12	Hmoob tej zej, tej zos.	*Hmong's village and city.*
13	Lawv tej liaj, tej teb.	*Their rice paddy and farm.*
14	Nws tej tsiaj, tej txhu.	*His animals and rice.*
15	Muaj qoob, muaj loo.	*Have crops and fruits.*
16	Tej kab, tej ntsaum.	*The insects and ants.*
17	Tej niam, tej txiv.	*The mothers and fathers.*
18	Tej hlob, tej yau.	*The old and young.*
19	Tej pog, tej yawg.	*The grandma and grandpa.*
20	Tej Mab, tej Sua.	*The foreigners. Normally, Hmong say "Mab Sua" only.*
21	Xav mus, xav los	*To ponder, to think about something back and forth.*

For example:
Koj tej niam, tej txi.
Your mother and father.

Koj xaiv mus, xaiv los.
You choose back and forth.

Lawv hais zoo, hais phem.
They say good and bad.

Sorry about my English translation above because I am not good at English; however, I want you to know at least little bit of what each line means. Perhaps there is no proper way to translate the Hmong words without losing its native juice, so my best choice is to not confuse you with English words that make sense to you but have no direct translation for Hmong words on the left. For example, the Hmong words, "*xav mus, xav los*" means to "*think go, think come*" in a direct translation, but the meaningful English would be something like "*to ponder, to be undecided*" but the closest to the Hmong words would really be "*to think back and forth*" of something during an undecided stage.

Simple Phrase and Sentence

Well, I hope by now you are as sagacious and mature as most two year old children because you have come a long way. I want to congratulate you on your Hmong learning journey, and I want to help you master the Hmong language. I believe the Hmong language is easy to learn as long as you have a good teacher. Like the old Chinese saying, "***When a student fails to learn it is the teacher's fault.***" Not sure about the exact wording, but that is not far from the truth. Therefore, I certainly hope I have been a good teacher to you thus far. From here on, we will try to learn just like most young and inquisitive children do – interacting and conversing with each others.

So let's start with some simple greetings because you can apply what you learn here in real life. First, remember the **first** and **second** pronouns, **koj** thiab **kuv**, because we will be using these two pronouns heavily. In this exercise, we will have two people named: **Noog** and **Paj** (*bird* and *flower*).

Hmong	English
Noog: Nyob zoo ohs Paj.	**Noog:** Hello Paj.
Paj: *Nyob zoo ohs, Noog.*	***Paj:*** *Hello Noog.*
Noog: Ntev loo lawm txij thaum wb sib ntsib. Koj nyob li cas lawm xwb?	**Noog:** It has been a while since we met. How have you been?
Paj: *Kuv nyob zoo thiab hos koj ne?*	***Paj:*** *I am fine and how about you?*
Noog: Kuv nyob zoo, thiab kuv tseem niaj hnub ua hauj lwm li qub.	**Noog:** I am good, and I am still working every day as usual.
Paj: *Kuv tseem kawm ntawv, tabsis tshuav ib xyoos xwb ces kuv kawm tag lawm.*	***Paj:*** *I am still in school, but one more year only and I will be done then.*
Noog: Zoo heev. Rau siab kawm vim kev kawm yog ib yam tseem ceeb rau koj lub neej lawm yav pem suab.	**Noog**: Very good. Keep up the hard work because education is very important for your future.
Paj: *Muaj tseeb. Zoo siab tau ntsib koj dua.*	***Paj:*** *Indeed. Happy to see you again.*
Noog: Kuv los tib yam. Mus zoo koj.	**Noog:** Same here. Goodbye.
Paj: *Koj thiab ohs.*	***Paj:*** *And you, too.*

Nyob zoo, koj lub npe hu li cas? *Hello, what is your name?* Kuv hu ua Teeb xeem Xyooj. *My name is Teng last name Xiong.* Kuv zoo siab tau jib koj. *I am happy to meet you*. Wb mam li sib tham dua lwm zaus. *We will chat again next time.* Sis ntsib dua lwm zaus. *See you again next time.*

More Basic Phrases

No	Hmong	English
1	Kuv **tshaib plab.**	*I am **hungry.***
2	Koj puas xav **noj mov**?	*Would you like to **eat**? Or Would you like to eat rice?*
3	**Tshaib plab** kawg li tiag.	*Very **hungry** indeed.*
4	Koj **nyiam** noj ab tsi?	*What would you **like** to eat?*
5	Kuv xav noj ib phaj **mov kib**.	*I would like a plate of **fried rice.***
6	Koj ne?	*And you?*
7	Kuv mam li noj ib taig **fawm.**	*I will eat a bowl of **pho** (a bowl of noodle soup).*
8	Koj lub **npe** hu li cas?	*What is your **name**?*
9	**Kuv lub npe** hu ua Noog.	***My name** is Noog.*
10	Koj **muaj pes tsawg xyoo**?	***How old are** you?*
11	Kuv muaj *ob caug* **xyoo**.	*I am twenty **years** old.*
12	**Cia wb** so nov.	***Let us** rest here.*
13	Ua tsaug.	*Thank you.*
14	Koj **nyiam** tuaj nov heev los?	*You **like** to come here a lot?*
15	**Wb**, zaum no yog kuv **thawj zaug** xwb.	***No**, this is my **first time** only.*
16	Hos koj ne?	*How about you?*
17	Kuv twb tuaj nov **ntau zaus** lawm.	*I have been here **many times** already.*
18	**Zoo.** Qhov chaw no muaj zaub mov **qab.**	***Good**. This place has **good** food.*
19	Yog, kuv **hnov** neeg hais li thiab tiag.	*Yes, I **heard** people say something like that.*
20	**Chav dej** nyob qhov twg?	*Where is the **bathroom**?*
21	Ncaj qha tov ces lem rau koj **sab xis.**	*Straight there and then turn to your **right.***
22	**Koj puas tseem** kawm ntawv?	***Do you still** go to school?*
23	Wb, tsuas ua hauj lwm **txhua hnub.**	*No, just working **every day.***
24	Koj nyob qhov twg **tuaj?**	*Where are you **from?***
25	Kuv nyob teb chaws **Suav** tuaj ohs.	*I am from **China.***
26	Huag, pev mas **deb heev.**	*Wow, that is **very far**.*
27	Siv **peb hnub** mam tuaj txog hos.	*Took **three days** to get here.*
28	Hos koj ne?	*And how about you?*
29	Kuv nyob teb chaws **no** xwb.	*I am from **this** country only.*
30	Zoo heev.	*Very good.*

No	Hmong	English
1	Kuv **mob.**	*I am **sick.***
2	Tu siab tau **hnov** li.	*Sorry to **hear** that.*
3	Koj puas noj **tshuaj** li?	*Are you taking any **medications**?*
4	Wb, tsuas **vam tias** kuv yuav zoo xwb.	*No, just **hoping** I will get better only.*
5	Koj mob tau **hov ntev** lawm?	***How long** have you been sick?*
6	**Ob hnub** lawm.	***Two days** already.*
7	Zoo, kuv vam tias koj yuav **zoo sai.**	*Well, I hope you will feel **better soon.***
8	**Ua tsaug.** Kuv mam li pw thiab so.	***Thank you.** I will sleep and rest.*
9	Yog, so txaus ces **yuav pab.**	*Yes, enough rest **will help.***
10	Koj puas **nco qab** ab tsi ua rau koj mob?	*Did you **remember** what made you sick?*
11	**Tsis paub.** Yam kuv noj kawg ces yog ib tug **ntses kib.**	***Don't know.** The last thing I ate was a **fried fish.***
12	Ntawv zoo li yuav tsis ua rau koj **mob.**	*That seems like it would not make you **sick.***
13	Kuv **tsis xav** li thiab.	*I **don't think** so either.*
14	**Tej zaum** nws yog ib phaum kab mob xwb.	***Perhaps** it is just some virus going around only.*
15	Kuv xav li **thiab.**	*I think so, **too.***
16	Zoo, ua tib zoo tu koj **tus kheej** nawb.	*Well, take good care of **yourself** okay.*
17	Kuv mam li **sim.**	*I will **try.***
18	Mus zoo koj ohs.	*Goodbye to you.*

Short Greetings

No	Hmong	English
1	Koj tuaj thiab los.	*You come, too.*
2	Aws, tuaj thiab los mas.	*Yes, come, too.*
3	Nej tuaj **yuav ab tsi** ohs?	*You come here to **buy what**?*
4	Peb tuaj yuav **txhuv** xwb.	*We come to buy **rice** only.*
5	Nej ne?	*And you?*
6	Peb tuaj yuav txhuv **thiab.**	*We come to buy rice, **too.***
7	Nej mam li **lawv qab** ohs.	*You come later (or leave later on).*
8	Aws, sib ntsib **dua** nawb.	*Yes, see you again.*

Lawv qab means *to follow or to go after someone or to leave at a later time.*

Typical Hmong Greetings

No	Zaj	Paj
1	Koj tuaj thiab los, Paj.	Aws, kuv tuaj thiab ohs.
2	Koj lam tuaj ncig ua si xwb los?	Kuv tuaj nrhiav seb lawv puas muag kub xwb.
3	Auv, kuv pom lawv muag nyob pev thiab los mas.	Nyob hov deb nov naj?
4	Ze ze xwb ohs. Koj mus nov rau pev ces koj yeej pom lawv nyob kiag ntawm sab xis xwb los mas.	Ua tsaug nawb.
5	Tsis ua li cas ohs.	Sis ntsib dua ohs.

Equivalent English Translation

No	Zaj	Paj
1	You come here, too, Paj.	Yes, I come here, too.
2	You come here just for fun?	I come to see if they sell gold.
3	Oh, I saw they sell gold over there.	How far is it from here?
4	Very close. You go straight from here and you should see them on the right.	Thank you.
5	Not a problem.	See you again.

Some Hmong like to use some of the following words to end their phrases or sentences:
Ham tsis los mas, laiv, hos, nas, naj, ne, nev, los mas, los, ohs, nab, maj

Hmong Asking – **Person A**	Answer – **Person B**
1. Nws niaj hnub mus ua teb xwb **los?**	*Ham tsis los mas.*
*2. Lawv puas paub lus Hmoob zoo **naj**?*	*Tsis paub no thiab **laiv.***
3. Nws puas kam ua ntxiv lawm **maj**?	Nws zeem li lawm **hos.**
*4. Koj mob li cas tiag **ohs**?*	*Kuv pheej khaus caj pas xwb naj.*
5. Koj noj puas qab thiab **nab**?	Tsis qab li **ohs.** *Or* qab heev li **tiag.**
*6. Ua cas koj ho ua li ntawv **maj**?*	*Es koj twb kom kuv ua li ntawv **ne.***

Again, the above words are just a few to show you how strange Hmong sentences can be. You really do have to be born in Hmong and/or live with them long enough to really know how to speak and understand sentences like these. However, once you know these ending words, you can use them, too. For example: *Koj muaj pes tsawg xyoo lawm **naj**? Koj puas muaj nyiaj **nab**? Kuv hlub koj heev **laiv**. Koj puas kam pab kuv **ohs**? Tau kawg **los mas**. Ua tsaug ntau nawb. Txhob ua tsaug ohs.*

The above phrases are very common in Hmong, but you won't hear them from the less fluent Hmong speakers, and the words above fall into the "**friendly**" conversation category. So let's take a look at the following examples:

Normal question	Friendly version
1. Koj puas xav mus tsev?	Koj puas xav mus tsev ***ohs?***
2. Koj lub npe hu li cas?	Koj lub npe hu li cas ***nab?***
3. Koj puas paub nws zoo?	Koj puas paub nws zoo ***ohs?***
4. Nws ua li tiag.	Nws ua li tiag ***hos.***

Typical Phone Conversations

No	Hmong	English
1	Nyob zoo ohs, koj yog leej twg ni?	*Hello, who are you?*
2	Oev, kuv yog Paj ohs.	*Oh, I am Paj.*
3	Kuv xav nrog Zaj tham no es nws puas nyob **tsev** lawm ne yod?	*I would like to talk to Zaj so is he **home**?*
4	Nws nyob thiab los mas. Koj **tos** ib pliag ohv.	*Yes, he is home. You **wait** a moment okay.*
5	Ua tsaug ntau nawb.	*Thank you very much.*
6	Tsis ua li cas ohs.	*Not a problem.*

Shopping Phrase

No	Hmong	English transliterated
1	Nej puas muag *nqaij* **os**?	Do you sell **duck** *meat*?
2	Peb muag **thiab los mas.**	We sell them, **too**.
3	Nej muag ib tug **pes tsawg** *nab*?	You sell *each one* **how much**?
4	Peb muag ib tug yog **yim duas.**	We sell each for **eight dollars.**
5	Yog li kuv xav yuav **ob** tug ohs.	If so I would like to buy **two.**
6	Ces tus tswv muab ob tus os rau koj. Nws hais tias, "Yog ***kaum rau*** duas thiab ***yim caum*** xees." Ces koj cev daim nyiaj $20 rau nws. Nws txais thiab rov tau *peb duas* thiab *ob caug xees* los, thiab nws hais tias, "Ua tsaug nawb."	Then the owner handed you the two ducks. He said, "It is ***sixteen*** dollars and ***eighty*** cents." You then handed him a $20 bill. He took and returned *three dollars* and *twenty cents*, and he said, "Thank you."

$0.80 cents is the 5% tax.

Lo uas "*ob caug*" yog lus tshiab. Lo qub thiab Hmoob paub tiag mas yog "*nees nkaum*" no.
To ask for ***how much***, you would say, "Pes tsawg no?" Or "Yog pes tsawg?"

Body Parts

No	Hmong	English	Hmong Example
1	aub *ncaug*	saliva	*Koj nti* ***aub ncaug*** *rau peb coj mus kuaj.*
2	*caj* dab	neck	*Neeg coj xauv ntawm lawv lub* ***caj dab.***
3	caj ntswm	nose bridge	*Koj tus* ***caj ntswm*** *siab heev.*
4	*caj* qwb	nape (of the neck)	*Nws cov plaub hau ntev npog nws lub* ***caj qwb*** *tag.*
5	cev	body	*Lub qhov rooj tsis haum nws lub* ***cev.***
6	di ncauj	lips	*Mob nws daim* ***di ncauj.***
7	hauv *siab*	chest	*Koj ntog tsoo koj lub* ***hauv siab*** *doog tas.*
8	hniav, *kaus* hniav	tooth, teeth	*Koj pab txhuam tus me nyuam cov* ***hniav.***
9	kua *ntswg*	mucus	*Cov* ***kua ntswg*** *tawm hauv ob lub qhov ntswg los.*
10	mis	breast	*Ib tus neeg muaj ob lub* ***mis.***
11	ncauj, *qhov* ncauj	mouth	*Yus* ***ncauj*** *tsis txhob loj~. Don't have a big mouth.*
12	nplaig	tongue	*Koj rov tom koj tus* ***nplaig*** *los ntshav.*
13	nrob qaum	back	*Thov koj pab khawb kuv lub* ***nrob qaum.***
14	ntsej muag	face	*Ib tus neeg muaj ib lub* ***ntsej muag.***
15	ntsiab muag	pupil	*Ua zoo tsis txhob pub raug koj lub* ***ntsiab muag.***
16	plaub hau	hair	***Plaub hau*** *tuaj saum neeg lub taub hau.*
17	plaub muag	eyebrow	*Koj cov* ***plaub muag*** *dub heev.*
18	plaub *qhov ntswg*	nose hair	*Nws txiav nws cov* ***plaub qhov ntswg.***
19	plhu	face, cheek	*No~ es ua rau nws ob sab* ***plhu*** *liab tag li.*
20	*pob* tsaig	chin	*Nws ntog tsoo nws lub* ***pob tsaig****.*
21	*pob* yeeb	Adam's apple	*Txiv neej thiaj li muaj lub* ***pob yeeb.***
22	qhov muag	eye	*Neeg muaj ob lub* ***qhov muag.***
23	qhov ntswg	nostril	*Cov ntswg tawm hauv ob lub* ***qhov ntswg*** *los.*
24	taub hau	head	*Mob nws lub* ***taub hau.***
25	taub ntswg	upturned nose, tip	*Koj lub* ***taub ntswg*** *siab heev.*
26	tawv muag	eyelid	*Mob nws daim* ***tawv muag.***
27	xib tes	palm	*Koj tuav lub qe rau hauv koj lub* ***xib tes.***
28	xub ntiag	chest, front of	*Tus me nyuam pw hauv nws lub* ***xub ntiag.***
29	xub pwg	shoulder	*Nws kwv yav cav saum nws lub* ***xub pwg****.*

30	ceg	leg	*Neeg muaj ob txhais **ceg.***
31	*hauv* caug	knee	*Puas mob koj ob lub **hauv caug**?*
32	hlab ntaws	umbilical cord	*Koj niam tseem khaws koj txoj **hlab ntaws.***
33	leeg	tendon	*Mob nws cov **leeg.***
34	*luj* taws	heel	*Nws siv nws ob lub **luj taws** mus kev xwb.*
35	*ncej* puab	thigh	*Tus qaib muaj ob tus **ncej puab.***
36	nqaij	flesh, *meat*	*Nws ntog tsoo nws thaj **nqaij** doog tas.*
38	*nqaij* rog	fat	*Tus npua muaj **nqaij rog** ntau heev li.*
39	nqaij zog*	muscle	*Txiv neej muaj **nqaij zog** ntau dua poj niam.*
40	*ntiv* taw	toe	*Koj cov **ntiv taw** lo av dhau hwv.*
41	pij ntaws	belly button	*Khaus nws lub **pij ntaws.***
42	*plab* hlaub	calf	*Nws ntog tsoo nws lub **plab hlaub.***
43	plab mos	abdomen	*Mob nws lub **plab mos** lossis **plab mog.***
44	plaub qau	male pubic hair	*Cov **plaub qau** yog cov tuaj nyob ze ntawm qau.*
46	plaub qhov tsos	armpit hair	*Nws txiav nws cov **plaub qhov tsos.***
47	pob ntseg	ear	*Neeg muaj ob lub **pob ntseg.***
48	pob tw	buttocks	*Tus me nyuam tso zis ntub nws lub **pob tw** tag lawm.*
49	qhov ntsej	ear hole	*Koj tsis muaj **qhov ntsej** los ua cas hu koj tsis hnov?*
50	qhov quav	anus hole	*Cov quav tawm hauv lub **qhov quav** los.*
51	*qhov* raws	the area behind the knee, *knee pit*?	*Puas mob koj ob lub **qhov raws**?*
52	qhov tsos	armpit	*Nws muab nws ob txhais tes ntsaws hauv **qhov tsos.***
53	qhov zis	the hole of a penis or vagina	*Lub **qhov zis** yog lub qhov uas thaum yus tso zis es zis tawm hauv los.*
54	quav	feces, stool	*Tus kws kho mob xav tau koj cov **quav** no.*
55	*roob* hlaub	shank, tibia	*Nws dawm yav cav es tsoo nws lub **roob hlaub.***
56	taw	foot	*Sab khau tsis haum nws txhais **taw.***
57	tawv	skin	*Miv khawb nws daim **tawv** ntawm tes to tag.*
58	txha	bone	*Neeg muaj ntau yav **txha.***
59	txiv mis	nipple	*Ib lub mis muaj ib lub **txiv mis.***
60	zis	urine	*Tus kws kho mob xav tau koj cov **zis** no.*

* a new word I invented

Internal Organs

No	Hmong	English	Hmong Example
1	caj pas	throat	*Khaus~ nws **caj pas** thiaj ua rau nws hnoos heev.*
2	hlwb, *paj* hlwb	brain	*Cov neeg ntse **hlwb** khiav zoo dua.*
3	hnyuv	intestine	*Muaj ob hom **hnyuv**: Hnyuv **laus** thiab hnyuv **mos.***
4	hnyuv *laus*	big intestine	***Hnyuv laus** yog cov hnyuv uas **loj** thiab dub.*
5	hnyuv *mos*	small intestine	***Hnyuv mos** yog cov hnyuv uas **me.***
6	hnyuv *tws*	appendix	*Lawv txiav nws yav **hnyuv tws** pov tseg lawm.*
7	*kua* tsib	bile	*Cov **kua tsib** muaj nyob hauv lub **tsib,** thiab iab heev.*
8	**leeg** *nrob qaum*	spinal cord	*Mob nws cov **leeg nrob qaum.***
9	**mob** *hnyuv tws*	appendicitis	*Ib yam **mob** nyob ntawm yav **hnyuv tws.***
10	noob qes	testicles	***Noob qes** npua loj dua noob qes qaib.*
11	nru	uvula	*Mob nws tus **nru** es nws thiaj li hais tsis tau lus.*
12	ntshav	blood	*Tus doctor xav tau koj cov **ntshav** coj mus ntsuam.*
13	ntshav *dawb*	white blood cells	*Koj cov **ntshav dawb** ntau dhau lawm no.*
14	ntshav *liab*	red blood cells	*Koj cov **ntshav liab** tsawg zog lawm no.*
15	ntsws	lung	*Tsis txhob haus luam yeeb thiaj tsis mob **ntsws.***
16	paum	vagina	*Poj niam muaj **paum** tabsis txiv neej muaj **qau.***
17	plab	stomach	*Puas mob koj lub **plab** ohs?*
18	plawv	heart	*Neeg muaj ib lub **plawv** uas yog xa ntshav.*
19	ple, kaus ple	clitoris, gland clitoris	*Poj niam thiaj li muaj **ple** lossis **kaus ple** xwb.*
20	po	spleen	*Ib tus neeg muaj ib tus **po.***
21	qa	throat	*Mob nws lub **qa** es nws thiaj li nqos tsis tau mov.*
22	qau	penis	*Txiv neej thiaj li muaj **qau.***
23	quav	feces, stool, poop	*Tus nees tso **quav** rau hauv kev.*
24	raum	kidney	*Ib tus neeg muaj ob lub **raum.***
25	siab	liver	*Neeg muaj ib daim **siab.***
26	tsev me nyuam	uterus, womb	*Poj niam thiaj li muaj lub **tsev me nyuam** xwb.*
27	tsib	gallbladder	*Ib tus neeg muaj ib lub **tsib.***
28	**txha** *nrob qaum*	spine	*Puas mob koj tus **txha nrob qaum**?*
29	zais *zis*	bladder	*Nws tso zis ntau vim nws lub **zais zis** loj heev.*

Household Items

No	Hmong	English	Hmong Example
1	chav	room	*Nej lub tsev muaj tsib **chav** pw diam.*
2	*chav* dej	bathroom	*Kuv lub tsev muaj ib **chav dej** xwb.*
3	*chav* pw	bedroom	*Koj lub tsev muaj ntau **chav pw.***
4	*chav* ua noj	kitchen	*Kuv nyiam cov tsev uas muaj **chav ua noj** loj thiab dav.*
5	cib laug	dust pan	*Muab lub **cib laug** los rau kuv.*
6	*dab* da dej	bathtub	*Ib lub tsev yeej muaj ib lub **dab da dej.***
7	diav	spoon	*Neeg siv **diav** los hais mov noj.*
8	dos	onion	*Peb nyiam siv **dos** thiab qej los xyaw nqaij kib.*
9	hwj txob	black pepper	*Noj fawm yuav tau rau **hwj txob.***
10	khaub ruab	broom	*Koj pab yuav ib rab **khaub ruab** rau kuv nawb.*
11	lauj kaub	pot	*Neeg siv **lauj kaub** los hau zaub thiab nqaij.*
12	ntsev	salt	*Neeg nyiam noj **ntsev** xyaw nqaij.*
13	*phab* ntsa	wall	*Ib lub tsev yeej muaj ntau sab **phab ntsa**.*
14	phaj	plate	*Koj pab muab **phaj** los rau peb tau noj mov.*
15	qej	garlic	*Kuv tsis nyiam noj **qej** nyoos.*
16	qhov *rai*	window	*Kuv nyiam cov tsev muaj ntau lub **qhov rai.***
17	qhov *rooj*	door	*Nws lub tsev muaj plaub lub **qhov rooj.***
18	qws txob	pestle	*Tus **qws txob** yog siv los tuav kua txob hauv lub **tshuaj khib**.*
19	riam	knife	*Neeg siv **riam** los txiav ntoo thiab hlais nqaij tej.*
20	roj, roj ua noj	oil, cooking oil	*Neeg siv **roj** los kib zaub thiab nqaij.*
21	rooj	table	*Los peb noj mov saum lub rooj.*
22	ruv	roof	*Lub tsev siab ces lub **ruv** thiaj li siab.*
23	tais	bowl	*Koj pab muab ib lub **tais** los rau kuv rau zaub.*
24	tog	chair	*Neeg siv **tog** los zaum.*
25	tsev	house, home	*Nej muaj ib lub **tsev** loj thiab dav heev.*
26	tshuaj khib	mortar	*Lub **tshuaj khib** yog lub tais uas neeg siv los tuav kua txob.*
27	txee	shelf	*Neeg ua **txee** los rau tais thiab diav.*
28	yias	pan, frying pan	*Neeg siv **yias** los kib nqaij thiab zaub.*

Grocery Items

No	Hmong	English	Hmong Example – English
1	dej	water	*Nej cov **dej** nyob qhov twg? Where is your water?*
2	hnab	bag	*Ib **hnab** txiv pes tsawg ohs? How much is a bag of fruits?*
3	hnyuv	brat or sausage	*Nej muag ib ya **hnyuv** pes tsawg ohs?*
4	koos poom	can (food cans)	*Nej muag ib **koos poom** pes tsawg nab?*
5	mov	rice (cooked)	*Ib tais **mov** pes tsawg? One bowl of rice is how much?*
6	mov ci**	bread	*Nej puas muaj **mov ci** lossis **khaub cij** nab?*
7	npua*	pork	*Nej puas muaj nqaij **npuas**? Do you have pig meat (pork)?*
8	*nqaij* nyuj	beef	*Nej puas muaj nqaij **nyuj?** Do you have cow meat (beef)?*
9	ntses*	fish	*Nej muag ib tus **ntses** pes tsawg? How much is one fish?*
10	ntsev	salt	*Nej cov **ntsev** nyob qhov twg? Where is your salt?*
11	nyiaj	money	*Kuv tsis muaj **nyiaj** txaus. I don't enough money.*
12	qaib	chicken	*Nej muag ib tus **qaib** pes tsawg? How much is one chicken?*
13	*qaib* ntxhw*	turkey	*Nej puas muag **qaib ntxhw**? Do you sell turkey?*
14	roj	oil, cooking oil	*Nej cov **roj kib zaub** nyob qhov twg?*
15	*roj* pob kws	corn oil	*Nej puas muaj **roj pob kws**? Do you have corn oil?*
16	*roj* zaub	vegetable oil	*Kuv xav yuav **roj zaub** es nej puas muaj nab?*
17	taub mis	gallon of milk	*Nej muag ib **taub mis** pes tsawg ohs?*
18	taub ntoos	papaya	*Nej puas muaj **taub ntoos**? Do you have papaya?*
19	them	pay	*Kuv mus them qhov twg? Where do I go pay?*
20	tshis*	goat	*Nej puas muag nqaij **tshis**? Do you sell goat meat?*
21	txhuv	rice (uncooked)	*Nej puas muag **txhuv**? Do you sell rice?*
22	*txhuv* nplaum	sticky rice	*Peb muag **txhuv nplaum** xwb. We sell sticky rice only.*
23	*txhuv* txua	non-sticky rice	*Nej puas muaj **txhuv txua**? Do you have non-sticky rice?*
24	*txiv* kab ntxwv	orange	*Ib hnab **txiv kab ntxwv** pes tsawg ohs?*
25	*txiv* tsawb	banana	*Nej muag ib kuam **txiv tsawb** pes tsawg?*
26	yaj*	sheep, lamb	*Nej puas muaj **nqaij yaj**?*
27	zaub	vegetable	*Nej muag ib pob **zaub** pes tsawg?*

* Mostly, Hmong use the word nqaij, *meat,* along with the animal, i.e., **nqaij** *npua*, **nqaij** *qaib* etc...
** Most Hmong know the Lao word "khaub cij" only.

Agricultural Products

No	Hmong	**English Word** – *Hmong Example*
1	nplej	Rice grains that still have the palea or chaff, rice seeds. *Nej muag ib hnab **nplej** pes tsawg?*
2	pob kws	Corn, cornstalk. *Lawv muaj ib txhab **pob kws.***
3	kua txob, hov txob	Pepper. *Nej puas cog **kua txob** thiab?*
4	zaub paj	Cauliflower. *Peb muaj ib thaj teb **zaub paj.***
5	taum	Bean. *Nej puas muaj **taum?***
6	zaub ntsuab	Green vegetables. *Koj muaj ib thaj teb **zaub ntsuab.***
7	dos	Onion. *Xyoo no nej puas cog **dos** lawm?*
8	tauj qaib	Lemongrass. *Nej puas muag **tauj qaib**?*
9	qhiav	Ginger. *Leej twg thaj teb **qhiav** no nab?*
10	taum ntaj	Long bean. *Nej puas muaj cov noob **taum ntaj**?*
11	taum pauv	Soybean. *Koj thaj teb **taum pauv** puas zoo thiab?*
12	qos yaj ywm	Potato. *Nej puas cog **qos yaj ywm** lawm?*
13	taub ntoos	Papaya. *Peb muaj ib thaj teb **taub ntoos.***
14	tsawb	Banana. *Nej puas muaj cog **tsawb** thiab?*
15	dib ntsuab	Cucumber. *Nej puas muaj noob **dib ntsuab**?*
16	dib pag	Yellow melon, melon. *Nej puas cog **dib pag** thiab?*
17	dib liab	Watermelon. *Peb mus yuav **dib liab** los muag xwb.*
18	noob	Seed. *Nej puas muaj **noob** dib?*
19	qos	Yam, tuber, potato. *Nej puas cog **qos** lawm thiab?*
20	pum hub	Mint. *Koj puas tseem muaj **pum hub lawm**?*
21	qos liab	Red potato. *Nej thaj teb **qos liab** puas zoo thiab?*
22	lws suav	Tomato. *Peb muaj ib thaj teb **lws suav.***
23	zaub pob	Cabbage. *Nej puas muaj noob **zaub pob**?*
24	kab tsib	Sugarcane also *sugar cane*. *Peb muaj ib thaj teb **kab tsib.***
25	dib iab	Bitter melon. *Kuv niam cog tau ib tsob **dib iab.***
26	txiv txhais	Mango. *Ntawm peb tsev muaj ntau tsob **txiv txhais.***
27	lws, txiv lws	Eggplant. *Nej puas cog tau **txiv lws** thiab?*
28	taub hwb	Gourd. *Nej muag ib lub **taub hwb** pes tsawg?*

Illness and Disease

No	Hmong	**English Word** – *Hmong Example*
1	mob	Hurt, pain. *Koj* ***mob*** *qhov twg?*
2	mob *plab*	Stomach*ache*. *Nws* ***mob plab*** *thiab ntuav.*
3	mob *taub hau*	Head*ache*. *Nws* ***mob taub hau*** *thiab hnoos.*
4	raws *plab*	Diarrhea. *Nws* ***raws plab*** *thiab ntuav.*
5	zawv *plab*	Diarrhea. *Nws* ***zawv plab*** *thiab hnoos.*
6	kem *plab*	Stomachache caused by digestion problems. *Tej zaum koj* ***kem plab*** *xwb.*
7	ntuav	Vomit, throw up. *Nws* ***ntuav*** *thiab zawv plab.*
8	hnoos	Cough. *Nws* ***hnoos*** *thiab ntuav tau peb hnub los lawm.*
9	los *ntswg*	Runny nose. *Nws hnoos thiab* ***los ntswg.***
10	mob *khaub thuas*	Cold, common cold. *Koj mob* ***khaub thuas*** *xwb.*
11	qis	Sprain. *Koj ua koj txhais taw* ***qis*** *lawm.*
12	lov	Break, like a broken bone. *Nws ntog ces ua rau nws txhais taw* ***lov.***
13	doog	Bruise. *Koj ntog tsoo koj txhais tes* ***doog*** *tas.*
14	kub, kub *hnyiab*	Burn, by fire or hot liquid. *Nws ua hluav taws* ***kub*** *nws txhais tes.*
15	hlab	Burn, by hot liquid. *Nws ua dej kub* ***hlab*** *nws txhais tes.*
16	daj ntseg	Pale, pallor. *Nws mob tau ib hlis ces ua rau nws* ***daj ntseg*** *heev.*
17	qoob	Pox, chicken pox. *Nws mob cov* ***qoob.***
18	rwj	Cyst. *Nws mob ib lub* ***rwj*** *rau ntawm nws sab ncej puab.*
19	cos	Wart. *Nws mob ib lub* ***cos*** *ntawm nws txhais taw.*
20	ruas	Leprosy. ***Ruas*** *yog ib yam mob nyob rau ntawm tej ntiv tes thiab ntiv taw.*
21	hlwv	Blister. *Nws ntov ntoo ib hnub nkaus es ua rau nws tes tawm* ***hlwv*** *tas.*
22	xeev *siab*	Nausea. *Tus poj niam xeeb me nyuam ces ua rau nws* ***xeev siab*** *heev.*
23	ntshav siab	High blood pressure. *Koj rog thiaj li ua rau koj cov* ***ntshav siab*** *heev.*
24	mob *ntshav qab zib*	Diabetes, diabetic. *Koj muaj mob* ***ntshav qab zib.***
25	mob *hnyuv tws*	Appendicitis. ***Mob hnyuv tws*** *ces kawg muab txiav tawm xwb.*
26	qaug *dab peg*	Epilepsy, seizure. *Tsis muaj leeg twg xav mob* ***qaug dab peg****.*

Unlike English, Hmong does not have many separate words for different types of pains. Therefore, the way the Hmong describe a specific **ache** or **pain** is similar to some of the English words **head***ache*, **stomach***ache*, and **tooth***ache*. In other words, each pain starts with the Hmong verb "**mob**" and followed by whatever the part (*object, noun*) that is aching or painful.

Basic Conversation Regarding Illness

No	Hmong	English
1	Nyob zoo.	Hello.
2	*Mob* koj qhov twg?	Where does it *hurt*?
3	Mob kuv _______(hais koj qhov chaw uas mob)	Hurt my ________(say the area it hurts)
4	Mob tau *hov ntev* los lawm?	*How long* have you had the pain?
5	Twb mob tau *tsib hnub* los lawm.	It has been *five days* already.
6	Tam sim no koj puas noj *tshuaj* ab tsi li?	Are you currently taking any *medicines*?
7	Wb, tsis noj li.	No, taking nothing.
8	1 txog 10, 10 yog mob heev, 1 yog tsis mob li; koj qhov mob yog pes tsawg?	1 to 10, 10 being very painful, what number is your pain?
9	Kuv xav tias yog 8.	I think it is 8.
10	Thaum twg yog koj tso zis zaum kawg?	When did you last urinate?
11	Tag kis no li thaum 8:00 sawv ntxov.	This morning around 8:00 A.M.
12	Hos tso quav ne?	What about bowel movement?
13	Nag hmo xwb.	Last night only.
14	Puas mob lwm qhov li thiab?	Does it hurt anywhere else?
15	Wb.	No.
16	Koj tus kws kho mob yog leej twg?	Who is your family doctor?
17	Kuv tsis muaj li.	I don't have one.
18	Puas muaj tej yam tshuaj uas koj tsis haum?	Are you allergic to any medications?
19	Tsis muaj.	Have none *or nothing*.
20	Koj puas tau raug phais dua li?	Have you had any surgeries in the past?
21	Tsis muaj.	Have none.
22	Sib zog qus pa.	Take a deep breath.
23	Peb yuav tso ib co ntshav.	We will take some blood.
24	Ib xuaj moo ces peb mam li paub.	One hour and we will have the answer.
25	Koj yuav tau pw nov ib hmos.	You will have to stay here for one night.
26	Tus doctor mam li lo saib koj ib pliag no.	The doctor will come to see you shortly.

Have you = *Koj puas tau?* Do you have = *Koj puas muaj?* When = *Thaum twg?* What = *Ab tsi?* Pain or hurt = *Mob.* *Squeeze = Nyem.* Open your mouth = *Rua koj lub qhov ncauj. Say Ah = Hais As.* *Does it hurt = Puas mob?* Do you remember = *Koj puas nco?* Do you know = *Koj puas paub?*

World and Country

No	Hmong	English Word – *Hmong Example*
1	ntuj	Universe, sky. *Neeg tsis paub tias lub **ntuj** loj thiab dav npaum li cas.*
2	ntiaj tab	Earth. *Lub **ntiaj teb** no kheej, muaj av, thiab muaj dej.*
3	qaum ntuj	Above the universe, a planet above the sky.
4	qab ntuj	Below the universe, a place below the sky. *Nws yog neeg qaum ntuj.*
5	ceeb tsheej	Heaven. *Vaj Tswv nyob saum **Ceeb Tsheej.***
6	hiav txwv	Ocean. *Dej **hiav txwv** loj thiab ntau tshaj av ntau npaug.*
7	hav zoov, zoov	Forest. *Neeg tsis txuag **hav zoov** ces tej tsiaj qus yuav tsis muaj chaw nyob.*
8	liaj ia	Farm, farm land. *Hmoob nyiam nyob tej teb chaws uas muaj **liaj ia** xwb.*
9	zej zos, zos	Village, city, town. *Nej tej **zej zos** ntxim nyob heev li.*
10	xeev	State. *Teb chaws Meskas muaj 50 lub **xeev.***
11	teb chaws	Country. *Hmoob yog ib haiv neeg tsis muaj **teb chaws.***
12	dej, hav dej	Water, river. *Tus dej loj thiab ntev tshaj plaws yog tus **dej** hu ua Mississippi.*
13	av	Land, soil, dirt. *Nej muaj ib thaj **av** dav thiab zoo heev.*
14	huab cua	Weather. *Teb chaws **Hawaii** muaj **huab cua** zoo heev li.*
15	laj kam	Employment, job. *Thaum tsis muaj **laj kam** ua ces neeg tsis muaj nyiaj siv.*
16	hauj lwm	Job, work. *Thaum tsis muaj **hauj lwm** ua ces neeg tsis muaj nyiaj siv.*
17	vaj tse	House, home. *Nej muaj **vaj tse** zoo heev li.*
18	Huab Tais	King, God. *Thaib teb tseem muaj tus **Huab Tais Thaib.***
19	kev cai	Law, rule. *Txawv teb chaws ces muaj txawv **kev cai.***
20	pej xeem	Citizen, people. *Cov **pej xeem** feem coob xaiv tau tus nom tshiab lawm.*
21	nom tswv	Government, officials. *Tej **nom tswv** hlub thiab pab tej pej xeem heev.*
22	yaj sab	Bucolic, in a rural or country. *Kuv nyiam nyob **yaj sab** xwb.*
23	ciam	Boundary, limit. *Txhua lub teb chaws yeej muaj **ciam** tas lawm.*
24	nroog	County, region. *Kuv nyob hauv lub **nroog** Manitowoc, **xeev** Wisconsin.*

These are just a few of the most common terms people normally use during a typical conversation. Lub ntiaj teb no muaj ntau lub teb chaws. Ib lub teb chaws twg yeej muaj neeg nyob puv nkaus li. Muaj qee lub teb chaws kuj tseem muaj ntau hom neeg nyob ua ke thiab. Zoo li lub teb chaws Meskas nws muaj 50 lub xeev, thiab muaj ntau hom neeg. Tej huab tej cua los kuj txawv vim lub teb chaws Meskas mas loj thiab dav heev li. Nram qab teb xws li *Florida* ces sov thiab los nag heev, tabsis pem qaub teb xws li *Montana* thiab *North Dakota* mas kuj no thiab tseem los daus ntau nyob rau lub caij *ntuj no – winter.*

Directions and Orientation

No	Hmong	English	Hmong Example
1	**deb** npaum li cas?	how **far**?	*Nej nyob **deb npaum li cas**?*
2	dhau	past, over	*Koj tuaj kom **dhau** tus dej.*
3	hauv	in, inside, within	*Peb nyob **hauv** lub zos loj.*
4	laug, sab laug	left, left side. *Sab = side, laug = left.*	*Nyob ntawm koj **sab laug.***
5	lem, tig	turn	*Koj **lem** sab xis. Koj **tig** sab xis.*
6	**luag** teb	**northern** end *of a farm. Teb = farm.*	*Nyob pem **luag** teb.*
7	lwm	other, *different, next*	***Lwm** lub zos muaj neeg coob.*
8	*ncaj* qha	straight, directly	*Koj mus **ncaj qha** xwb.*
9	nrav, nram, *nrad*	down there, south, southern	***Nram** lub xeev Texas.*
10	ntawm, *ntawd*	at, by, where	*Kuv nyob **ntawm** tus choj.*
11	**ntev** npaum li cas?	how **long**?	*Yuav mus **ntev npaum li cas**?*
12	**ntug** zos	**the edge of** a city or town	*Kuv nyob ntawm **ntug zos.***
13	pev, pem, *ped*	up there, north, northern	***Pem** lub xeev Minnesota.*
14	**plawv** zos	**middle of** a city or town, center	*Kuv nyob hauv **plawv zos.***
15	qab	below, south of, under, underneath	*Qab ke, qab zos, qab teb ltn...*
16	qab teb	south, southern, down there	*Nram **qab teb** mas sov heev.*
17	**qab** zos	**south** or **southern** of a city	*Nws nyob nram **qab zos.***
18	qaum teb	north, northern, up there	*Sab pem **qaum teb** muaj daus.*
19	**qaum** zos	**north** or **northern** of a city	*Lawv nyob pem **qaum zos.***
20	rov qab	turn back, come back, turn around	***Rov qab** los kom pom tus choj.*
21	teeb liab	red light, a stop-and-go light that is.	*Los kom dhau ob lub **teeb liab.***
22	tiv, tim, *tid*	eastern regions having similar longitude	*Nws nyob **tim** Michigan.*
23	tov, tom, *tod*	western regions having similar longitude	*Nws nyob **tom** lub zos Av Liab.*
24	tus dej	a river. dej = water	*Koj tuaj kom dhau **tus dej.***
25	txawv	different	*Nws nyob **txawv** zos tuaj.*
26	txog	to, reach	*Tuaj kom **txog** ntawm tus choj.*
27	xis, sab xis	right, right side. Xis = right	*Nyob ntawm koj **sab xis.***
28	ze	near, nearby	***Pes tsawg** hnub mam tuaj txog?*

Well, only use this page if you don't have any GPS device to help you navigate okay.

Geographical Locations

To make life easier, let's use a map that I drew of the United States, and let's pretend you are in the **center,** *hauve plawv*, of the map – somewhere near **Nebraska** that is.

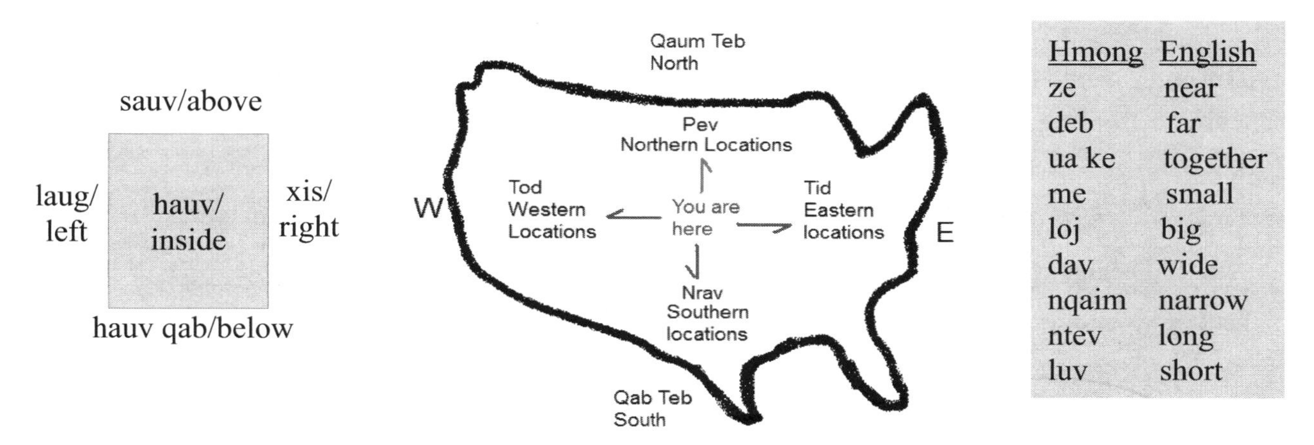

Hmong	English
ze	near
deb	far
ua ke	together
me	small
loj	big
dav	wide
nqaim	narrow
ntev	long
luv	short

The *default word* for any unknown country locations is "**tiv** or **tim**", and "**tov** or **tom**" for closer locations such as cities and towns. For example: *Nyob tom lawv zos.*

As you can see, I labeled *North* = **Qaum** teb, *South* = **Qab** teb. For *East* is called sab **hnub tuaj** (the side where the sun rises), and *West* is called sab **hnub poob** (the side where the sun goes down).

1	Pev, pem, ped	Refer to any ***northern*** locations	For example: *Minnesota, Canada*
2	Nrav, nram, nrad	Refer to any ***southern*** locations	For example: *Texas, Florida*
3	Tiv, tim, tid	Refer to any ***eastern*** locations	For example: *New York, Maine*
4	Tov, tom, tod	Refer to any ***western*** locations	For example: *Colorado, California*

As long as you get the city or state name correct, don't worry too much about North or South, and East and West because most people do know where things are. If you start calling "**pem**" **Texas** when you are living in **Minnesota** then people just think you just came from Laos that is all. If you are not sure about its proper location, you can always use the word "tiv or tim." For example, tim Thaib teb, tim Suav teb, thiab tim Meska, and use "**tom**" for closer cities and/or states within your own country.

Practice

Nws nyob ______ Minnesota tuaj. _______ Texas mas sov heev li. Cov neeg _____ Thaib teb.
Lawv nyob _________ **W**. Nws nyob _________ Florida mas sov heev. Koj nyob __________ **E**.
Canada nyob ______ teb thiab no heev. ________ California. Nyob rau __________Kentucky.
________ Thaib teb mas sov kawg. Nej rov mus ________ Nplog los? _____ lub peb zos.

Hmong Clans

There are *roughly* 18 Hmong clans or last names the Hmong people use worldwide; however, these are Chinese last names and the Hmong adopted them many decades ago when Hmong still lived in China. Additionally, some of the Hmong people who live in the United States also have changed their last names to other names and some have different spellings than what listed here.

No	Hmong	English spelling	Hmong Example
1	Faj	Fang	*Faj yog ib xeem Hmoob.*
2	Ham	Hang, Ha	*Lawv yog xeem Ham.*
3	Hawj	Her, Herr	*Xeem Ham yuav tsis tau xeem Hawj.*
4	Khab	Khang, Kha	*Nws tus poj niam yog xeem Khab.*
5	Koo	Kong	*Nws lub xeem yog Koo.*
6	Kwm	Kue	*Hmoob Kwm yuav tsis tau Hmoob Thoj.*
7	Lauj	Lor, Lo	*Nws lub npe hu ua Paj, xeem Lauj.*
8	Lis	Lee, Ly	*Koj yog xeem Lis.*
9	Muas	Moua	*Peb tus vauv yog xeem Muas.*
10	Phab	Pha, Phang	*Lawv lub zos muaj ib xeem hu ua Phab.*
11	Thoj	Thao, Thor	*Hmoob Thoj yuav tsis tau Hmoob Kwm.*
12	Tsab	Chang, Cha.	*Kuv niam hu ua Ntxhi xeem Tsab.*
13	Tsheej	Cheng	*Nej puas yog xeem Tsheej?*
14	Tswb	Chue	*Nws yog xeem Tswb.*
15	Vaj	Vang, Va	*Nai Phoo Vaj Pov yog xeem Vaj. General Vang, Pao.*
16	Vwj	Vue, Vu	*Kuv tus niam tij yog xeem Vwj.*
17	Xyooj	Xiong, Song	*Kuv txiv hu ua Txoov Neeb xeem Xyooj.*
18	Yaj	Yang, Ya	*Thawj tus Hmoob uas kawm tiav Ph.D. yog hu ua Yaj Daus.*

According to the Hmong culture and marriage practice, a person can not, or should not, marry another person who has the same last name. Additionally, some of the clans listed below also don't encourage their children to marry each other due to their closed and brotherly relationships in the past.

1	Kwm, Khab and Thoj are related.
2	Lauj and Khab are related.
3	Ham and Hawj are related.

Hmong First Names

Thanks to Charles Tsu Vue

Name	English	Sex	Meanings
Aiv	Ai	F	small
Cawv	Cher	M	alcohol
Cua	Choua	F	wind
Dawb	Der	F	white
Diav	Dia	F	spoon
Dib	Dee	F	cucumber
Foom	Fong	M	bless
Hwj	Hue	M	bottle, control
Kab	Ka	F	insect
Kaus	Kao	M	umbrella
Kub	Kou	M	gold
Nkauj	Gao	F	song, young female
Npauj	Bao	F	butterfly, moth
Npawv	Ber	M	chubby
Npib	Bee	F	coin
Nplooj	Blong	M	leaf
Nruas	Doua	M	drum
Ntaj	Dang	M	sword
Ntsuab	Joua	F	green
Ntxawg	Ger	M	last son
Ntxawm	Yer	F	last daughter
Paj	Pa	F	flowers
Tsav	Cha	M	drive, rule
Tswb	Chue	M	bell
Txiab	Chia	M	scissors
Vaj	Va	F	King
Zeb	Ge, Jay	M/F	rock, stone, Peter

Name	English	Sex	Meanings
Hlau	Hlao	M	metal, hoe
Hli	Hlee	F	moon
Hnub	Nou	F	sun
Leej	Leng	M	row, effective
Liab	Lia	F	red
Liag	Liang	F	rice sickle
Mab	Ma	F	foreigner
Maiv	Mai	F	girl
Mos	Mao	M/F	young, soft
Neeb	Neng	M	shaman
Nyiaj	Nhia	B	silver, money
Pov	Pao	M	protect
Siab	Shia	M	tall
Suav	Shoua	M	Chinese
Teeb	Teng	M	light
Teem	Teng	M/F	short
Tooj	Tong	M/F	brass
Tub	Tou	M	son
Vam	Wa	M	prosperous
Xis	See	F	like
Xyoob	Shong	M	bamboo

Hmong first names fall into five categories:
1. The last name of others: Vaj, Lis, Yaj
2. Household items: Diav, Riam, Vab
3. Animals: Ntxhw, Zaj, Nab, Noog
4. Planets: Hnub, Hli, Huab, Cua
5. Plants: Paj, Dib, Nplooj, Xyoob

Traditionally, the last names stay the same for men but women will adopt their husbands' last names. These are just a few, and the younger generations do take first names from other nationalities from the country they live, i.e., in the United States: **Peter** Yang, **Thomas** Xiong, and **Lisa** Vang etc...

Family and Friends

No	Hmong	English	Hmong Example
1	yim, yig	family	*Ib **yim** neeg, ib **yig** neeg.*
2	cuab	family	*Yus lub **cuab** lub **yig.***
3	*tsev* neeg	family. tsev = house, neeg = people.	*Kuv **tsev neeg** muaj 6 leej.*
4	*niam* tsev	house wife	*Nws yog ib tug **niam tsev** zoo.*
5	txiv tsev	house husband	*Koj yog ib tus **txiv tsev** zoo.*
6	*me* nyuam	child, kid	*Wb muaj 4 tug **me nyuam.***
7	tus hlub*	honey, loved one	*Koj yog kuv tus **hlub.***
8	neej tsa	wife's relatives	*Kuv cov **neej tsa** yog xeem Yaj.*
9	kwv tij	husband's relatives	*Kuv cov **kwv tij** yog xeem Xyooj.*
10	txiv	father, man, male	*Kuv **txiv** hu ua Txoov Neeb Xyooj.*
11	niam	mother, woman	*Kuv **niam** hu ua Ntxhi xeem Tsab.*
12	yawm txiv	grandfather-in-law	*Peb **yawm txiv** hu ua Xaiv Khwb Tsab.*
13	niam tais	grandmother-in-law	*Peb **niam tais** hu ua Ntxhoo Lauj*
14	dab laug	brother-in-law – wife's brothers.	*Nws yog kuv tus **dab laug.***
15	niam dab laug	brother-in-law's wife	*Nws yog kuv tus **niam dab laug.***
16	yawm yij, yij	brother-in-law – sister's husdband	*Kuv muaj peb tus **yawm yij.***
17	niam hluas	wife's younger sister	*Kuv tus poj niam yog tus **niam hluas.***
18	txiv hlob	uncle who is older than one's dad	*Kuv muaj ob tug **txiv hlob.***
19	txiv ntxawm	uncle who is younger than one's dad	*Peb muaj coob leej **txiv ntxawm.***
20	tij laug, tij	older brother	*Kuv tus **tij laug** hu ua Tswv Tooj Xyooj*
21	kwv	younger brother – called by guys.	*Kuv muaj ob tug **kwv**: Ntshiab thiab Vaj.*
22	kwv *ntxawg*	youngest brother – called by guys.	*Kuv tus **kwv ntxawg** hu ua Ntshiab no.*
23	muam	sister – called by brothers only	*Kuv muaj peb leeg **muam.***
24	muam *ntxawm*	youngest sister – called by brothers.	*Kuv tus **muam ntxawm** hu ua Khu no.*
25	viv ncaus	sisters – called by ladies only.	*Nws muaj **viv ncaus** coob heev.*
26	nus	brother – called by sisters only.	*Kuv yog kuv cov muam tus **nus** nrab.*
27	phooj ywg	friends	*Koj muaj **phooj ywg** coob heev.*

One of the word young Hmong men like to use is "**npawg**" which is similar to "**buddy**" in English, and it is used to call other men. For example: *Npawg, koj mus qhov twg ohs?*

Courtship and Dating

No	Hmong	English	Example
1	hlub	to love, love	*Zaj **hlub** Paj heev li.*
2	nco	miss, to think of	*Koj puas **nco** kuv lawm thiab?*
3	tshua	miss, to think of	*Peb **tshua** txog koj heev.*
4	khawm	to hug, to hold	*Koj puas kam kuv **khawm** koj nab?*
5	**tuav** *tes*	**to hold** *hands*	*Koj puas kam kuv **tuav** koj tes ohs?*
6	plhws	**touch** using the palm	*Kuv **plhws** nws lub taub hau.*
7	kov	to touch, caress	*Kuv **kov** nws es nws thiaj li cem kuv.*
8	hnia	to kiss	*Tus hluas nraug **hnia** tus hluas nkauj.*
9	puag	to hug	*Koj **puag** kuv ib pliag puas tau?*
10	saib	see, watch, visit, to look at	*Tag kis kuv mam li tuaj **saib** koj.*
11	duab	picture	*Koj puas muaj **duab** xa tuaj rau kuv saib?*
12	kho siab	the feeling of missing someone, homesick, love*sick*	*Nyob ib leeg cas yuav **kho siab** ua luaj li.*
13	deev	sexual intercourse, sex	*Tsis txhob lam **deev** yog yus tsis hlub tiag.*
14	dag	to lie, joke, tease, trick	*Nws **dag** koj xwb es tsis txhob chim.*
15	tseeb	true, real, fact	*Yeej muaj **tseeb** li nws hais.*
16	ntxias	persuade, seduce, coax	*Nws **ntxias** kom peb muab nyiaj rau nws.*
17	yuav	to marry, buy	*Koj puas kam **yuav** kuv nab?*
18	hluas *nkauj*	girlfriend. hluas = young	*Koj puas kam ua kuv tus **hluas nkauj**?*
19	hluas *nraug*	boyfriend. nraug = guy	*Koj puas kam ua kuv tus **hluas nraug**?*
20	txij nkawm	spouse, couple	*Neb yog **txij nkawm** los ntev lawm.*
21	qhaib	to reserve a person as to prearrange for marriage, engaged.	*Nws nqa ib choj nyiaj tuaj **qhaib** lawv tus ntxhais rau nws tus tub.*
22	koj niam*	honey, a wife	***Koj niam**, wb mus ua teb ohs.*
23	koj txiv*	honey, a husband	***Koj txiv**, koj ua mov rau kuv noj nawb!*

* Hmong use these two words a lot, especially the older couples. Don't go by the literal translation because the word "**koj niam**" literally means "**your mom**" and "**koj txiv**" means "**your dad**." The other way Hmong use to call their spouse is the *first name* of their very *first child*. For example, I would call my wife "*Maiv Nyiaj* niam" instead of "koj niam" and not by her first name. However, each generation is different and I think the younger folks like to call their spouses by their first name because my wife told me that when I called her "*koj niam*" makes her feel *very old.*

Marriage and Wedding

No	Hmong	English	Hmong Example
1	sib yuav	to marry each other	Nkawv ***sib yuav*** tau ob hlis los lawm.
2	txiv	husband	Koj *tus* ***txiv*** yog leej twg?
3	poj niam	wife, woman	Nws yog kuv *tus* ***poj niam.***
4	vauv, nraug vauv	groom, bridegroom	Nej *tus* ***vauv*** tshiab yog leej twg?
5	nyab, nkauj nyab	bride, daughter-in-law	Peb *tus* ***nyab*** tshiab hu ua Paj *xeem* Yaj.
6	me nyuam	child, baby, kid	Neb *puas tau muaj* ***me nyuam*** ohs?
7	lub neej	family, life	Tuav koj ***lub neej*** kom zoo.
8	tsev neeg	family	Saib *yus* ***tsev neeg*** kom muaj nqis.
9	neej tsa	wife's relatives	Koj muaj ***neej tsa*** coob heev.
10	pe	to kneel as to bow	Tus vauv ***pe*** lawv ib hnub nkaus.
11	tshoob	wedding	Peb mus hais ***tshoob*** ib hmos nkaus.
12	tshoob kos	wedding	Hmoob tej ***tshoob kos*** tsis yooj yim.
13	dej caw	alcohol, drinks	Ib txhia Hmoob nyiam haus ***dej caw*** ntau heev thaum muaj *tshoob kos.*
14	phij cuam	to give, esp., wedding gifts	Lawv ***phij cuam*** khoom ntau kawg li.
15	phij laj	best man	**Lis Xyooj** yog kuv tus ***phij laj.***
16	niam tais ntsuab	bridesmaid, but from the groom's side or family.	**Mab Tsab** yog kuv tus ***niam tais ntsuab.***
17	mej koob	marriage mediators, wedding negotiators	Kuv tug ***mej koob*** yog kuv tus yawm yij ***Vaj Txoo*** *xeem* ***Yaj***
18	**nqi** tshoob	wedding dowry or **price**	Hmoob tus ***nqi tshoob*** yog *tsib txhiab.*
19	nus muag	brothers and sisters	Peb yog ***nus muag*** xwb.
20	viv ncaus*	sisters, cousins	Nej yog kuv cov ***viv ncaus.***
21	txhooj	a wedding dowry standard	Nej puas muaj tus ***txhooj*** tshoob?

* Called by girls only. Viv ncaus = *sister cousins*, kwv tij = *brother* cousins.

Hmoob kev sib yuav ces muaj xws li nram no:

1. Tus tub mus them nqi tshoob rau tus ntxhais niam thiab txiv, thiab them nqi noj haus.
2. Thaum hais tshoob tiav ces tus ntxhais mus nrog tus tub nyob – mus ua ***nyab*** lawm.

Khoom phij cuam ces feem ntau yog los ntawm tus ntxhais niam, txiv thiab nws tej neeg txheeb ze.
Ib txhia Hmoob kuj tsis sau nqi tshoob lawm vim lawv tsis ntseeg tias sau nyiaj yog ib qho kev *pab* tub thiab *txhawb* ntxhais. In other words, **free does not** mean **valueless** nor **money** equals **love.**

Funeral

No	Hmong	English	Hmong Example
1	tuag	die, dead	*Lawv yawg **tuag** nag hmo lawm no.*
2	tag sim neej	die, deceased	*Nws yawg tau **tag sim neej** lawm.*
3	tu siav	pronounced dead, dead	*Nws **tu siav** kiag lawm nawb.*
4	tsis nrog *nej* nyob lawm	is not living with *you*, is dead	*Hais rau nej paub tias nej yawg **tsis nrog** (nej, nws, peb, koj) **nyob** lawm no ohs.*
5	faus	to bury	*Tag kis, lawv muab tus tuag coj mus **faus.***
6	sam sab	to bury the deceased	*Tag kis lawv mam li coj nws lub cev mus **sam sab.***
7	zais	to bury, to hide the body.	*Tag kis lawv muab tus tuag coj mus **zais.***
8	hleb	coffin	*Lawv twb mus yuav tau ib lub **hleb** lawm.*
9	toj ntxas	cemetery	*Nej yuav coj nws mus faus rau lub **toj ntxas** twg?*
10	ntxa	a cemetery lot	*Neeg nyiam cog paj rau cov tuag tej **ntxa.***
11	nyiav	wail, a mournful cry	*Ib txhia Hmoob **nyiav** nrov dhau hwv.*
12	quaj	cry	*Nws tuag mas ua rau neeg **quaj** zom zaws.*
13	hlub	love	*Kev **hlub** yog los ntawm kev ntxub.*
14	tsev txias	a funeral home	*Peb mus nrog lawv zov hmo tim **tsev txias.***
15	zov hmo	to be at a funeral as to help entertain the deceased's family members.	*Peb mus nrog lawv **zov hmo** tim tsev txias.*
16	***ntees*** tuag	a funeral ***event***	*Peb mus tim lawv lub **ntees tuag.***
17	kav xwm	the person who is in charge of activities at a funeral.	*Nws yog lawv ib tus **kav xwm.***
18	xyom *cuab*	the men who help at a funeral and usually are relatives of the deceased – same clan.	*Lawv yog cov **xyom cuab.***
19	qua ntxa	a cemetery lot	*Nws tsis nyiam nws lub **qua ntxa.***
20	tsawb*	a dead body, a deceased	*Tej chaw no zoo cog **tsawb** kawg li.*

* Tsawb yog ib lo lus uas Hmoob nyiam siv thaum tus neeg tseem muaj sia, thiab nws tseem mus nrhiav tej *qua ntxa* xwb. Piv txwv li, tej chaw no zoo *cog tsawb kawg*. Txhais tau tias tej chaw no zoo chaw lossis zoo ua ntxa heev. Tej lo lus no yog siv ua *paj lug hais* xws li kom dab txhob paub lossis ua rau yus txhob tuag vim yus twb mus nrhiav tau chaws lawm. Tabsis tiam tshiab no ces neeg mus *tam* chaw tag lawm los kuj ho tsis txawj tuag li lawm thiab – *txawv ntuj ces txawv dab lawm thiab.*

Wrapping Things in a Grammatical Way

I believe grammar should be a book on its own; however, as an author, I want you to learn the basic grammar so you will be able to construct simple sentences. The English is transliterated to help you understand **Hmong** and not *English.*

	Hmong Pronoun	+ Verb		English Pronoun	+ Verb
1.	Koj	*noj.*	⇔	*You*	*eat.*
2.	Kuv	*pw.*		*I*	*sleep.*
3.	Nws	*hais.*		*He/she*	*say.*
4.	Peb	*pom.*		*We*	*see.*

Hmong	English
Kuv **nyiam** *ua*	I **like to** *verb*
haus	drink
mus	go
pw	sleep
pab	help

Hmong	English
xav	would like to
nyiam	like to
paub	know how to
yuav	will
yuav tsum	have to

	Hmong	+ Verb	+ **Object**		English	Verb	+ **Object**
1.	Koj	noj	*mov.*	⇔	You	eat	*rice.*
2.	Kuv	mus	*tsev.*		I	go	*home.*
3.	Nws	mob	*tes.*		He/she	hurt	*hand.*
4.	Peb	pom	*koj.*		We	see	*you.*

Regardless of the past, present and/or future, and singular or plural, verbs don't change, for example:

Kuv	⇒	*haus*	⇒	Objective
Nws		*mus*		
Koj		*pom*		
Nej		*pab*		
Lawv		*noj*		

Negative Forms

	Hmong	+ **tsis**	+ Verb	+ **Object**		English	+ **do not**	+ Verb	+ **Object**
1.	Koj	*tsis*	noj	*mov.*	⇔	You	*do not*	eat	*rice.*
2.	Koj	*txhob*	mus	*tsev.*		You	*do not*	go	*home.*
3.	Nws	*tsis*	mob	*tes.*		He/she	*does not*	hurt	*hand.*
4.	Peb	*tsis*	pom	*koj.*		We	*do not*	see	*you.*

Interrogative Forms

	Hmong	+ verb	+ ab tsi/li cas		English	+ verb	+ what/why/how?
1.	Koj	noj	*ab tsi?*	⇔	You	eat	*what?*
2.	Kuv	pw	*ab tsi?*		I	sleep	*why?*
3.	Nws	hais	*ab tsi?*		He/she	says	*what?*
4.	Koj	ua	*li cas?*		You	do	how?

ab tsi and **dab tsi** are being used interchangeably

Hmong	**English transliterated**	**English**	**Proper translation**
Koj noj **yam** twg?	*You eat* ***kind*** *what?*	You eat ***what kind?***	*What kind* do you want to eat?
Koj pw **hmo** twg?	*You sleep* ***night*** *what?*	You sleep ***what night?***	*What night* did you sleep?
Koj hais **lo** twg?	*You say* ***word*** *which?*	You say ***which word?***	*Which word* did you say?
Koj pom **thaum** twg?	*You see* ***when*** *what?*	You see ***when?***	*When* did you see?

Keep in mind that the above phrases can be written as follows, too.

Hmong	**English**
Yam twg koj noj *lawm*?	***What kind*** did you eat *already*?
Hmo twg koj pw?	***What night*** did you sleep?
Leej twg koj paub?	***Who*** did you know?
Thaum twg koj pom?	***When*** did you see?

Key Words for Interrogative

ab tsi, twg, *and* **li cas**

Koj hais ***ab tsi***?	**What** did you say?
Koj yog leej ***twg***?	**Who** are you?
Koj noj ***li cas***?	**How** do you eat?

Next and Will

Lwm +	noun +	pronoun +	mam li +	verb		Next +	noun +	pronoun +	will +	verb
1. Lwm	*tiam*	koj	mam li	*mus.*	⟺	Next	*life*	you	will	*go.*
2. Lwm	*hmo*	peb	mam li	*tuaj.*		Next	*night*	we	will	*come.*
3. Lwm	*xyoo*	lawv	mam li	*paub.*		Next	*year*	they	will	*know.*
4. Lwm	*zaus*	peb	mam li	*ua.*		Next	*time*	we	will	*do.*

piv = to compare
sib piv = compare to each other

Comparisons

tshaj = more or exceed
dua = more, greater
zuj zus = increasingly

Tib yam. Nkawv zoo ***tib yam***. *They both are the **same**.*
Sib xws. Nej phem ***sib xws***. *You are **equally** bad.*
Dua. Koj hais lus Askiv ***zoo dua*** kuv. *You speak English **better than** me.*
Tshaj. Koj pluag ***tshaj*** nws. You are *more* poor **than** him/her.
Yim huab. Koj ***yim huab*** kawm ces koj ***yim huab*** paub. ***The more** you learn **the more** you know.*

Dua and **tshaj** means **more** than. **Phem** *dua* means ***worse** than*. **Zoo** *dua* means ***better** than.* **Phem tshaj** means *worse than*, and **zoo tshaj** means *better than*. In other words, the word "dua and tshaj" means **more** or **increasing** in degree of the verb being used. Literally, the words "phem dua" means "bad more", and "zoo tshaj" means "good more." So it is more like more bad, more good etc...

Another word that Hmong use a lot is the "**sis**" or "**sib**", and it means a ***reciprocal*** action, and it involves **two** or **more** people. For example:

sis and **sib** are being used interchangeably to mean *in a reciprocal* way or among everyone.

Nkawv **sis** hlub heev. *They love each other a lot.*
Nej **sis~** hlub heev. *You love, love one another a lot.*
Sib pab = help each other. **Sib** hu = call each other. **Sib** ceg = yell at each other.

Txhua. Peb mus ua hauj lwm **txhua** hnub. *We go to work **every** day.*
Tas mus li. Koj mus kawm ntawv **tas mus li.** *You go to school **all the time.***
Tas li. Koj noj mov **tas li** xwb. *You eat **all the time** only.*
Kuv nco koj **tas li.** *I think of you **all the time** or **always.***

txhua = every
tas li = always
qee zaus = sometime

Tsuas tab. Peb **tsuas tab** pom nws pw tas li. *We **always** see him sleeps all the time.*
Pheej tab. Koj **pheej tab** cem kuv xwb. *You **always** yell at me.*
Tsuas pom. Ua cas **tsuas pom** koj pw **tas li** xwb? *Why **always** see you sleep **all the time**?*
Txog. About or of. Nws tham **txog** koj. *He talks **about** you.* Nws hu **txog** koj. *He calls **upon** you.*
Rau. Peb muab **rau** nws. *We give **to** him.* Kuv muab **rau** koj. *I give to you.*
Kheev lam. Wish that, hope. ***Kheev lam** kuv muaj nyiaj ntau mas.* Wish that I have a lot of money.
Xav kom. Wish that, hope that. ***Xav kom** kuv muaj nyiaj ntau xwb.* Wish I have a lot of money.
Kav liam. Disregard, ignore, forget about it. ***Kav liam** koj txhob tuaj.* Forget it you don't have to come.
Puam chawj. Disregard, ignore, forget it. ***Puam chawj** koj txhob mus.* Forget it you don't have to go.
Kav chawj. Disregard, ignore, forget it. ***Kav chawj** nws seb nws yuav ua li cas.*

Everything You Need to Know

Consonants

B*	b***h*** bl bl***h***
C	c***h***
D	d***h***
F	
G*	g***h***
H	**h***l* **h***m* **h***ml* **h***n* **h***ny*
J*	j***h***
K	k***h***
L	
M	ml
N	nc nc***h*** nk nk***h*** np np***h*** npl npl***h*** nq nq***h*** nr nr***h*** nt nt***h*** nts nts***h*** ntx ntx***h*** ny
P	p***h*** pl pl***h***
Q	q***h***
R	r***h***
S	
T	t***h*** ts ts***h*** tx tx***h***
V	
X	xy, xz[1]
Y	
Z	

[1] As in English word **Z***oo*

Vowels

a, ai, au, aw, e, ee, i, ia, o, oo, u, ua, w, h[2]

Tones

J, S, V, M, G, B, D̄

Numbers**

0 = voj*
1 = ib
2 = ob
3 = peb
4 = plaub
5 = tsib
6 = rau
7 = xya
8 = yim
9 = cuaj
10 = kaum
20 = nees nkaum
30 = peb caug
40 = plaub cuag
50 = tsib caug
60 = rau caum
70 = xya caum
80 = yim caum
90 = cuaj caum
100 = ib puas
tens = caum
hundreds = puas
thousands = txhiab
10,000 = vam

* voj, qhoov.
** A few only
[2] Silent vowel

Classifiers**

Hmong	Use for
daim	flat objects
leej/g	human
lub	a/the
rab	tools
tug/s	animals
txoj	stringlike

Pronouns

Hmong	English
kuv	*I*
koj	*you (1)*
wb	*we (2)*
nkawv	*they (2)*
peb	*we (>2)*
neb	*you (2)*
nej	*you (>2)*
lawv	*they*
nws	*he,she, it*
yus	*one*
luag	*others*

Prepositions**

Hmong	English
ntawm	*by, at*
hauv	*inside*
nrauv	*outside*
sauv	*above*
dhau	*over*
pev	*up there*
nrav	*down there*
tiv	*eastern there*
tov	*western there*
ntawv	*over there*
hauv qab	*below*
rau	*to*
ze	*near*

Conjunctions

Hmong	English
thiab	*and*
hiab	*and*
vim	*because*
lossis	*and/or*
losyog	*or*
yeeb vim	*because*
twb yog	*because*
rau qhov	*because*
tabsis	*but*
tabmas	*but*

Interjections**

Hmong	English
ab	*hey*
nab	*here*
hwb	*here*
hoeb	*hoh*
hoeb yoej	*n/e*
oeb	*oh*
uib	*uih*
tuag	*die*
aws	*yes*
wb	*no*

Grammar**

Pronoun	verb	object
Kuv	nyiam	koj.
I	*like*	*you.*
Kuv	haus	dej.
I	*drink*	*water.*
Kuv **xav** verb...		
I ***would like to*** *verb...*		

Pronoun	verb	noun
Koj	nyiam	ab tsi?
You	*like*	*what?*
Koj	noj	li cas?
You	*eat*	*how?*
Koj	hais	ab tsi?
You	*say*	*what?*

Pronoun	**not**	verb	object
Kuv	tsis	nyiam	koj.
I	*do not*	*like*	*you.*
Kuv	tsis	haus	dej.
I	*do not*	*drink*	*water.*

Pronoun	**will**	verb	object
Kuv	yuav	nyiam	koj.
I	*will*	*like*	*you.*
Kuv	yuav	haus	dej.
I	*will*	*drink*	*water.*

Pronoun	verb	quantity	classifier	object	adjective	adverb
Kuv	nyiam	ib	lub	tsev	loj	heev.
Koj	yog	ib	tus	neeg	zoo	heev.
Kuv	muaj	coob	leej	kwv	zoo	heev.
Koj	muaj	ob	thaj	teb	tiaj	heev.

Verbs**

Hmong	English
mus	*go*
los	*come*
paub	*know*
hais	*say*
qhia	*tell*
pab	*help*
yuav	*buy*
muag	*sell*
them	*pay*
noj	*eat*
haus	*drink*
nyiam	*like*
hlub	*love*
ntxub	*hate*
nco	*think of*
nug	*ask*
teb	*answer*

Hmong vowel(English sound), **a**(ah) **ai**(ai) **au**(ao) **aw**(er) **e**(ay) **ee**(eng) **i**(ee) **ia**(ia) **o**(aw) **oo**(ong) **u**(oo) **ua**(oua) **w**(w)
 Hmong tone markers: ko**J** mu**S** ku**V** nia**M** nee**G** sia**B** zoo to**D**

What is a Mono*syllabic* Language

The word "mono" means *oneness*, and that means we can't write two or more syllables as one word or unit – *phoneme*. However, as I mentioned in the beginning of this book that I don't believe Hmong is a *true monosyllabic* language because there are a few words that do have more than *one syllables*, i.e., **tabsis**. Nonetheless, for the most part, the Hmong language is very monosyllabic. So let's learn the smallest meaningful syllable in the Hmong language in order to understand its syntax and content. To help you understand, let us **compare how** computers parse data stored on disks **to how** the Hmong people parse their monosyllabic syntax. By looking at the bits pattern, computers know the result, and by looking at the Hmong mono words pattern, the Hmong people understand its *content*.

Result	bit4	bit3	bit2	bit1		How computer counts
1				1	=	1
3			1	1	=	2 + 1
7		1	1	1	=	4 + 2 + 1
15	1	1	1	1	=	8 + 4 + 2 + 1

Result	word4	word3	word2	word1		How Hmong people read
tsa				tsa	=	tsa
neej tsa			neej	tsa	=	neej + tsa
tij neej tsa		tij	neej	tsa	=	tij + neej + tsa
kwv tij neeg tsa	kwv	tij	neej	tsa	=	kwv + tij + neej + tsa

Piv txwv: **Nyob zoo ib tsoom *kwv tij neej tsa sawv daws***. This is how the founders suggested for writing the Hmong RPA language. Perhaps some of us might not agree, but monologically, it does make sense if we want to maintain its monosyllabic constructs. It is, however, very tempting to combine words such as, **sawv daws**, **yooj yim**, **xos liam**, **phooj ywg** etc... Likewise, we would prefer to write **15** instead of 1,1,1,1, but that is not possible to put **15** in *one* bit.

So I will offer you what I suggested in my **Lus Hmoob Txhais** Dictionary.
Only combine words if one of the syllables has no meaning on its own or has a single consonant.
Tabsis, tiamsis, lossis, xwsli, sispab, sishlub, xosliam, kwvtij, sawvdaws etc...

Do not combine words that have more than one consonants, for example:
txhiajtxhais, ntsuabxiab, ceebtsheej. And not classifier or compound words, for example:
Haivneeg, sauntawv, txojmoo, leejtwg. Haiv = nation, neeg = people. Sau = write, ntawv = letter, and txoj = a/the – a classifier, and moo = news, leej = classifier and twg = who.

Therefore, "**Who calls me**" is similar to the Hmong "**Leej twg hu kuv**", but the word "**who**" does not equal to the Hmong words "**leejtwg.**" Why? Because "**leej**" is a classifier and "**twg**" is analogous to the English "**who.**" Otherwise, we will have to combine words like "*cov twg, pawg twg, haiv twg*" etc...

Well, this is little deep to be included in this book but as an author and teacher, I rather give you more than offering you less because I want you to be *very knowledgeable* in the Hmongology.

Time For a Short Story

Zaj dab neeg no muaj lub npe hu ua ***Tub Zaj Ntshaw Kawm Lus Hmoob.***

Puag thaum ub ohv... muaj ib tug me nyuam tub nws lub npe hu ua **Zaj** no. Nws yug los ces nws niam thiab txiv nkawv tsuas qhia lus **Askiv**, English, rau nws xwb lauj. Yog li, nws tsuas paub tias hauv lub ntiaj teb no tsuas muaj neeg Meskas thiab hais lus Askiv xwb. Thaum nws loj thiab hlob tuaj ces nws niam thiab txiv xa nws mus kawm ntawv hauv **tsev kawm**, school. Zaj txawm mus pom ib cov neeg dub hau thiab hais lus Askiv tsis meej thiab txaus~ luag – with accent and funny in English. Nws mam li los nug nws niam thiab txiv ces nkawv mam li piav tias, "Xyoo 1975 muaj ib haiv neeg hu ua Hmoob no tau tawg rog tuaj nyob rau lub teb chaws Meskas. Cov neeg no muaj plaub hau dub, me thiab hais ib hom lus txawv lus Askiv uas yog hu ua lus Hmoob no."

Ces tub Zaj mam li nug nws niam thiab txiv tias, "Yog li, kuv xav paub lawv cov lus es kuv yuav mus kawm qhov twg?" Zaj txiv txawm teb niag dag ntsuav rau Zaj tias, "Me tub awh, yog koj xav kawm lus Hmoob ces koj mus tham ib tug hluas nkauj Hmoob xwb los mas!" Zaj txawm teb nws leej txiv tias, "Txiv, es yuav ua li cas mus tham tau naj yog yus twb tsis paub txuas lus nrog nws ua ntej yus yuav muaj tau kev phooj ywg!" Zaj leej niam thiab txiv nkawv txawm sib ntsia sib ntsia tag ces leej niam txawm teb Zaj tias, "Me tub, koj txhob txhawj mog. Yog koj xav kawm tiag ces tag kis kuv mam li mus nug seb hauv peb lub zos no puas muaj leeg twg paub thiab kam qhia lus Hmoob rau koj mog."

Ces leej tub mas nim luag his~ thiab has~, thiab sas loo los khawm kiag leej niam. Zaj txawm hais rau nws niam tias, "Ua tsaug ohs niam. Qhov kuv xav kawm lus Hmoob mas vim yog kuv ntseeg tias Tswv Ntuj tsim tau peb ntau haiv neeg los nyob ua ke; uas zoo li ib lub vaj txiv uas muaj ntau hom txiv nyob ua ke. Yog tias peb sib txuas tau lus, ces yuav ua rau peb sib paub, sib pab, muaj kev haum xeeb thiab sib hlub tshaj li yav dhau los lawm." Leej niam teb Zaj tias, "Me tub, ua cas nyob~ es koj lam yuav mus txawj xav deb thiab xav dav ua luaj li ko naj?" Zaj txawm teb nws leej niam tias, "Niam, koj mus nug Vaj Tswv ces nws qhia koj xwb los mas."

The fiction story above is pretty close to what a real Hmong conversation would be like.
The moral of the story is that an American boy, named Zaj, pronounced Zhah, who went to school without knowing that there are other people who don't look like himself and speak a different language – Hmong. Zaj then wanted to learn Hmong so he can interact with the Hmong people because he believes that God created this universe like an orchard with a variety of fruit trees. Zaj's real inspiration and hope is that if all human kinds would know each other's language we would be able to communicate and have better relationship far more than what we are having today. Needless to say, Zaj's parents were shock at their son's unusual wisdom and his interest to learn Hmong.

Again, translating one language into another is like taking an apple and trying to make it taste like an orange. So good luck with that. For the most part, most languages do have very similar words but for some, the number of inner layers and tastes are so inexplicable, and the only way you will know and/or experience the real thing is to learn and live in that culture and environment yourself.

Indeed, humans have many languages, but for God, there is only one language:
The human language with a lot of synonyms – JX

Phrase Translation of the Previous Short Story

No	Hmong	Equivalent English
1	muaj ib tug *me nyuam* tub	there was a little *baby* boy
2	nws lub npe hu ua **Zaj** no	his name is called Zaj (*Zha in English)*
3	nws yug los ces nws *niam thiab txiv*	when he was born his *mother and father*
4	*tsuas qhia* lus Askiv	*only taught* English
5	*rau nws* xwb lauj	*to him* only
6	*Yog li*, nws tsuas paub tias	*therefore*, he only knew that
7	hauv lub *ntiaj teb* no	in this *world*
8	*tsuas muaj* **neeg** Meskas thiab hais lus Askiv xwb	*only has* American **people** and speak English only
9	*Thaum nws* loj thiab hlob tuaj	*When he* got big and grew older
10	ces nws niam thiab txiv *xa nws* mus kawm ntawv	then his mother and father *sent him* to school
11	Zaj txawm mus pom ib *cov neeg*	Zaj then met *some people*
12	dub hau thiab hais lus Askiv *tsis meej*	with black hair and speak English *not clear*
13	Nws mam li *los nug nws niam* thiab txiv	He then *came ask his mom* and dad
14	ces nkawv mam li *piav tias*	and they then *explain that*
15	*xyoo* 1975 muaj ib ***haiv neeg***	In *year* 1975 there were some people (***nationality***)
16	hu ua Hmoob no tau tawg rog **tuaj nyob** rau lub teb chaws *Meskas*	called Hmong came here as refugees **to live** in *America*
17	*Cov neeg* no **muaj** plaub hau dub	*These people* **have** black hair
18	*me thiab hais* ib hom lus txawv lus Askiv	*small and speak* a different language than English
19	uas yog *hu ua* lus Hmoob no	and it *is called* Hmong
20	Ces tub Zaj mam li *nug nws niam thiab txiv* tias	And son Zaj then *asked his mom and dad*
21	Yog li, *kuv xav paub* lawv cov lus es kuv yuav **mus kawm** qhov twg?	Therefore, *I would like to know* their language and where would I **go learn**?
22	Zaj txiv txawm teb niag *dag ntsuav* rau Zaj tias,	Zaj's dad then replied in a *jokingly* manner to him that,
23	Me tub awh, yog koj *xav kawm lus Hmoob*	Son, if you *want to learn Hmong*

No	Hmong	Equivalent English
24	ces koj *mus tham* ib tug hluas nkauj Hmoob xwb los mas!	then you *go date* a Hmong girl that is all!
25	Zaj txawm teb *nws leej txiv tias,*	Zaj replied to *his father that,*
26	"Txiv, es yuav ua li cas mus tham tau naj	"Father, and how is that going to happen
27	*yog* ***yus*** *twb tsis paub* txuas lus nrog nws **ua ntej**	*if* ***one*** *already could not* communicate with her **before**
28	yus yuav muaj tau *kev phooj ywg*!"	one would have a *friendship*!"
29	*Zaj leej niam* thiab txiv nkawv txawm sib ntsia sib ntsia tag ces	*Zaj's mom* and dad then looked at each other and then
30	*leej niam* txawm teb Zaj tias,	*the mother* answered Zaj that,
31	"*Me tub*, koj **txhob txhawj** mog.	"*Son*, you **don't worry** okay.
32	Yog koj xav kawm *tiag* ces tag kis kuv **mam li**	If you want to learn for *real* then tomorrow I **will**
33	mus nug seb hauv peb lub *zos* no puas muaj leeg twg paub	go ask to see if anyone in our *town* knows
34	*thiab kam qhia* lus Hmoob rau koj mog."	*and willing to teach* Hmong to you okay."
35	*Ces leej tub mas* nim luag his~ thiab has~,	*And the son then* was laughing he he and ha ha,
36	thiab sas loo los *khawm* kiag leej niam.	and quickly jumped to *hug* this mother.
37	Zaj txawm *hais rau nws niam* tias,	Zaj then *said to his mother* that,
38	*Ua tsaug ohs, niam*. Qhov kuv xav kawm lus Hmoob	*Thank you, mother.* The reason I would like to learn Hmong
39	mas vim yog kuv ntseeg tias *Tswv Ntuj tsim tau peb*	is because I believe that *God had created us*
40	ntau *haiv neeg* los nyob **ua ke**;	many *nationalities* to live **together**;
41	uas zoo li ib lub *vaj txiv* uas muaj ntau **hom txiv**	which is like an *orchard* with many different **kinds of fruit trees**
42	*Yog tias peb sib txuas tau lus*, ces yuav ua rau peb sib paub,	*If we can communicate*, then it will make us know each other,

Well, you get the point. I wish I can finish the translation, but you have the summary already. The reason I provided you this little translation is to help you understand that the translation is hard since the words in both language do not always have the same meanings.

Time to Write a Letter in Hmong

Chaw nyob

Hnub

Nyob zoo ohs Paj,

Kuv sau[0] **tsab ntawv**[1] no **tuaj qhia**[2] rau koj paub tias kuv **nyuam qhuav**[3] kawm nyeem thiab sau ntawv Hmoob **los ntawm**[4] ib phau ntawv hu ua, "*Learn Hmong the Jay Way*" no **tiav**[5] lawm. **Yog li**[6], kuv mas zoo siab heev li **es**[7] kuv thiaj li sau ntawv tuaj qhia rau koj paub xwb.

Thaum twg[8] koj tau txais tsab ntawv **nov**[9] lawm no ces thov koj **sau tuaj**[10] qhia kuv paub thiab. **Tsis tag li**[11], kuv vam thiab ntseeg tias koj **tseem**[12] **ntsib kev**[13] noj qab thiab nyob zoo li **yav**[14] **dhau los**[15].

Kuv sau ntawv **tuaj ntsib**[16] koj li no xwb es wb **mam li**[17] **sib ntsib dua**[18] **nyob rau**[19] **lwm**[20] **zaus**[21].

Tshua txog[22],

Sau npe

Key Words to Understand

chaw nyob = address
hnub = date
0. kuv sau = I write
1. tsab ntawv = a letter
2. tuaj qhia = to inform, to tell
3. nyuam qhuav = recently or just
4. los ntawm = from
5. tiav = finish, complete. *lawm = already*
6. yog li = therefore
7. es = so

8. thaum twg = when, whenever
9. nov = this
10. sau tuaj = write back. *sau los = write home.*
11. tsis tag li = not only that
12. tseem = still
13. ntsib kev = have or in a way of (*condition*)
14. yav = period or interval of time
15. dhau los = in the past
16. tuaj ntsib = come to *meet, chat, visit*
17. mam li = will
18. sib ntsib dua = meet again
19. nyob rau = in, within
20. lwm = next
21. zaus = time
22. tshua txog = thinking of

No	Hmong	**English Transliterated**, examples and Remarks (*tos = wait for*)
1	Kuv **nyob** tos koj.	I **live** wait *for* you. *Nyob tos = live and wait for.*
2	Kuv **tos** koj.	I **wait** *for* you. *Kuv tuaj* ***tos*** *koj = I come* ***to get*** *you (pick up).*
3	Rov qab **tuaj** saib koj.	**Come** back to see you. Rov = turn, qab = back (*return*)
4	Kuv **vam** thiab *ntseeg* tias.	I **hope** and *believe* that. *Kuv ntseeg koj = I believe you.*
5	Noj **qab** thiab *nyob* zoo.	Eat **well** and *live* fine. *Being healthy that is.*
6	**Ntsib** koj li no xwb.	**Meet** you like this only. *Kuv tuaj ntsib koj = I come to meet you.*
7	Koj **tib** kuv.	You **reject** me. *Tib = refuse, deny, reject.*
8	Kuv zoo siab **heev.**	I am **very** happy. *Koj tsis zoo siab = You are not happy.*

Simple Phrase Translation

Hmong **bold** word = English **bold** word, and Hmong *italic* word = English *italic* word

Hmong Phrase	Equivalent English
1. **Yog** tsis *hlub* koj.	1. **If** do not *love* you.
2. **Yuav mus** hlub *leej twg*?	2. **Will go** love *whom*?
3. Koj yeej **yog** tus *kuv nyiam*.	3. You **are** the one *I like*.
4. **Thov** *koj ntseeg* kuv thiab.	4. **Please** *you believe* me, too.
5. *Vim kuv* yeej yog koj tug tiag tiag.	5. *Because I* am yours for real.
6. Kuv yuav ua *li cas* es koj thiaj li ***ntseeg kuv?***	6. *What* should I do so you will ***believe me***?
7. Yog kuv *qhib* tau kuv lub siab rau **koj pom**.	7. If I can *open* my heart for **you to see**.
8. Thiab **nthuav** rau koj saib li ib *phau ntawv.*	8. And **open** for you to see like *a book.*
9. Kom **txhua yam** kuv *hais*.	9. So **everything** I *say.*
10. Koj **thiaj** pom tias tsis yog *dag*.	10. You **then** see that it is not a *lie*.

Yuav *verb* + *verb*:
Yuav *mus noj.*
Yuav *tuaj pab.*
Yuav *paub qhia.*

Hmong Phrase	Equivalent English
1. Koj yog *leej twg*?	1. *Who* are you?
2. Koj *npe* hu li cas?	2. What is your *name*?
3. Kuv *zoo siab* tau **ntsib** koj.	3. I *am happy* to **meet** you.
4. Kuv los *tib yam.*	4. I am the same – *same here.*
5. Koj muaj pes tsawg xyoo?	5. How old are you?
6. Kuv muaj **peb caug** xyoo.	6. I am **thirty** years old.
7. Hos koj ne?	7. How about you?
8. Kuv muaj **peb caug tsib** xyoos.	8. I am **thirty-five** years old.
9. Zoo siab tau nrog koj **tham**.	9. Nice **talking** to you.
10. **Sib ntsib dua** nawb.	10. **See you later** okay.

What you see here are very simple construct. For example, the first line could be written as follows:
*1. Koj yog **leej twg** ne yom?*
2. Koj yog leej twg nab?
3. Koj yog leej twg ohs?
4. Koj yog leej twg?
And the response could be:
1. Kuv yog npe naj.
2. Kuv yog ____ ohs.
3. Kuv yog ____ los mas.
4. Kuv yog ____ ntag.

Hmong Phrase – interrogative	Equivalent English
1. Koj **puas** verb? *noj, haus, mus etc...*	1. Do you ***verb?*** *Just about any verbs...*
2. *Koj **puas noj?***	2. Do you *eat?* *More like "Do you want to eat?"*
3. Koj puas **tau** *verb?*	3. Have you ***verb?***
4. *Koj puas **tau noj?***	4. Have you *ate?*
5. Koj **puas tau xav** *verb*?	5. **Are** you **ready** *to **verb**?*
6. *Koj puas tau* **xav *noj?***	6. Are you ready *to eat?*
7. Koj puas **txawj** *verb?*	7. Do you **know how to *verb*?**
8. *Koj puas* **txawj *noj?***	8. Do you **know *how to*** *eat?*
9. Koj puas **txawj verb** *object?*	9. Do you **know how to verb *object***?
10. *Koj puas* **txawj sau** *ntawv?*	10. Do you **know how to write** *letter?*

Puas tau generally means ***have done*** and/or ***did do***. For example:
Koj ***puas tau mus***?
Did you ***go***? Or
Have you ***gone***?

Some of the English translations might not be proper; however, the Hmong parts are correct. When translating Hmong into English, there are various English word choices, synonyms, that one can use. For example, the Hmong word "**pab**" can mean **assist**, **aid**, **support**, and **help** etc...

Short Phrase Translation

Hmong **bold** word = English **bold** word, and Hmong *italic* word = English *italic* word

Hmong Words	English transliterated	Hmong Words	English transliterated
1. Tuaj los.	1. Greeting, "hello or come, too"	11. Koj puas **pom**?	11. Do you **see**?
2. Mus **twg**?	2. Go **where**?	12. **Tsis** pom.	12. **Not** see. *No.*
3. Pab **kuv**.	3. Help **me**.	13. **Saib** koj sab xis.	13. **Look** on your right.
4. Aws.	4. Yes *or okay.*	14. Pom lawm.	14. See now.
5. Yog los mas.	5. That is right *or correct.*	15. **Zoo** heev.	15. Very **good**.
6. Leej twg nab?	6. What person *or who?*	16. Ua li cas?	16. What happens?
7. Yog **kuv** naj.	7. It is **me**.	17. Vim tias.	17. Because.
8. Yog koj los?	8. Is it you?	18. Piav los soj.	18. So explain.
9. Yog los mas.	9. Yes, it is.	19. Tau kawg.	19. Okay *or fine*.
10. Zoo **heev**.	10. **Very** good.	20. Yog lawm.	20. Correct *or right.*

Hmong Words	English transliterated	Hmong Words	English transliterated
1. **Paub** koj.	1. **Know** you.	11. **Cia** koj mus.	11. **Let** you go.
2. **Tiag** los?	2. For real? – questioning	12. Pab koj **ua**.	12. Help you **do**.
3. Tiag hos.	3. For **real**. – confirming.	13. **Saib** koj noj.	13. **Watch** you eat.
4. Thov **zam**	4. Please **forgive.**	14. **Lawv** koj qab.	14. **Follow** you.
5. Tsis ua li cas.	5. Not a problem.	15. **Ua** koj **ntej**.	15. **Before** you.
6. **Yog tias** koj.	6. **If** you.	16. **Tseg** rau koj.	16. **Save** for you.
7. **Xav** *paub.*	7. **Would like to** *know.*	17. Puas txaus?	17. Enough? *Is it enough?*
8. Xav tiag hos.	8. Would like for real.	18. **Tshuav** thiab.	18. Still **have**. *Some left.*
9. **Tej zaum**	9. **Maybe** *or perhaps.*	19. **Tag** lawm.	19. All **gone** *or done.*
10. **Tsis** paub.	10. **Don't** know.	20. Tsis **muaj**.	20. Don't **have**.

Hmong Words	English transliterated	Hmong Words	English transliterated
1. **Qhia** kuv.	1. **Tell** me *or teach me.*	15. Noj kom **tsau**.	15. Eat until **full**.
2. Tsis **kam**.	2. Not **allow** *or no.*	16. Yus tsev ohs.	16. One's home.
3. Qhia kiag los.	3. Just tell.	17. Txhob *txaj muag.*	17. Don't be *shy.*
4. **Txhob** nug.	4. **Don't** ask.	18. Tsis **txaj muag**.	18. Not **shy**.
5. Vim li cas?	5. Why?	19. **Thov** Vaj Tswv.	19. **Ask** God *or pray.*
6. **Ntshai** ab tsi?	6. **Fear** what?	20. Leej **Txiv**.	20. The **Father**.
7. **Ab tsi** maj?	7. About **what**?	21. Leej **Tub**.	21. The **Son**.
8. **Dag** xwb.	8. Just **joking**.	22. Leej Ntsuj **Plig**.	22. The Holy **Spirit**.
9. Koj mas...	9. You...	23. Mary.	23. Mab Liab.
10. Siab phem!	10. Bad heart. *Wicked heart.*	24. Tib neeg.	24. Humans.
11. Pom zoo.	11. Agree.	25. Jesus Christ.	25. Yexus Khetos.
12. Xis neej.	12. Feeling well *or healthy.*	26. Ceeb Tsheej.	26. Heaven.
13. Muaj **mob**.	13. Have **illness** *or **sickness**.*	27. Dab Teb.	27. Hell (*Ghost country*)
14. Siab zoo.	14. Good heart. *Kind-hearted.*	28. Plig.	28. Spirit.

Short Phrase Translation

Hmong **bold** word = English **bold** word, and Hmong *italic* word = English *italic* word

Hmong Words	English transliterated	Hmong Words	English transliterated
1. **Nrog** hlub.	1. **Help** love.	11. **Tseem** zoo li qub.	11. **Still** the same.
2. **Pab** qhia.	2. **Help** teach.	12. Yog li.	12. Therefore.
3. Kheev lam.	3. Wish that.	13. Tu siab heev.	13. Have a broken heart.
4. Muaj **tseeb.**	4. Happening for **real.**	14. Ua ib siab.	14. Decide to.
5. Ntshe yuav.	5. Perhaps will.	15. Rov los.	15. Come back.
6. Tsis xav **tuag.**	6. Not wanting to **die.**	16. Pab **tib neeg.**	16. Help **human beings.**
7. Mus ib sim.	7. Forever.	17. Thiaj li tau **txais.**	17. So will **receive.**
8. Tabsis mas.	8. But.	18. Vaj Tswv.	18. God.
9. **Yog** npau suav.	9. **It is** a dream.	19. Tej **koob hmoov.**	19. **Blessing** *or luck.*
10. **Tsim los** ces.	10. **Wake up** and.	20. **Xwb** mog.	20. **Only**.

Hmong Words	English transliterated	Hmong Words	English transliterated
1. **Xyaum** hais.	1. **Learn** to speak *or say.*	11. **Paub** xwb.	11. **Know** only.
2. Lus Hmoob.	2. Hmong language.	12. Lwm txoj **kev.**	12. Different **path.**
3. Tsis **nyuaj.**	3. Not **difficult.**	13. **Lwm** xyoo.	13. **Next** year.
4. Tabsis.	4. But.	14. Lwm **tiam.**	14. Next **life.**
5. Nws kuj tsis.	5. It is not.	15. **Pauj** tsis tau.	15. Can't **repay.**
6. Yooj yim thiab.	6. Easy either.	16. Koj txoj **kev pab.**	16. Your **assistance.**
7. Yog li.	7. Therefore.	17. Thov kom **Ntuj.**	17. Ask that **God.**
8. Yuav tau.	8. Must *or ought to.*	18. Foom koob hmoo.	18. **Bless** *or bless upon.*
9. Ua siab ntev.	9. Be patient.	19. **Rau** koj.	19. ***To*** *you.*
10. Thiaj li yuav.	10. Then will.	20. Mus zoo.	20. Goodbye.

Hmong Words	English transliterated	Hmong Words	English transliterated
1. Koj **yog**.	1. You **are**. *Also you're right.*	11. **Hauv** no tau.	11. **In** here for.
2. **Leej twg** nab?	2. **What** person *or who?*	12. Peb **hlis** xwb.	12. Three **months** only.
3. Kuv **yog**.	3. I **am**. *Also I am right.*	13. **Hos** koj ne?	13. **And** you?
4. Dib Vaj.	4. Dee Vang.	14. Kuv yeej **ib txwm**.	14. I **always**.
5. Es koj **nyob**.	5. And you **live**.	15. Nyob hauv **no**.	15. Live in **here**.
6. Qhov twg **tuaj.**	6. Where **from**?	16. **Twb** nyob nov tau.	16. **Already** live here for.
7. **Nyob** hauv no.	7. **Live** in here.	17. 30 **xyoo** lawm.	17. 30 **years** already.
8. Cas **tsis pom.**	8. Why **not see.**	18. Ua li los.	18. Is that so.
9. Koj **dua li.**	9. You **before** *or in the past.*	19. Zoo li zoo *tau*.	19. As good as *possible*.
10. Kuv **los** nyob.	10. I **came** live *or have lived.*	20. Ua li.	20. Okay.

The Hmong line, "**zoo li zoo**" means "**as good as**", for example: Kuv ua **zoo li zoo** tau lawn. This syntax is also true for verbs, i.e., **pab**, **pub**, **phem**, **hlub** etc... The word "**tau**" is usually placed after such usage and it means "*able or possible*." However, this same line can be written like this, too: "Kuv ua **zoo** *rau koj* **li zoo** tau" and it means "I do **as good** *for you* **as** possible."

Short Phrase Translation

Hmong **bold** word = English **bold** word, and Hmong *italic* word = English *italic* word

Hmong Words	English transliterated	Hmong Words	English transliterated
1. Kuv lees.	1. I admit.	11. Kuv **tseem** *verb...*	11. I **still** *verb...*
2. Kuv muaj.	2. I have.	12. Kuv **yuav** *verb...*	12. I **will** *verb...*
3. Kuv liam.	3. I accuse.	13. Kuv **mam li** *verb...*	13. I **will** *verb...*
4. Kuv dag.	4. I lie (*or trick, joke)*	14. Kuv **twb** *verb...*	14. I **already** *verb...*
5. Kuv *paub* **zoo**.	5. I *know* **well**.	15. Kuv **xav** *verb...*	15. I **would like to** *verb...*
6. Kuv tso cai.	6. I allow *or let.*	16. Kuv **pheej tab**...	16. I **always**...
7. Kuv **thov** koj.	7. I **beg** you.	17. Kuv **niaj hnub**...	17. I **every day**...
8. Kuv **txib** koj.	8. I **ask** you (*to do a chore*)	18. Kuv **los** tsis *verb...*	18. I, **too**, not *verb...*
9. Thov *dag zog*.	9. Ask for *manpower, strength.*	19. Kuv **haj yam** *verb...*	19. I **more** *verb...*
10. Kuv tso mus.	10. I let go, *release, set free.*	20. Kuv **yeej** *verb...*	20. I **really** *verb...*

Hmong phrase	English transliterated
1. Kuv **haj yam** hlub koj.	1. I **more** love you. *I love you* ***more*** *that is.*
2. Kuv **kwv yees** xwb.	2. I am **guessing** only.
3. Kuv **liam** *tias* koj dag.	3. I **accuse** *that* you lie.
4. Koj **dag** tias koj *muaj*.	4. You **lie** that you *have*.
5. Koj *mus* tsev **tau**.	5. You *go* home **okay**. *You may go home.*
6. Kuv **tso cai** rau koj mus.	6. I **allow** you to go.
7. Kuv **thov** koj txhob mus.	7. I **beg** you not to go.
8. Koj **zam** txim rau kuv.	8. You please **forgive** me.
9. Kuv **pub** rau koj xwb.	9. I **give** to free you only. (*freely that is)*
10. Koj **ua piam** lawm.	10. You **damaged** or *ruined* it.

Hmong phrase	English transliterated
1. Leej twg thiaj li **paub**?	1.Who would **know**?
2. Tus neeg lub **npe** hu ua Paj no.	2. A person whose **name** is Paj.
3. Nws nyob lub **zos** twg?	3. She lives in what **city**?
4. Nws nyob **hauv** zos no xwb.	4. She lives **in** this city only.
5. **Tag kis** koj puas *khoom?* Or *xyeej.*	5. **Tomorrow** are you *available*? Or free?
6. Khoom thiab los mas.	6. Yes, I am available *or free.*
7. Lub **sij hawm** twg?	7. What **time**?
8. **Thaum** tav su.	8. **At** noon. *More like* ***"when"*** *noon in Hmong.*
9. Ua li.	9. Okay.
10. **Mam li** ntsib koj thaum ntawd.	10. **Will** see you then. Or meet you **at** then.
11. Txuag yus txoj **sia**.	11. Save one's **life** (*as to not overwork*)
12. **Txuag** yus ntsej muag.	12. **Save** one's face.
13. Cuaj khaum. *Koj cuaj khaum* ***dhau***.	13. Being stingy. *You are* ***too*** *stingy.*
14. Txuag **nyiaj**.	14. Save **money**.

Short Phrase Translation

Hmong **bold** word = English **bold** word, and Hmong *italic* word = English *italic* word

Hmong Words	English transliterated	Hmong Words	English transliterated
1. **Nruab** hnub	1. **During** the day.	11. Tshua txog.	11. Thinking of.
2. Tav twg?	2. When *or at what time?*	12. Yooj yim.	12. Easy.
3. Kab li.	3. Perhaps *or around.*	13. **Nyuaj** kawg.	13. Very **difficult**.
4. **Ze** li.	4. **Near** *or* ***close*** *to.*	14. Ua siab ntev.	14. Be patient.
5. Rov **hu**.	5. **Call** again, call back.	15. Siab **luv**.	15. **Short** temper.
6. Hais **dua**.	6. Say **again** *or repeat.*	16. Siab **kub**.	16. **Hot** temper, rush.
7. Hais ntxiv.	7. Say more *or continue.*	17. Maj.	17. Hurry, rush.
8. Xaus li no.	8. End like this *or the end.*	18. Siab **qeeb**.	18. **Slow**, not hurry at all.
9. **Lwm** zaus.	9. **Next** time.	19. Ua siab txias.	19. Calm down, cool down.
10. **Niaj** hnub.	10. **Every** day.	20. Yoog xwb.	20. Going along, follow.

Hmong phrase	English transliterated
1. Tav twg koj **mam li** tuaj?	1. When **will** you come?
2. Tej zaum 11 teev **sawv ntxov** li ntawd.	2. Perhaps 11:00 **morning** like that.
3. Kuv mam li **rov** *hu* rau koj.	3. I will *call* you **back**.
4. Thov hais **dua** soj.	4. Please say **again**.
5. Kuv **niaj** *hnub* mus ua num xwb.	5. I **every** *day* go to work only.
6. Koj *kawm* lus Hmoob puas **yooj yim**?	6. You *learn* Hmong is it **easy**?
7. Nws nyuaj **kawg** hos.	7. It is **very** difficult.
8. **Yuav tau** ua siab ntev xwb.	8. **Must** be patient only.
9. Yog li los mas.	9. That is correct.
10. Koj puas *xav* **kawm**?	10. Do you *want to* **learn**?

Hmong phrase	English transliterated
1. **Cia** *lwm* xyoo tso.	1. **Wait** until *next* year.
2. **Tos** lwm *zaus* tso.	2. **Wait** until next *time*.
3. **Yuav** phau ntawv no mus *kawm.*	3. **Buy** this book to *study or learn.*
4. Thiab **saib** Hmoob movies xwb.	4. And **watch** Hmong movies only.
5. Tsis txhob **maj**.	5. Don't **hurry** *or* ***rush***.
6. *Cia* kuv **qhia** koj.	6. *Let* me **teach** you.
7. *Hais* lus Hmoob tsis nyuaj.	7. *Speaking* Hmong is not difficult.
8. Tabsis ho *muaj* **cim**.	8. But then *have* **tones**.
9. Uas muaj cov **suab** siab thiab qes.	9. That have **pitches** high and low.
10. **Xws li**, "Yau^{b} yau$_{m}$"	10. **Such as**, "**YO**-yo"
11. **Ua cas** koj hais lus *qab zib* ua luaj?	11. **Why** do you talk so *sweet*?
12. **Vim** kuv nyiam koj.	12. **Because** I like you.
13. **Thov** Vaj Tswv rau koj.	13. **Pray** God for you.
14. **Saib taus** *lwm tug neeg* thiab.	14. **Respect** *other people*, too.

Some Differences between Hmong Der and Mong Leng Dialects

Like I said before, the majority of these two dialects are the same, and roughly about 30 percent that are different. For more information about the difference between these two dialects, please refer to my **Hmong Dictionary** on pages 581-587. For now, I would like to just briefly mention some basic differences. Also, the word "**Der**" is short for *Hmong Der*, and "**Leng**" is short for *Hmong Leng*.

Consonants*

Hmong Der	Hmong Leng	Der Example	Leng Example	English Meaning
d	dl	dev	dlev	dog
hm	m	Hmoob	Moob	Hmong / Mong
hn	n	hnub	nub	sun
nt	nt, ndl	**ntuj**, dej ntws	**ntuj**, dlej ndlwg	**universe**, **sky**, water runs

Vowels*

Hmong Der	Hmong Leng[1]	Der Example	Leng Example	English Meaning
o	o *and* u	mov, tus os	mov, tug us	rice, duck
a	aa	txav, av	txaav, aav	move, dirt
ia	a	txiav, iav	txav, av	cut, a mirror
ai	ai *and* a	hais lus, tais, diav	has lug, tais, dlav	speak, bowl, spoon
u	u *and* oo	hu, mus	hu, moog	call, go

[1] Not always used as indicated, however.

Pronouns*

Hmong Der	Hmong Leng	Der Example	Leng Example	English Meaning
nej	mej	nej mus	mej moog	you go *(you all)*
nws	nwg	nws ***los***	nwg ***lug***	he/she/it comes *(returns)*
lawv	puab	lawv tuaj	puab tuaj	they come *(visiting)*

The pronouns "koj" and "kuv" are the same in both dialects.

Verbs*

Der	Leng	Der	Leng	Der	Leng	Der	Leng	Der	Leng
me	*miv*	pom	*pum*	ncaj	*ncaaj*	zam	*zaam*	xav	*xaav*
hais	*has*	sov	*suv*	iab	*ab*	zov	*zuv*	ziab	*zab*

* Only a few listed here. It will require more than one page to fully discuss the difference between these two dialects.

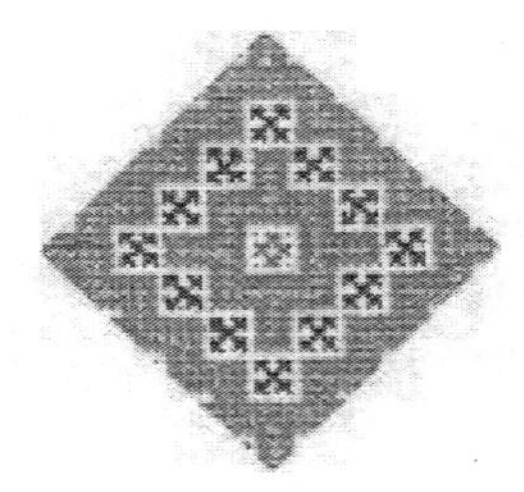

Summary

Well, I sincerely want to congratulate you on your long and arduous journey, and thank you so much for your tenacity and patience. You have come a long way and only if I could I would part with you of what I know about the Hmong language, but unfortunately that is not possible. Therefore, I am trying to indirectly transfer to you of what I know about the Hmong language by writing this book. With that being said, if you have mastered the information I provided here, you should be able to properly read, write and understand the Hmong language.

Writing this book has been a very interesting journey and the most challenging endeavor for me due to *my lack of good English grammar* and a formal education in linguistics. The problems I often faced was to find a succinct and direct way to explain or instruct using proper English grammars so learners will comprehend. Nonetheless, I have decided to challenge myself to write this book in hope that it will be useful to learners who wish to learn the Hmong language from a non-linguistic point of view by using simple English terms and simple explanation. In addition, I do realize that this book covered many areas and some parts might be *too overwhelming* for beginners; however, I want this book to be as useful as possible for everyone.

Additionally, you can always visit my website, www.HmongDictionary.com, for more information about the Hmong language as well as looking up Hmong words and definitions. Also, there are useful audio and programs available on the website, i.e., Hmong Dictionary software and other tools where you can download. Together, let's keep improving and teaching the Hmong language so that the native juice of the Hmong fruits will not perish but flourish for many generations to come.

Last but most importantly, I want to say a big "**Thank You**" for your patronage and continued support of the www.HmongDictionary.com, and without your support and encouragement this book would not even exist!

Wishing you the very best of luck in your Hmong learning journey.

Jay Xiong
Author of the *Lus Hmoob Txhais,* a Hmong-Hmong Dictionary, ISBN: 0-9726964-1-5
Owner and Creator of the www.HmongDictionary.com